A TIME OF
OUR CHOOSING

A TIME OF OUR CHOOSING

AMERICA'S WAR IN IRAQ

TODD S. PURDUM

AND THE STAFF OF

The New York Times

TIMES BOOKS

HENRY HOLT AND COMPANY

NEW YORK

TIMES BOOKS
HENRY HOLT AND COMPANY, LLC
Publishers since 1866
115 WEST 18TH STREET
NEW YORK, NEW YORK 10011

Library of Congress Cataloging-in-Publication Data
Purdum, Todd S.
    A time of our choosing : America's war in Iraq / Todd S. Purdum and the
staff of the New York Times.
      p.   cm.
    Includes index.
    ISBN 0-8050-7562-3
    1. Iraq War, 2003.   2. Iraq War, 2003—Press coverage—United States.
I. New York Times. II. Title.
DS79.76.P87   2003
956.7044'3—dc22   2003061268

FIRST EDITION 2003

Designed by Cathryn S. Aison

Printed in the United States of America

1 3 5 7 9 10 8 6 4 2

To the memory of Michael Kelly,
1957–2003,
a great storyteller who died telling this one.

And to the men and women of The New York Times
whose brave work around the world
made this book possible.

Only the soldier really lives the war. The journalist does not. He may share the soldier's outward life and dangers, but he cannot share his inner life because the same moral compulsion does not bear upon him. The observer knows he has alternatives of action; the solider knows *he* has none. It is the mere knowing which makes the difference.

—Eric Sevareid, CBS radio broadcast, 1945

CONTENTS

MAPS

AUTHOR'S NOTE

The cover of this book describes it as the work of Todd S. Purdum and the staff of *The New York Times,* and the back of the jacket lists the names of the dozens of individuals on whose work it is based. That is not an act of politesse but a reflection of the plain truth. I am the author of this narrative, but I have constructed it on behalf of the newspaper, and in collaboration with my colleagues who covered the war and its prelude and aftermath, from Washington to the United Nations, Europe and the Middle East. My explicit assignment was to draw the work of my colleagues into a single narrative—adding additional reporting of my own—so that this book could stand as a synthesis of the paper's comprehensive reportage. My colleagues have also generously shared with me their notes and firsthand impressions, so that this book includes details not previously published. In writing the text, I have drawn freely from the ideas, analyses, impressions—and occasionally even verbatim phrases—already printed in the pages of the *Times.* It would be hard to improve on the prose of John F. Burns or Jim Dwyer, for example, so I have sometimes not even tried. All nonfiction authors depend on the work of others, but I have done so more than most, and I gratefully reflect my immeasurable debt in fuller detail in the acknowledgments at the back of this book. Because so much of the material in this book comes by design from work that previously appeared in the *Times,* I do not provide citations to specific articles. Material from other books and publications, however, is listed in the endnotes. I am solely responsible for any errors of fact, emphasis or interpretation.

• • •

IT SHOULD ALSO BE NOTED that there is no universally recognized method of transcribing Arabic into English, which explains why this book, and other books on related topics, contain inconsistencies in their transcriptions of Arabic words and names. Family preferences and historical usages have meant that the same letters in Arabic can come out in two or even three different ways in English. This book follows the spellings most commonly used in *The New York Times.* Thus, for example, Nasiriya, not Nasiriyah, and Muhammad Said al-Sahhaf, not Mohammed Saeed al-Sahaf.

Todd S. Purdum

A TIME OF
OUR CHOOSING

PROLOGUE

It began with the dawn. Like a convoy of armor-plated dinosaurs come suddenly to life, the column of seventy-ton Abrams tanks and twenty-five-ton Bradley fighting vehicles barreled up the six lanes of Highway 8, the Hilla Road into southern Baghdad. In the stifling heat of early spring, the moving line of metal rolled toward the heart of Saddam Hussein's capital city, some sixty vehicles in all. "The tanks, the tanks are close!" a young Iraqi girl cried out.

Barely thirty-six hours earlier, troops from the United States Army's Third Infantry Division had stormed and held a strategic outpost at Baghdad's international airport, but the city of five million people was by no means fully encircled, or even under siege. Yet here were 761 soldiers from the division's 2nd Brigade blasting their way through neighborhoods—first industrial, then residential—just five miles from the center of town. They called it a "Thunder Run," and when commanders told their troops the plan, they thought the officers were kidding, so audacious did the idea seem. The Iraqi information minister was warning of suicide bombings to block the American advance—a wave of "martyrdom operations in a very new, creative way." Sure enough, during the morning, at least three Iraqi civilian vehicles tried to crash into the line, and an Iraqi man in a white headband with explosives strapped to his chest was shot dead in his car a few feet shy of an American armored personnel carrier.

But now it was the Americans who were creative—and the Iraqis who were rocked back with surprise on this Saturday morning. In no time, however, Iraqi fighters began hitting the American tanks with all they had. Under skies smoky from the days of punishing American bombing raids, Republican Guard units and guerrilla fighters in plain clothes fired on the advancing Americans from squat rooftops and highway overpasses, from behind trees and walls, from sandbags at intersections and from machine guns mounted in the beds of white Nissan pickup trucks known as "technicals." Rocket-propelled grenades, 57-millimeter antiaircraft guns and fire from Kalashnikov rifles pocked and charred the massive American armored convoy. Many of the Iraqi weapons were Soviet- and Chinese-made. But some were American, a bitter reminder of the days in the 1980s when Saddam was not Washington's sworn enemy but a useful counterweight against Islamic fundamentalism in Iran.

At one point, Iraqi fire hit the track on a giant M1A1 Abrams tank, and the Americans tried to tow it, but it caught fire and had to be blown up instead, to prevent the enemy from using it. For their part, the Americans blew up at least thirty Iraqi trucks and an armored personnel carrier and killed, by their estimate, 1,000 to 3,000 Iraqis in just over three hours of bloody, harrowing fighting. An American tank commander, sitting exposed in his open hatch, was killed when a grenade or mortar shell exploded in his face. A grenade hit Specialist Joseph A. Aiello's tank, and Sergeant Daniel R. Thompson, riding two tanks behind, saw the Iraqi who fired it as he fell backward. The Iraqi had no legs, but somehow managed to fire before Sergeant Thompson's tank commander killed him in a burst of machine-gun fire.

Specialist Aiello, a gunner, never stopped firing, but struggled to pick targets in the confusing swirl of civilians and Iraqi soldiers. "It was hard to shoot, because you don't want to shoot the civilians," he said. "It was hard to pick out the threat." One Iraqi family stopped their car on the highway's median, apparently hoping to endure the blistering gauntlet of death and destruction they had driven into. But their hope was misplaced. A large Iraqi truck, mounted with an anti-aircraft gun, hurtled toward the American column and was fired at. It careered onto the median, struck the family's car and burst into flames. As the Americans passed, a man, a woman and three children—the youngest an infant—struggled to move, horribly burned.

By 9:30 A.M. it was over, and the Americans curved west toward the airport, leaving a trail of destruction in their wake. The Third Infantry had earned its nickname, "The Rock of the Marne," when, outnumbered, it repulsed a German advance near Chateau Thierry in World War I. In World War II, it bore the brunt of brutal combat in campaigns from North Africa to the Nazi mountain retreat at

Berchtesgaden; one of its members, Audie Murphy, was the most decorated soldier of that war. The division's song is a proud claim: "Wouldn't give a bean to be a fancy pants marine / I'd rather be a dogface soldier like I am."

This Saturday morning was something else again.

"I was a tank commander in the Persian Gulf war," said the raid's leader, Lieutenant Colonel Eric C. Schwartz, commander of the 2nd Brigade's 1st Battalion, 64th Armor, a third-generation veteran whose grandfather had been gassed in World War I, whose father had flown Navy helicopters in Vietnam. This morning, as always, Schwartz was wearing a pair of red socks, his family's good-luck charm. "After today I feel like I fought five Desert Storms," he said.[1] "It was three hours of organized chaos."

It was that, and more. Like James H. Doolittle's daring 1942 bombing raid over Tokyo, the Third Infantry's "Thunder Run" through Baghdad that Saturday morning was less important militarily than symbolically. Barely two weeks into a war that had already seen one of the swiftest armored advances in military history, the Third Infantry's sweeping "reconnaissance in force" was a way to test Iraqi defenses. But more than anything, it was a way to proclaim to the Iraqi president, Saddam Hussein, and to the world, that American troops were at his very doorstep, whatever his propaganda machine might say. In that sense, it succeeded spectacularly. An Iraqi colonel taken into custody that morning told his captors he had been led to believe that American forces were still 100 miles away.

"This is supposed to be his city, yet we drove right through it," Colonel David Perkins, the commander of the 2nd Brigade, said that day of Saddam. "This shows we can go anywhere in the city at a time of our choosing."[2] Four days of sometimes fierce fighting later, Baghdad would fall to American forces.

WHETHER HE KNEW IT OR not, Colonel Perkins's words neatly distilled the whole history and philosophy of the United States' second war in the Persian Gulf. Just hours before the war began, President George W. Bush himself used the same phrase—"a time of our choosing"—to sum up his determination to drive Saddam Hussein from power, twelve years after the end of the first Gulf war, when his father, the first President Bush, agreed to the cease-fire that left the Iraqi dictator in power.

The story of what happened in those twelve years—and in six weeks of active combat in March and April 2003—is the story of what the elder Bush once called, in another context, "a world transformed." When hijackers used loaded jetliners to attack the Pentagon and destroy the World Trade Center on September 11, 2001, they transformed not only the second Bush presidency, but fifty years of seemingly settled American foreign policy as well. The impact of the worst terrorist attack in American history, combined with a decade of increasing Iraqi defiance of United Nations resolutions requiring disarmament, galvanized an aggressive group of defense intellectuals who had argued for years that Saddam was a menace that could no longer be contained. These thinkers were now scattered in government posts and had the power to carry out their ideas.

The extent of Saddam Hussein's efforts to develop and deploy nuclear, chemical and biological weapons may never be fully known. Nor may the extent and nature of his ties, if any, to the Al Qaeda terrorist organization, which planned and carried out the 9/11 attacks. The range of President Bush's motives in choosing military action to dislodge Saddam will doubtless be debated by historians for generations to come. But even with the hindsight of just a few months, this much is clear: Iraq became the first test case in the Bush administration's evolving new foreign-policy doctrine of America's right not only to preeminence in world affairs, but to preemption, by military might if necessary, of whatever threats it perceives to its security at home and abroad.

At its most aggressive, this doctrine holds that the web of international institutions, alliances and security arrangements—and the policy of deterrence against the former Soviet Union—that largely sustained United States foreign policy in the fifty years after World War II is no longer adequate in the face of shadowy global terrorist organizations and the states that aid or support them. "After September the 11th, the doctrine of containment just doesn't hold any water, as far as I'm concerned," is how President Bush characterized the new stance in a news conference with Prime Minister Tony Blair of Great Britain a few weeks before the war began.

And so, with only a handful of active allies, Washington went to war against Iraq without the support of the United Nations, over the objections of two of its most important European allies—France and Germany—and in the face of mass popular opposition abroad, significant dissent at home and deep strains of disagreement within the Bush administration itself. It was in some ways a new kind of war, swift in its execution, light and flexible in its tactics, making strategic use of Special Operations forces, real-time intelligence and precision targeting. The air power was massive—about ten times that of the first Persian Gulf war, more than 1,000 sorties a day at the peak. So was the ordnance, some 30,000 bombs and missiles dropped or launched, close to 70 percent of them precision-guided. Targets that once took days of planning to hit were struck in mere minutes.

No WAR IN HUMAN HISTORY was chronicled more extensively in real time, with reporters, photographers and television crews as close to combat in the constantly shifting front lines as they have ever been, with communications equipment that enabled them to broadcast the war live, round the clock and around the world, from legendary places whose names are familiar to Americans mostly from Sunday school and sixth-grade social studies classes. They lived, ate and slept with troops who loaned them gear, confessed their fears, endured airless days and chill nights in barren deserts and dangerous cities in the brutality, blood and confusion of what Lieutenant Colonel Rick Carlson of the Army's 101st Airborne Division dubbed "the country of NQR: not quite right."

Yet often the story was told only in flashes, "soda-straw snapshots," in the words of General Richard B. Myers, the chairman of the Joint Chiefs of Staff. A conflict that lasted just days seemed at times to drag on for months, only to end as abruptly—and in some ways as ambiguously—as it had started. What really happened? Why did the United States choose war? Why did the war unfold along the path it did? And what did America's military victory mean for the future of Iraq, the Middle East, international institutions and American foreign policy itself? Was the United States now safer, or was it more vulnerable? Had the war inspired a new generation of anti-American sentiment in the Muslim world, new resentments among old allies and new terrorists bent on attacking Americans with suicide bombers or even makeshift nuclear bombs?

The war dislodged one of the most ruthless, repressive regimes of the modern era, as the mass graves and grim survivors' stories made all too clear. It held out the promise of more representative government in a fractious, multiethnic state that has never truly been a nation so much as an artificial colonial construct pieced together at the end of World War I. But it also unleashed new and unpredictable forces in Iraq and in the region, and it raised new questions about the limits of American power throughout the world. Even though the United States accomplished its immediate goal of toppling Saddam Hussein's government, winning the peace, at least in the early stages, was proving more difficult than winning the war. Iraq's vital infrastructure was in shambles, from years of neglect, battle damage and postwar looting, and its people were understandably frustrated, even bitter. In the months after President Bush pronounced the end of major combat operations, guerrilla fighters and loyalists of Saddam's regime continued a campaign of steady attacks against American forces. By the end of August, the fighting in Iraq had taken the lives of more than 270 Americans—more than 175 of them lost to hostile fire—and more than 45 British troops. Unknown thousands of Iraqi soldiers and civilians were killed. The effort cost tens of billions of dollars, not counting the ultimate costs of reconstruction.

And even for commanders at the end of that hot and dusty Saturday when the Third Infantry crashed into Baghdad, the questions were clearer than the answers.

"We're there," said Lieutenant Colonel Dave Pere, a senior Marine operations officer. "We're the dog that caught the car. Now what do we do with it?"[3]

AMERICA'S TERMS

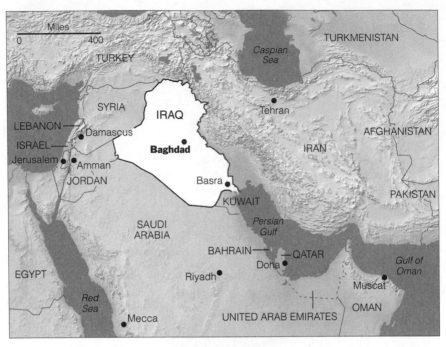

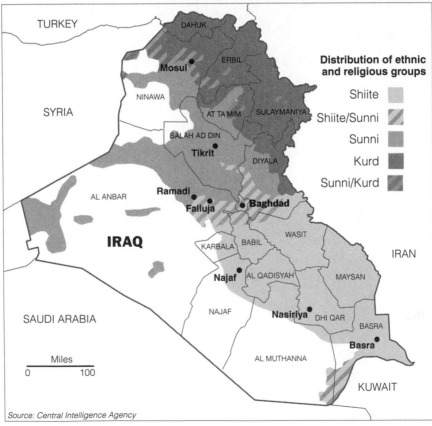

Chapter 1

TWELVE YEARS IN THE MAKING

Camp David, Maryland
Saturday, September 15, 2001

In the secure isolation of the Catoctin Mountains outside Washington, D.C., a grim group of the world's most powerful people sat bundled in windbreakers and fleece jackets against the morning chill. Four days earlier, jetliners loaded with fuel had slammed into the Pentagon and flattened the World Trade Center, killing unknown thousands of people in the worst terrorist attack in American history. Now President George W. Bush and his top advisers were meeting for a daylong discussion on how to respond to what the president had described in unblinking terms as "an act of war." Already the chief suspect was clear: a Saudi-born exile named Osama bin Laden, head of the worldwide Al Qaeda terror network, which had found shelter and support from the brutal Taliban regime in Afghanistan and flourished in secretive cells from Pakistan to Germany. The director of Central Intelligence, George J. Tenet, had come armed with detailed briefing books on how to wage a campaign against this newly obvious, though hardly new, threat.

But around the long table in the functional-woodsy conference room of Laurel Lodge, the specter of another, better-known villain hovered. Ten years earlier, many of the same officials sitting at Camp David that morning had helped the president's father, the first President George Bush, plan and execute the Persian Gulf war to drive Saddam Hussein's Iraqi forces out of Kuwait. Vice President Dick Cheney had been secretary of defense, Secretary of State Colin Powell had been chairman of the Joint Chiefs of Staff, National Security Adviser Condoleezza Rice had been a Russia expert on the White House staff, and the deputy defense secretary, Paul Wolfowitz, had been undersecretary of defense for policy.

On this Saturday morning, none of the officials around the table could yet know what role Iraq had played, if any, in the horrific attacks days before. But at least one of them, Wolfowitz, had suspicions, and he piped up. That morning's *New York Times* had carried an editorial chastising Wolfowitz for having spoken at the Pentagon in the aftermath of the attacks about "ending states who sponsor terrorism."[1] The *Times* intoned: "That may work as a form of intimidation but we trust he does not have in mind invading and occupying Iraq" and other countries. In fact, even as the newspaper's readers were absorbing that editorial, Wolfowitz was advocating just such a course to his colleagues at the presidential retreat. During a break in the seven-hour meeting, or in the middle of it—accounts from participants differ—Wolfowitz expounded on the Iraqi threat, and President Bush listened. Wolfowitz argued that toppling Saddam was an achievable goal, and he estimated that there was a 10 to 50 percent chance that the Iraqi leader had been involved in the 9/11 attacks. By going after Iraq, Wolfowitz argued, America's resolve would be taken seriously. Secretary of State Powell, however, argued strongly for keeping the "focus on the ball" of Al Qaeda and the Taliban and not pulling a "bait and switch." Wolfowitz's boss, Defense Secretary Donald Rumsfeld, took no public position. Vice President Cheney, too, was skeptical, saying that by going after Saddam "we lose our rightful place as good guy." The next morning, when he was asked on NBC's *Meet the Press* if there was any Iraqi connection to the attacks, the vice president answered with a flat "no." But a seed had been planted.[2]

On Sunday morning, after the other officials had left Camp David, Bush summoned Rice, a trusted confidante who had tutored him on foreign policy throughout his campaign, to his cabin.

"Here's what I want to do," he said. The assault on terrorism would come in phases, opening with a more focused attack on Osama bin Laden, his followers and their Afghan protectors, but eventually extending to any terrorist organization or nation with the "global reach" to harm the United States. Rice's hastily taken notes turned out to be the first tentative draft of a sweeping new foreign policy outlook that would come to be known as the Bush Doctrine.

GEORGE WALKER BUSH HAD COME to the presidency at the age of fifty-four with strikingly little knowledge of or exposure to the world beyond the United States and Mexico. In fact, he had rarely traveled abroad as an adult: one of his trips was to China in the 1970s when his father was the American envoy in the early days of Washington's opening to the mainland; when his father was president, he led a delegation to Gambia for a celebration of its independence; and in 1998 he visited one of his twin daughters in Italy before joining other governors on a tour of the Middle East. He had met with perhaps 150 foreign diplomats and trade officials in six successful years as governor of Texas. But neither he nor his much more experienced rival in the 2000 election, Vice President Al Gore, expected foreign policy to be a major issue after a decade in which the end of the Cold War had given way to a series of regional conflicts—a period that the columnist George Will later summed up as a "holiday from history." Bush's campaign emphasized education and a package of sweeping tax cuts that he said would spark a domestic economy that was beginning to flag after a run of unprecedented expansion. Asked in the second presidential debate of the 2000 campaign to describe his philosophy for projecting American power, Bush responded in terms that sounded startlingly like Gore. "If we are an arrogant nation," he said, "they will resent us. If we're a humble nation, but strong, they'll welcome us." As a candidate, Bush was famously unprepared to answer detailed questions on foreign policy, and when asked in one interview about the Taliban leadership in Afghanistan, answered, "Oh, I thought you said some band. The Taliban in Afghanistan. Absolutely. Repressive." He scorned "nation-building" as a woolly-headed ambition that risked diluting America's priorities and diverting its military into insoluble conflicts around the world.

At the same time, however, Bush surrounded himself with a cadre of harder-headed foreign policy advisers dubbed the Vulcans, after the Roman god of fire, a statue of whom was a landmark in Birmingham, Alabama, Condoleezza Rice's hometown. This team included both Rice and Wolfowitz, along with such veteran players as Richard L. Armitage, Richard Perle, and Robert B. Zoellick. Significantly, it did not include either the cautious, moderate Colin Powell or Brent Scowcroft, the first President Bush's pragmatic national security adviser. Powell had considered but declined a run for president himself in 1996, and had emerged as the nation's most prominent black Republican, having written a best-selling autobiography and led a nonprofit public-service group called America's Promise. When Powell gave his public support to Bush's candidacy in the summer of 2000, it was universally understood that he would become secretary of state if Bush were elected, but his relationship with the new president remained more professional and correct than personal, and his careful, internationalist approach was already shaping up to be at odds with that of many of Bush's other advisers and the president himself.

What Bush lacked in detailed knowledge of foreign affairs, he made up for in decades of family exposure to the hard realities of modern American electoral politics. During his father's presidential campaign and presidency, Bush took on a role as loyalty enforcer and studied the take-no-prisoners political gamesmanship of Lee Atwater, the legendary Republican political consultant. He had absorbed the painful lessons of his father's lack of "the vision thing," and once declared that the challenge of the presidency was to "have a strategy and set the debate."[3] A former owner of the Texas Rangers baseball team, Bush liked to think of himself as a "gut-player," whose instincts were true, even when his knowledge might be shaky. If Bush sometimes shrunk from articulating a clear vision of his foreign policy goals, many of his advisers, in their writings and speaking, did not. They did not agree on all issues, but pulsing through the thinking of many was the conviction that nation-states, acting in self-interest—not international organizations, alliances or increasingly interlinked economies—constituted the crucial elements of global politics. Wolfowitz, citing the "remarkable record" of coalition-building during the Cold War, argued that leadership means "demonstrating that your friends will be protected and taken care of, that your enemies will be punished, and that those who refuse to support you will live to regret having done so."[4]

The intellectual Wolfowitz was an unlikely soul mate for Bush. He grew up in Ithaca, New York, the son of a Cornell University mathematics professor who had emigrated from Warsaw in 1920 and told his children how lucky they were to have escaped the horrors of Hitler. As a teenager, Wolfowitz was a John F. Kennedy Democrat and marched on Washington in Martin Luther King's great pilgrimage for civil rights in 1963.

After considering a career in mathematics, Wolfowitz earned his doctorate in political science at the University of Chicago, a cradle of what came to be called neo-conservative thinking on foreign policy and a hotbed of the anti-détente school during the Cold War. After three years' teaching at Yale, he came to the Arms Control and Disarmament Agency at the end of the Nixon administration, where he was part of a group that espoused the contrarian view that the Soviet Union should not merely be contained, as American policy had held since the late 1940s, but instead challenged on every front. He fell into various jobs as an analyst at both the State and Defense Departments, and ultimately wound up working for Dick Cheney in the first Bush administration as undersecretary for policy, the Pentagon's brainstormer-in-chief. A decade later, Rumsfeld hired him as the Pentagon's number-two official after working with him on a congressional commission on missile defense. Morton Abramowitz, a veteran diplomat, called Wolfowitz "the preeminent house intellectual." Conversant in six foreign languages, Wolfowitz was the kind of unrepentant wonk who kept Civil War histories by his bedside, and a painting of the Battle of Antietam—the single bloodiest day in American history—in his third floor, E-Ring Pentagon office.

As a young Defense Department analyst, Wolfowitz had directed a secret assessment of Persian Gulf threats that listed Iraq as a menace to its neighbors and a threat to American interests—and this was in 1979, a dozen years before the Persian Gulf war. In 1992, he oversaw the writing of a new "Defense Planning Guidance" for Cheney, a broad outline of what the military should be prepared for. An early draft argued that, with the collapse of the Soviet Union, Washington should be ready to assure that no new superpower could arise to challenge America's enlightened dominion, and that the United States should be "postured to act independently when collective action cannot be orchestrated." The guidance was accompanied by scenarios sketching out possible wars, including another war with Iraq. The draft was leaked to *The New York Times*—without his ever having read it, Wolfowitz later said—and sparked a storm of criticism as being overly bellicose. But now, in the aftermath of the 9/11 terrorist attacks, ideas similar to these were coalescing at the highest levels of the Bush administration's thinking.

For all his fire-breathing pronouncements, Wolfowitz in person was low-key and engaging, if sometimes politically tone-deaf with colleagues, showing up at meetings uninvited or offering his views in the presence of his superiors without being asked. He still described himself as a "bleeding heart" on social issues, and friends said his hard-line foreign policy views sprang from a relentless optimism about the improvability of the human condition. But Wolfowitz could also be so intellectually unshrinking as to seem unfeeling. "We know the costs of Vietnam," he said in an interview in 2002. "They were horrendous. But we don't know what that part of the world would have looked like today if it hadn't been."

The 1991 Persian Gulf war had been designed, by Colin Powell and others, to be the precise opposite of Vietnam: a clear-cut conflict, with limited aims, defined goals, massive force and broad international support. At the head of a coalition of some thirty-four nations, American forces had succeeded in a campaign that lasted just forty-two days, with only 100 hours of ground combat. Coalition forces drove Iraqi troops out of Kuwait back north toward Baghdad, but did not try to topple Saddam Hussein's dictatorial regime, already well known for extraordinary viciousness and brutality. To have done so would have splintered the international coalition, exceeded the United Nations resolutions that had backed the war in the first place and risked exploding a volatile country already riven by centuries of ethnic and religious rivalries and hatreds.

"If we'd gone to Baghdad and got rid of Saddam Hussein—assuming we could have found him—we'd have had to put a lot of forces in and run him to ground someplace," Cheney told the BBC in 1992. "He would not have been easy to capture. Then you've got to put a new government in his place, and then you're faced with the question of what kind of government are you going to establish in Iraq? Is it going to be a Kurdish government or a Shia government or a Sunni government? How many forces are you going to have to leave there to keep it propped up, how many casualties are you going to take through the course of this operation?"[5]

So at Powell's urging, with Cheney's acceptance and the first President Bush's approval, the war was stopped—a decision that would be hotly debated, by the participants and critics, for much of the following decade. The assumption in 1991 was that Saddam's regime, defeated militarily and humbled politically, would collapse of its own weight or be toppled in a coup. Ten years later, not only had that not happened, but Saddam had defied or eluded numerous United Nations resolutions requiring him to destroy weapons of mass destruction or forsake oil revenues—and had further squeezed, bled and tortured his own populace.

Less than two years after the end of the first Bush administration, however, Wolfowitz was already expressing regrets about the outcome of the Persian Gulf war. In a 1994 review of *Crusade,* Rick Atkinson's book on the conflict, Wolfowitz argued: "With hindsight, it does seem like a mistake to have announced, even before the war was over, that we would not go to Baghdad, or to give Saddam the reassurance of the dignified cease-fire ceremony at Safwan."[6] In this view, Wolfowitz was far from alone. Twice the administration of President Bill Clinton had conducted major air strikes, first in 1993 in retaliation for an assassination plot against the first President Bush and then, five years later, as punishment for Iraq's non-cooperation with international weapons inspectors. And on other occasions, American and British bombers hit targets, including Iraqi air defense sites, in enforcement of "no-fly" zones established to protect Kurds in the north and Shiite Muslims in the south of Iraq—most recently in August 2001. In 1998, Congress and Clinton had declared that supporting "regime change" in Baghdad was the official policy of the United States.

But support for the web of United Nations economic sanctions against Iraq had eroded in the face of obvious suffering by Iraqi civilians, and an effort by the Bush administration in 2001 to tighten and revive sanctions in a way that would focus on the regime, not the Iraqi people, was bogged down in disagreement at the UN. The Bush administration was in the midst of an overall review of policy toward Iraq, one that seemed headed toward strengthening the air patrols and reinforcing support for the range of Iraqi opposition groups hoping to topple Saddam.

During the 1990s, a cadre of influential thinkers on foreign policy and politics had begun to argue vocally for tougher American action to hold Iraq to account. Their motives were varied and complex. Some, like Wolfowitz, saw a post-Saddam Iraq as a potential beachhead of democracy in the Middle East. Others, like Rumsfeld, took the more pragmatic view that Saddam was simply too brutal, mischievous and dangerous to tolerate. As it happened, many who took this view were also strong supporters of Israel and argued that as the Middle East's only true democracy and strongest American strategic ally, the Jewish state could never be fully secure—nor could a lasting Middle East peace settlement be achieved—as long as regimes like Saddam's menaced the region.

For Wolfowitz in particular, the goal of a democratic—or at least more representative—government in Iraq had the parallel aim of shaking up and remaking the map of the entire Arab Middle East, where antidemocratic oligarchies like Saudi Arabia and Egypt faced (and even fomented) strong anti-American sentiment among their own populations. This theory held that only by breaking the prevailing pattern— and spreading the gospel of free institutions, government transparency and rule of law—could these societies be transformed and America's strategic and security interests be protected. It was a bold and risky idea, for several reasons, not least that only one Muslim nation in the Middle East, Turkey, had a working version of Western-style democracy—and Turkey was not an Arab country. Iraq, a pieced-together post-colonial construct of feuding ethnic and religious factions, had no democratic tradition at all, and many Middle East experts in the State Department and elsewhere believed that Iraq's prospects for developing into a Jeffersonian ideal were limited at best.

But Wolfowitz was not alone in his evangelism. On December 1, 1997, the conservative magazine *The Weekly Standard* featured the cover headline "Saddam Must Go," and one of the articles elaborating on that point was co-written by Wolfowitz. That same year, Wolfowitz joined the *Standard*'s editor, William Kristol, the former chief of staff to Vice President Dan Quayle, and others in forming a group called the Project for the New American Century, which promoted robust American engagement in the world. In 1998, in a letter signed by Wolfowitz, Rumsfeld and a number of other officials who would ultimately take senior jobs in the Bush administration, the group urged President Clinton to adopt a "full complement" of diplomatic and military measures to remove Saddam Hussein from power.

● ● ●

WHILE IRAQ DID NOT BECOME a front-burner issue in the early days of the second Bush presidency, the administration did offer abundant evidence that it intended to pursue an altogether more single-minded, and single-handed, brand of foreign policy.

The crux of this approach, espoused by a range of Bush advisers beginning with Vice President Cheney and including Condoleezza Rice and Donald Rumsfeld, was that the world was a dangerous place, and that America's paramount goal must be to protect its own interests as the dominant global power, without any rival. In the 2000 campaign, Bush and his advisers did not hesitate to fault Bill Clinton for failing to recognize such hard realities—and for what they saw as the Democratic president's gushing about "globalization." China was not a strategic partner, Bush argued, but a competitor. Rice, with her credentials as a Russia expert, declared at one point, "If we have learned anything in the last several years, it is that a romantic view of Russia—rather than a realistic one—did nothing to help the cause of stability in Russia."[7] For much of the 1990s, Clinton and his foreign policy team had argued that economic globalization was making traditional nation-states less powerful and less important, but Bush rejected this view as well, contending that states still sought to advance their own interests. "Power matters," Rice wrote in *Foreign Affairs* in 2000, "both the exercise of power by the United States and the ability of others to exercise it."[8] In his first major campaign speech on foreign policy, at the Reagan presidential library in California, Bush himself declared, "There are limits to the smiles and scowls of diplomacy. Armies and missiles are not stopped by stiff notes of condemnation. They are held in check by strength and purpose and the promise of swift punishment." What is more, Bush and Rice did not believe there was anything wrong with the United States flexing such muscles in support of its own goals, and Rice dismissed "the belief that the United States is exercising power legitimately only when it is doing so on behalf of someone or something else."

In exercising this power to protect its interests, Rice and the others held, America might well have to act alone. The network of post–World War II security alliances like the North Atlantic Treaty Organization (NATO) and the United Nations had their uses, but also their limits. In a world without a competing superpower, such alliances could well cramp America's freedom of action to defend what it saw as its own interests. The 1992 Pentagon policy guidance drafted in Wolfowitz's shop had declared that coalitions were all to the good if they served American needs, but it warned: "We should expect future coalitions to be ad hoc assemblies, often not lasting beyond the crisis being confronted and in many cases carrying only general agreement over the objectives to be accomplished."

Ivo Daalder and James Lindsay of the Brookings Institution summed up the philosophy as a "billiard ball view of the world, where the United States was the biggest (and most virtuous) ball on the table and could move every other ball when and where it wished." They also described the Bush mantra as "ABC—Anything But Clinton," as the new president and his aides set about undoing or reversing many of the policies and approaches of the previous administration. In truth, the new President Bush often seemed equally determined to break with the policies and thinking of his own father's administration as well.

The administration wasted no time putting its ideas into practice. In March 2001, Bush dropped a campaign pledge to curtail carbon dioxide emissions from power plants, and not long after, Rice told European ambassadors that the Kyoto Treaty on global warming was dead. The administration had also declared its opposition to a raft of international compacts, including a new protocol to the Biological Weapons Convention, the Comprehensive Test Ban Treaty and the International Criminal Court, and it had threatened to withdraw unilaterally from the 1972 Anti-Ballistic Missile Treaty with Russia if Moscow would not agree to changes that would allow development of a new American missile defense system.

The Bush administration also chose to stay conspicuously uninvolved in the Israeli-Palestinian conflict, which was then spinning out of control in a wave of violence following the collapse of the Camp David peace negotiations in 2000. Bill Clinton had made an Israeli-Palestinian settlement a major priority of his second term, only to fall short, and Bush, who remembered his own father's political difficulties in dealing with the situation, held it at arm's length. His basic posture amounted to unwavering support for the government of Israeli prime minister Ariel Sharon.

In August 2001, after Sharon had moved Israeli tanks into parts of the West Bank and Bush described Israel as under Palestinian siege, the government of Saudi Arabia, one of Washington's key Middle East allies, exploded. Crown Prince Abdullah, the de facto Saudi ruler, ordered his ambassador, Prince Bandar bin Sultan—the dean of the Washington diplomatic corps and an old personal friend of the Bush family—to deliver a terse message to the president through Rice. "It is clear you made a strategic decision to support Sharon irrespective of what he does and regardless of the impact it has on your interests and your friends in the region," the message warned, according to a paraphrase offered later by a Saudi official. "You leave us no alternative except to pursue policies based on our national interests, regardless of their impact on you." Bush promised the crown prince that he would soon give a speech calling for the creation of a Palestinian state. It was against this tense background that the planes wrought their devastation on the crystal clear morning of September 11. A disaster for America was also a diplomatic fiasco for Saudi Arabia, whose support for extremist education had helped spread anti-American hatred throughout the Muslim world. Of the nineteen hijackers, fifteen were Saudis.

IN THE DAYS AFTER THE Saturday meeting at Camp David, the administration's public focus remained on Al Qaeda and the Taliban. But in hindsight, it is clear that, at least in Wolfowitz's mind, Iraq bubbled just beneath the surface. When asked at the Pentagon on September 19 about possible links between Iraq and the 9/11 attacks, Wolfowitz had his eye instead on the future, saying that the president had indicated the response to the attacks would involve more than one event. "I think everyone has got to look at this problem with completely new eyes, in a completely new light," he added. Even as Wolfowitz took this view, Powell continued to urge caution, arguing, "We can't solve everything in one blow," according to a friend. But even Powell would later say it was always clear to him that the president's next target could well be Iraq.

Bush's own sense of himself and his presidency had been deeply affected by the attacks, friends and aides said. Again and again in that dark September, he would say that whatever he had done before would matter little, that history would judge them all on how they responded to this new challenge. The president was a person of deep and abiding faith, and often spoke unself-consciously in religious terms. One friend said that Bush now seemed to see the attacks as a test from God, and was determined not to be found wanting.

On the evening of September 20, Bush took the rostrum of the House of Representatives—the same chamber where Woodrow Wilson had solemnly vowed to make the world "safe for democracy" and Franklin D. Roosevelt had asked for a declaration of war on Japan. Forgotten was the rancorous 2000 presidential election, in which Bush had been selected the winner only after the United States Supreme Court halted a pending vote recount in Florida. The president now stood unchallenged astride the political landscape, basking in thunderous, bipartisan applause. Days earlier, in a memorial service at the National Cathedral for the victims of the attacks, Bush had issued a Wilsonian warning: "Our responsibility to history is already clear: to answer these attacks and rid the world of evil." This night, the president made clear just what he meant, articulating the outlines of a broad new philosophy that would come to guide his presidency: "From this day forward, any nation that continues to harbor or support terrorism will be regarded by the United States as a hostile regime." He made no mention of Saddam Hussein. He did not have to. Three days earlier, in a secret memorandum that ordered the military to begin planning for war in Afghanistan, he also directed commanders to begin planning for another potential target: Iraq.[9]

Chapter 2

THE AXIS OF EVIL

Washington, D.C.
Tuesday, January 29, 2002

"**W**e last met in an hour of shock and suffering," President Bush told Congress and the nation, delivering his first State of the Union Address to a packed House chamber in circumstances that were the opposite of ordinary. In the four months since Bush had last stood in this room, United States forces working with Afghan fighters from the Northern Alliance had routed the Taliban, though Osama bin Laden and some of his top Al Qaeda lieutenants were still unaccounted for. A new provisional leader of Afghanistan, Hamid Karzai, had been installed in Kabul, and painful rebuilding efforts were beginning. But the United States also remained on heightened alert for new terrorist attacks and for several weeks in October, a series of unsolved mailings of deadly anthrax bacteria to media organizations and public officials, including the Senate majority leader, Tom Daschle, had killed five people and sent fresh waves of fear rippling through the nation. Tonight, the president got down to business. "Our nation will continue to be steadfast and patient and persistent in the pursuit of two great objectives," he said. "First, we will shut down terrorist camps, disrupt terrorist plans and bring terrorists to justice. And second, we must prevent the terrorists and regimes who seek chemical, biological or nuclear weapons from threatening the United States and the world.

"Some of these regimes have been pretty quiet since September 11," the president went on, "but we know their true nature." Like a prosecutor unsealing an indictment, he read out a bill of particulars against three countries: North Korea, Iran and, finally, Iraq. He spared no details. "The Iraqi regime has plotted to develop anthrax and nerve gas and nuclear weapons for over a decade," he told lawmakers, some of whose offices had just reopened after weeks of anthrax decontamination. "This is a regime that has already used poison gas to murder thousands of its own citizens, leaving the bodies of mothers huddled over their dead children. This is a regime that agreed to international inspections, then kicked out the inspectors. This is a regime that has something to hide from the civilized world."

Then Bush uttered words that would provoke banner headlines around the world and come to transform his presidency. "States like these, and their terrorist allies, constitute an axis of evil, arming to threaten the peace of the world. By seeking weapons of mass destruction, these regimes pose a grave and growing danger." He added: "All nations should know: America will do what is necessary to ensure our nation's security. We'll be deliberate. Yet time is not on our side. I will not wait on events while dangers gather. I will not stand by as peril draws closer and closer. The United States of America will not permit the world's most dangerous regimes to threaten us with the world's most destructive weapons."

No presidential oratory had been more bellicose in the forty-one years since John F. Kennedy committed the United States to "pay any price, bear any burden" at the height of the Cold War, and the hard words implied a big new idea: America could no longer wait to be roused to action by attacks on its shores or its interests. It would act first. Bush's supporters praised him for candor, and likened his pronouncement to Ronald Reagan's denunciation of the Soviet Union as an "evil empire." Critics at home and abroad complained that Bush had lumped three delicate and difficult foreign policy problems into a one-size-fits-all formulation. As a metaphor, the "axis of evil" was florid, they said. As a doctrine? Impossible. But less than a week later, Secretary of State Powell assured the Senate Foreign Relations Committee that Bush's indictment was "not a rhetorical flourish—he meant it." It turned out that he meant it especially about Iraq, whose propaganda machine referred to this second President Bush as the "son of the viper."

By any measure, Saddam Hussein stood out in the pantheon of contemporary tyrants. His twenty-three years of iron dictatorship, two wars and casual brutality had left his country economically battered, militarily weakened and wretched with fear. Saddam had been soundly defeated in the Gulf war, but under the terms of the March 3, 1991, cease-fire, he retained the use of his military helicopters and the core of his best troops, the Republican Guard, some of which had eluded the allied steamroller or never been sent forward into the fight. In the war's aftermath, Saddam swiftly put down rebellions by Shiite Muslims in the south and Kurds (a non-Arab minority) in the north, and though he eventually acquiesced in a measure of autonomy for the Kurds, he retained an unshaken grip on the rest of Iraq. Over two decades, perhaps 200,000 Iraqi citizens—suspected traitors, would-be assassins, personal enemies, former friends—had disappeared into Saddam's dank gulag of prisons, never to be heard from again. The scope of the losses emerges from the story of Muhammad Muslim Muhammad, who at age fourteen in 1996 went to work as a gravedigger at a cemetery near the infamous Abu Ghraib prison, outside Baghdad, to fulfill his military service. Over the years, he buried perhaps 7,000 bodies, as many as eighteen a day at a peak time in 2001. He never told anyone. "I didn't open my mouth, or I would have ended up with these poor people here," he would say in 2003. Saddam's regime comprised about a dozen internal security services, employing perhaps 500,000 people in intelligence, police and security jobs. If the armed forces and paramilitary groups were factored in, the total approached 1.3 million, in a country of roughly 23 million people.[1]

In enforcing fealty to the leader, no tool of torture was too extreme. Nursing babies were held at arm's length from their imprisoned mothers and allowed to starve; eyes were gouged out and ears sliced off; the small bones in feet and hands were smashed with hammers; whole bodies were dunked in vats of acid in efforts to extract confessions or wreak punishment; and children were tortured in front of their parents. There were poisonings, hangings, beheadings, shootings. And always, in the smallest details of daily living, there was the fear. "Being in Iraq is like creeping around in someone else's migraine," the veteran BBC reporter John Sweeney once said. "The fear is so omnipresent, you could almost eat it."[2]

Even Saddam's own family had felt the fear firsthand. Hussein Kamel, the husband of Saddam's daughter Raghad, had been a favorite in the president's court, heading the Republican Guard and Iraq's weapons programs. Hussein Kamel's brother, Saddam, was married to another presidential daughter, Rana. But the Kamel brothers' prominence made Hussein's own two sons, Uday and Qusay, jealous, and they began winning increasing responsibilities of their own, with Uday in charge of virtually the entire Iraqi media and a pro-Saddam militia known as the Fedayeen Saddam, and Qusay taking control of the security forces that guarded the president. In 1995, the Kamel brothers and their wives and relatives fled to Jordan, apparently to escape the rising influence of Uday and Qusay. From Jordan, Hussein Kamel issued a public statement urging an overthrow of Saddam's regime. The call for an uprising prompted panic in Baghdad, but Saddam stayed cool, offering forgiveness to his sons-in-law and promising them safe return. Seven months after their defection they returned, only to be met at the border by Uday, who took his sisters back to Baghdad and promptly announced that they had divorced their husbands. Days later, members of the Kamels' family were brought in to kill the defectors at their sister's house in Baghdad, as Uday and Qusay watched from a nearby car.[3]

Qusay, the smarter and more emotionally stable of the sons, quickly began to emerge as his father's heir apparent, while the volatile Uday, a heavy drinker and so violent that he once bludgeoned his father's food taster to death, had almost unchecked power. He controlled the smuggling that sold Iraqi oil in violation of the United Nations sanctions, pocketing millions of dollars for himself.

After more than a decade of punishing economic sanctions, there was another brutal reality in a nation rich with oil: privation. In the oil boom of the 1970s, before Saddam's war with Iran, Iraq had had a thriving, vibrant, educated middle class, and Baghdad was a cosmopolitan crossroads of the Arab world. Now the country's economy was a shell of its former self and the fabric of society was in tatters. Hard figures are difficult to come by, and Iraqi claims have been dismissed as wildly inflated, but Kenneth M. Pollack, a former Iraq expert at the Central Intelligence Agency, estimated that close to a quarter million Iraqis may have died during the decade of sanctions, and a once proud and prospering middle class was squeezed into poverty. In 1989, an Iraqi dinar was worth more than $3. By 1998, $1 bought 1,500 dinars at money changers' rates in the bazaars. Professionals earned a base pay of 3,000 dinars a month, or about $2 at official exchange rates. Two pounds of chicken cost 1,100 dinars. Modern medicines were nonexistent or in horribly short supply. Ahmad Adnan, a ten-year-old with diabetes in Saddam Central Children's

Hospital, was too shy to tell a Western visitor what he'd like from a vendor's stall stocked with teddy bears and cookies. So he whispered it to his doctor: "One egg, please." Baydaa Ihsaan, in charge of what was left of international relations for the General Federation of Iraqi Women, said, "Just catching a cold or the flu now are things that terrify me. Life is like a nightmare. One day you have everything in your life, and the next day you open your eyes and there is darkness." By 2001, former engineers and high school teachers sold spit-roasted kebabs and cheap clothing from handcarts and rusty bed frames on the street, for the equivalent of two dollars a day.

The sanctions were intended to deprive Saddam's regime of weapons and hasten its collapse. None of the well-meaning Western powers who imposed them dreamed that Saddam would still be in power a decade later, using the sanctions to stoke Iraqi resentment at the outside world while selling oil in violation of them and enriching himself and his circle. Before a 1995 referendum on his tenure, members of the ruling Baath Party visited homes, taking care to ask if households had ration cards. The implication was clear: The wrong kind of vote could mean no food. Saddam, who called himself "the indispensable leader," received 99.96 percent of the vote.

HIS NAME MEANS "THE ONE who confronts." Saddam Hussein al-Tikriti was born on April 28, 1937, in a mud hut with a roof of reeds in the village of Awja, near the north-central Iraqi city of Tikrit, a town known for its violence and merciless clan reprisals. He never knew his father, who died or perhaps disappeared before he was born. His mother persuaded a local man to leave his wife and marry her, and Saddam Hussein's official biography claimed his stepfather would greet him each morning with the exhortation "Get up, you son of a whore, and look after the sheep!" At the age of ten, he ran away from home to live with his maternal uncle, Khairallah Tulfah, in Tikrit. Tulfah, an army officer, had supported a coup against the British-backed Iraqi monarchy in 1941 and spent five years in prison. He taught Saddam to distrust foreigners and filled him with admiration for the emerging pan-Arab nationalism of Gamal Abdel Nasser of Egypt.

In 1957, at age twenty, Saddam became a junior member of the fledgling Baath Party, which had been founded in Syria in resistance to centuries of occupation of Arab lands, first by the Ottoman Empire, then by the British and French. In 1959, Saddam, strapping and sturdy at six feet two inches, was part of a team that machine-gunned the car of General Abd al-Qasim, the military leader who had overthrown the Iraqi monarchy the year before. The attack did not succeed, and Saddam fled in a dramatic tale that has inspired many embellished versions, all of which involve his digging a bullet out of his own leg' with a knife. He wound up in Cairo, where he eventually went to law school on what amounted to a stipend from the Egyptian government and supplemented his income by selling cigarettes on the street. His favored redoubt was the Andiana Restaurant, where he had a reputation as a brawler. Years later, the restaurant's owner, Hussein Abdel Meguid, would exclaim: "I couldn't believe that such a bully, who was picking fights all the time, could grow up to be president of Iraq."[4]

The Baathists briefly seized power in 1963, at last toppling Qasim, but their control did not last, and it was not until after the Arab defeat in the 1967 war with Israel that the party gained power again. Saddam quickly became one of the new regime's enforcers, eventually emerging as the effective number two to President Ahmed Hassan al-Bakr. In 1979, he called together members of the Revolutionary Command Council and hundreds of other party leaders, announcing that he had uncovered a coup plot. Some sixty party leaders were taken away to be killed as Saddam videotaped the arrests. He was now in complete control of the country, and he set about turning the Baath Party into a personality cult and a tool of terror, styling himself as a second Saladin, the twelfth-century Tikriti who had staved off the European Crusaders. In a Muslim culture that made no fuss over birthdays, he marked his own with lavish public celebrations. His visage glared from huge posters, billboards and statues, even the gold faces of commemorative watches. His favorite movies included The Godfather, a tale of dynastic leadership, and The Old Man and the Sea, the story of one man's struggle against impossible odds.

Jerrold M. Post, a psychologist who has worked for American intelligence agencies, analyzed the Iraqi leader this way: "Saddam's pursuit of power for himself and Iraq is boundless. In fact, in his mind, the destiny of Saddam Hussein and Iraq are one and indistinguishable."[5] Saddam himself told the ABC television interviewer Diane Sawyer in 1990, "Saddam Hussein is present in any quantity of milk given to a child, and is present in any clean or new jacket that an Iraqi may wear."[6]

Saddam had barely taken power when he plunged Iraq into a brutal eight-year war with neighboring Iran, one of the longest wars of the twentieth century, which killed at least a million people and wounded two million more. Terrified that the Ayatollah Ruhollah Khomeini's Islamic revolution could threaten his power and Iraq's territorial integrity, Saddam waged a vicious campaign, with the first confirmed use of poison gas in combat since World War I. The beleaguered Kurds, accused by Saddam of sympathizing with Iran, bore the brunt of his wrath, never worse than on March 16, 1988, when waves of Iraqi aircraft dropped gas canisters on the city of Halabja, spraying its 50,000 residents with a misty fog of nerve and blister agents, including sarin, tabun, mustard gas, VX nerve agent, and perhaps the biological agent aflatoxin. There is no precise tally of the dead, but estimates range from 3,200 to 7,000, with 15,000 to 20,000 more injured, many of them horribly. In 2002, in a hospital in Halabja, a Kurdish woman named Hamida Hassan shivered in the cold. A white crosshatch of skin grafts covered her collarbone and shoulders; her breasts and stomach were twisted and scarred to her waist. "I am just a woman, no one will believe my words. But if you see my body, you will know whether Saddam Hussein has chemical weapons or not."

AT THE HEART OF BUSH'S warning to Congress was the fear that terrorists armed with weapons of mass destruction could mount an attack that would dwarf those on the World Trade Center and Pentagon. Far less clear—to the public and even to America's intelligence agencies— was just what sort of weapons Saddam Hussein still had, and just what ties his regime had, if any, to Al Qaeda or other shadowy groups that could cause imminent harm to Americans. Throughout the 1990s, United Nations weapons inspectors had destroyed 38,500 prohibited chemical warheads and millions of liters of chemical agents. In 1995

Iraq admitted producing large volumes of weapons-grade biological material, but inspectors never located this stockpile, which Iraq claimed to have destroyed. Iraq also claimed to have eliminated, of its own volition, 30,000 more chemical weapons and tons of chemical agents, but the inspectors could never verify that fact, either. The United States and Britain officially considered all such material as missing or "unaccounted for," while Iraq insisted it was gone. The inspectors believed that Iraq retained at least 157 aerial bombs and 25 missile warheads filled with germ agents, along with spraying equipment, and equipment to produce and dry germ agents—all claims that Iraq denied.[7]

Khidhir Abdul Abas Hamza, a longtime Iraqi nuclear scientist who defected in the 1990s and published a book called *Saddam's Bombmaker* in 2000, asserted that Saddam had personally directed the country's nuclear program from its inception (for ostensibly peaceful purposes) in 1971, and that by the eve of the Persian Gulf war twenty years later, Iraq had completed all the research and testing needed for an atomic weapon and was trying to make at least one crude bomb using uranium from civilian reactors. In June 1981, Israeli warplanes had destroyed a French-built nuclear reactor at Osirak, outside Baghdad, just weeks before it was to become operational. The plant had been a key to Saddam's illicit nuclear weapons program, and he responded to its destruction by demanding a redoubling of the effort, with new facilities to be built in multiple, heavily fortified locations that could be camouflaged.[8] Hamza said the effort could have produced a bomb in a few months, but was disrupted by the allied bombing campaign in Operation Desert Storm. That was sobering news to American officials, whose worst-case assessments had not envisioned Saddam as being so close to having a bomb. Hamza said that his colleagues had been lavishly rewarded for research successes and tortured by Saddam's secret police when they failed to deliver. Some experts questioned Hamza's accounts, suggesting his credibility had been colored by his strong anti-Saddam views, but despite Hamza's defection, the widely held assumption was that other Iraqi scientists had, at the very least, retained existing nuclear research and plans. Indeed, by the late 1990s, the consensus was that all Iraq lacked to make a nuclear bomb was fissile material, and it was unclear how far

Baghdad had gone toward producing centrifuges needed to process weapons-grade uranium.

In 1998, Iraq ordered half a dozen lithotripters, state-of-the-art machines used for pulverizing kidney stones without surgery—equipment it could purchase because the United Nations sanctions left an exemption for medical supplies. But in addition to the machines, Iraq also wanted 120 extra switches—far more than it would ever need as spare parts. Gary Milhollin, director of the Wisconsin Project, an American arms control research group, noted that the switches could also be used to detonate an atomic bomb.[9]

There were ample signs that, at a minimum, Saddam was trying to replenish his stockpile of prohibited biological and chemical weapons. In an August 2000 report to Congress, the CIA said that Iraq was continuing to rebuild former dual-use chemical and biological plants, including one that Iraq claimed was making castor oil for brake fluid. Castor beans also contain ricin, a toxic biological agent, and in the same report, the CIA warned that Iraq was also developing unmanned aerial vehicles that could be used to disseminate such agents. By not cooperating with the international inspectors, Saddam showed every indication that he had something to hide, and he paid a substantial price for his intransigence: Had inspectors been able to verify that Iraq had met its obligations to disarm, which would have caused the embargo to be lifted, Saddam might have reaped between $130 and $180 billion in oil revenues in the 1990s.[10] Though Saddam was not known to have used chemical or biological weapons against American forces in the Persian Gulf war, the consensus among military analysts was that he believed the mere threat of their use had helped deter the United States and its allies from marching on Baghdad and thus threatening his regime.

The problem was that no one could be sure what weapons Saddam still had, or how close he might be to getting more. Senior Bush administration officials like Vice President Cheney often complained about the ineffectiveness of UN inspections, but however incomplete the inspections might have been, the truth was that the presence of inspectors had forced Iraq to keep moving suspect equipment around, under the watchful gaze of American spy satellites. After the inspectors left the country in frustration in December 1998 (in anticipation of punitive American and British air strikes), "it was like losing your GPS guidance," in the words of one Pentagon official, referring to the military's navigational satellite system. For the next three years, the CIA and other intelligence agencies were essentially blinded, reduced to interpreting whatever new slivers of information they could glean about Iraq through the prism of what they had known when the inspectors left. The situation amounted to replacing sophisticated satellite guidance with old-fashioned dead-reckoning, and every scrap of information was seized on for whatever it might suggest.

But conclusions drawn from raw intelligence data, especially fragmentary data, are very often a reflection of the worldview and mindset of the people reviewing that information, and in the days and weeks after the September 11 attacks, many senior members of the Bush administration saw Iraqi actions through a prism of Saddam's history of misdeeds and malign intentions.

By all accounts, the administration was quick to suspect a possible link between Iraq and the anthrax attacks that had shaken the nation in the fall of 2001. Shortly after the death of the first anthrax victim, the administration ordered an intense, secret investigation to explore any possible link to Iraq, and continued to do so even after scientists determined that the form of anthrax sent through the mail was an American strain of the germ. Scientists scoured samples of the powder for signs of additives that would point to Iraq; they investigated whether Baghdad had somehow obtained samples of the so-called Ames strain of anthrax; they reviewed records from a United Nations investigation of Iraq's biological arms program in the 1990s. "We looked for any shred of evidence that would bear on this," one senior intelligence official said in late 2001. "It's just not there."

Evidence of an Iraqi link to the Al Qaeda attacks was equally hard to come by, the strong suspicions of Wolfowitz and others notwithstanding. In late October 2001, barely six weeks after the September 11 attacks, the Czech interior minister set off an international furor when he said that an Iraqi intelligence officer had met in Prague with Mohammed Atta, the suspected mastermind of the attacks, just five months before the hijackings. That raised fresh questions about whether Iraq's foreign intelligence service had established secret ties to Al Qaeda. But by December, Czech and American officials backed off, saying that the diplomat was a minor functionary who happened to have the same last name as a more senior Iraqi intelligence agent, and that he might have met with a different Mohammed Atta, or even with someone who simply looked like the hijacker. "There was definitely one meeting," one intelligence official in Washington said. "We don't know if it was significant. We certainly don't attribute to it the significance others attribute to it automatically. Just because there was a meeting doesn't mean it was connected to 9/11."

In his public statements that fall, Bush himself never claimed that there was a direct connection between Saddam Hussein and Al Qaeda. But he was already beginning to direct public attention to the Iraqi leader. In a prime-time news conference on October 11, he said of Saddam, "We're watching him very carefully," and in an interview with *Newsweek* in November, he described Saddam as "evil."

Bush's aides would later profess surprise that the president's characterization of the "axis of evil" had been the universal headline from his State of the Union speech, but it was clear that the phrase had taken hold. Just two weeks after Bush's clarion call, the most reluctant warrior on his team left little doubt that the administration was vigorously pursuing its new hard line. Peppered with questions by the Senate Budget Committee about the meaning of the president's words, Colin Powell for the first time drew a sharp distinction between the administration's outlook on Iran and North Korea and its attitude toward Iraq.

"With respect to Iran and with respect to North Korea, there is no plan to start a war with these nations," the secretary said. "With respect to Iraq, it has long been, for several years now, a policy of the United States government that regime change would be in the best interests of the region, the best interests of the Iraqi people, and we are looking at a variety of options that would bring that about." Powell knew his words would carry special weight, because in the preceding months he had expressed doubts about the wisdom of a second war in the Persian Gulf. So he used a nonurgent time element to make his point. The president, he said, "does not have a recommendation before him that would involve an armed conflict tomorrow." But it was becoming apparent that the day after tomorrow was coming.

Chapter 3

THE BUSH DOCTRINE

Camp Doha, Kuwait
Sunday, June 9, 2002

The cement and steel buildings of the desert military base were the same dusty shade as the sands that stretched under the summer sky, just thirty-five miles south of the Iraqi border. A thousand American troops had left the 110-degree heat of the day for a rally with Defense Secretary Donald Rumsfeld inside the cool base gym. "The global war on terrorism began in Afghanistan, to be sure, but it will not end there," Rumsfeld told the cheering troops. "It will not end until terrorist networks have been rooted out from wherever they exist. And it will not end until state sponsors of terror are made to understand that abetting terrorism is unacceptable, and will have deadly consequences for the regimes that do." Rumsfeld was beginning a tour of three crucial American allies in the Persian Gulf, to thank Kuwait, Bahrain and Qatar for their assistance and basing rights in the recent Afghanistan campaign.

But like the neighbor at a summer picnic who dominates discussion by his absence, Saddam Hussein was the unspoken topic of conversation. After all, Camp Doha was full of Abrams tanks, Bradley fighting vehicles and Patriot air-defense batteries, and the troops Rumsfeld addressed that day were among 8,000 American forces already stationed in the tiny emirate of Kuwait, including F-15 and F-16 flight crews who daily enforced the northern and southern no-fly zones in Iraqi skies. The Iraqi army's daily newspaper, *Al Qadissiya,* said Rumseld's trip was to promote "evil intentions toward Iraq."

"I am not going to get into the subject of an attack on Iraq," Rumsfeld told the reporters traveling with him. Before the secretary's party landed, a defense official said: "We're not at the stage where we're soliciting allies or something like that." But it was well known that Rumsfeld did not especially like to travel and his stops in the Gulf were no accident.

Even as Rumsfeld toured the Gulf, Secretary of State Powell was addressing members of the Asia Society in Manhattan on new opportunities for the United States. "All of my adult life was spent as a soldier preparing for a war with the Soviet Union, a war that, thank God, never came," Powell said. Now, he said, he saw a world transformed: Former adversaries like Russia and China were engaged in cooperative relationships with Washington and countries around the world were working "to advance global well-being on an unprecedented scale by freeing ordinary people to pursue their hopes and their dreams." It had been a hectic, mixed bag of a spring for Powell. He had overseen negotiation of the final details of a new arms control agreement with Russia—one he had prodded Bush to formalize in a treaty—and had attended the signing in the Kremlin. He had kept up pressure on India and Pakistan to defuse their standoff over the disputed Kashmir region, and was off that week to a meeting of foreign ministers from the eight leading industrial nations to talk about antiterrorism cooperation, Afghan reconstruction and the topic that occupied most of his time: the bitter Israeli-Palestinian conflict.

In April, violence in the Middle East had exploded in the wake of months of Palestinian suicide bomb attacks on Israel and the Sharon government's harsh reprisals and military occupation of large swaths of the West Bank and Gaza, which had been under virtual siege. After close to a year on the sidelines, President Bush had dispatched Powell to the region for ten days in April, in hopes of brokering some kind of tentative cease-fire. No sooner had Powell arrived in Jerusalem than another bomb went off in a crowded market in the city, and he warned the Palestinian leader, Yasir Arafat, that no progress was possible as long as violence continued. The administration had been moved to act in the Middle East for a number of reasons, perhaps none more important than the realization that building support for a war with Iraq would be more difficult as long as violence raged in Israel and the Palestinian territories. Saudi Arabia, Egypt and Jordan, the Arab states friendliest to Washington, had all made it clear that they would be hard-pressed to offer public support or military cooperation for any war on Iraq with their own populations outraged at near-daily scenes of Palestinian bloodshed.

Moreover, America's closest European allies, including British prime minister Tony Blair, pressed the Bush team to get more involved. In May, Powell had announced plans for a peace conference sometime in the summer, jointly sponsored by the United States, the European Union, Russia and the United Nations. But the words were barely out of his mouth before a senior White House official took pains to play down the planned session as only a "ministerial meeting," not a conference.

So the administration edged into a long hot summer, as the State Department, under Powell, tried to move toward peaceful resolutions through cooperation with allies, while the Defense Department, under Rumsfeld, sought just as vigorously to lay the groundwork for a war with Iraq, regardless of diplomatic niceties. Disputes between the State and Defense Departments are an old Washington story. As a military aide to Defense Secretary Caspar Weinberger in the Reagan years, Powell had been on the other side in Weinberger's struggles with George Shultz's State Department. But this was something different.

"The dilemma here is that these aren't just personal disagreements bred out of ambition and strong personality," said Richard C. Holbrooke, a veteran diplomat and former U.S. ambassador to the United Nations. "These are deep, philosophical differences between two very different views of America in the world. One is a traditional conservative view; the other is a radical break with fifty-five years of a bipartisan tradition that sought international agreements and regimes of benefit to us."

No two people in the capital better exemplified the polarizing tensions than President Bush's two senior cabinet officers themselves.

ONE WAS A FOUR-STAR general, twice wounded in Vietnam, a graduate of New York's City College and the first African-American ever to become national security adviser, chairman of the Joint Chiefs of Staff and secretary of state. The other was a peacetime naval aviator who never saw combat, captain of the wrestling team at Princeton, a congressman, White House chief of staff and corporate executive who became both the youngest and oldest secretary of defense in American history, the only man ever to hold the job twice. One was beloved by the rank-and-file career diplomats of the State Department, who believed he treated them with the professional respect they craved. The other was the frequent scourge of the Pentagon's uniformed commanders, many of whom resisted and resented the brusque management style they called "the wire brush treatment." The outlooks and worldviews of Colin Luther Powell and Donald Harold Rumsfeld were as different as their resumes.

The two men were close in age that summer: Powell was sixty-five and Rumsfeld seventy. By many measures, they enjoyed comparable stature as veteran players who had held multiple posts in Republican foreign policy and Washington power circles, and both had grown rich—Powell on the lecture circuit and through corporate boards, Rumsfeld as a top executive with G. D. Searle & Co. and General Instrument Corp. If Powell basked in worldwide public opinion polls that gave him the highest approval ratings of any American public official, Rumsfeld, too, had drawn high praise for his star turn as the public face of the successful military campaign against the Taliban.

But there was also, in the Powell-Rumsfeld equation, a lingering imbalance—one that did not favor Powell. Perhaps it was that when the two men first met in the 1970s, Rumsfeld was already serving his first tour as secretary of defense and Powell was just a lean young colonel in command at Fort Campbell, Kentucky, and Rumsfeld had never stopped thinking of him as a subordinate. Perhaps it was that Powell, who had so loyally served Bush's father, had a hard time connecting on a personal level with the second President Bush. Perhaps it was simply that Rumsfeld's cold-eyed views on topics from the Middle East peace process to Iraq were often closer to Bush's instinctual bold approach than Powell's innate caution was. In public, Powell and Rumsfeld insisted that their relationship was one of mutual respect, without acrimony. "There are always differences," Powell once said. "A president is well served by differences." But some of their key aides were openly hostile to one another, and Rumsfeld seemed to think nothing of popping off on nominally diplomatic topics, from the Israeli-Palestinian conflict to relations with longtime allies, while Powell was widely assumed to have frequent back-channel communications to senior commanders in the Pentagon who had served under him.

Powell was a past master at bureaucratic infighting and self-preservation. He had spent the vast bulk of his military career devising skillful, methodical, effective means of carrying out broad policies set by others, and was faulted even by many of his admirers for lacking an overall strategic vision. Seared by the experience of Vietnam, when politicians and military planners lost public support for a war by seeming to lack clear goals or a willingness to use all-out measures, Powell came to believe as a commander that military force should be used only after political objectives had been clearly established, and should then be applied overwhelmingly. This view had come to be known as the Powell Doctrine, and Powell hewed to it still. He believed reflexively in the value of longtime alliances like NATO, which had helped keep the peace in Europe for the half century after World War II. He liked to say that Saddam Hussein had "been a pain in my butt for twelve years," but was just as quick to list all the complications of trying to remove him by force.

By contrast, Rumsfeld described himself as "not into this detail stuff—I'm more concepty." He, too, was a skilled bureaucrat, but he was full of broad theories and strategic visions, from the need for an effective missile defense system to the conviction that the twenty-first-century military should be prepared to fight in novel ways, with lighter, more flexible forces and "floating coalitions" that might change with circumstances. He believed the Powell Doctrine was outmoded in a world of global positioning devices and other high-tech tools of war. As a former ambassador to NATO, he was skeptical about Western Europe's defense capacity and its willingness to spend money on necessary military modernization and interoperability of forces. His favored phrase of dismissal was "I have a minimum of high regard for . . ." and he did not hesitate to use it.

Over the years, both men had devised well-publicized sets of personal rules, maxims collected in the trenches of public life that summed up their leadership philosophies. Powell's rules, begun as slips of paper tucked under the glass top of his desk, ran the upbeat gamut from "It ain't as bad as you think—it will look better in the morning" through "Remain calm; be kind" to "Perpetual optimism is a force multiplier." Rumsfeld's collection was far larger, numbering more than 150; he had first put them together in 1974 and copyrighted them in 1980, last revising them on September 10, 2001, the day before the Pentagon was attacked. Grouped by topic from "Serving in the White House" to "Politics, Congress and the Press," they were sometimes original and sometimes the thoughts of others, ranging from "It's easier to get into something than to get out of it" to "When you're skiing, if you're not falling, you're not trying" to one of his favorites: "If a problem cannot be solved, enlarge it," coined by no less a military leader than Dwight D. Eisenhower. It was that spirit that motivated Rumsfeld on the morning of September 11, when American Airlines Flight 77 slammed into his building. The defense secretary's immediate reaction, according to notes taken by aides with him that day, was swift: "Best info fast. Judge whether good enough hit S.H. at same time"—meaning Saddam Hussein—"not only OBL," Rumsfeld's shorthand for Osama bin Laden. "Go massive. Sweep it all up. Things related and not."[1]

Ten months later, Rumsfeld's first-day instincts had hardened into a conviction that the next battle in the war on terrorism should come in Iraq. But fixing the precise moment at which President Bush himself decided that Saddam would have to be removed by force is more difficult. In March 2002, according to one report, the president stuck his head into a White House meeting on Iraq that Condoleezza Rice was having with some senators, and blurted out: "Fuck Saddam. We're taking him out."[2] By April, senior Pentagon and White House aides were letting it be known that plans were being sketched out for a possible major air campaign and land invasion, probably in early 2003, allowing time to create the right military, economic and diplomatic conditions.

In his State of the Union message, Bush had suggested that the Cold War doctrines of containment and deterrence were irrelevant in a world where the only strategy for defeating America's new enemies was to strike first. In a commencement speech at West Point on June 1, he was even more explicit. "If we wait for threats to fully materialize, we will have waited too long," Bush told the long gray lines of white-gloved cadets. "We must take the battle to the enemy, disrupt his plans, and confront the worst threats before they emerge."

The philosophy that Bush outlined was new enough to be called radical. The United States had long seen itself as a nation that did not go looking for trouble in the world, but met aggression when it came. (America "goes not abroad, in search of monsters to destroy,"

in the words of John Quincy Adams.)³ From Pearl Harbor to the first
Persian Gulf war to Afghanistan, Washington had always responded to
attacks, not launched them first. Now Bush declared, "The only path
to safety is the path of action. And this nation will act." He did not
mention Iraq by name but warned that "even weak states and small
groups could attain a catastrophic power to strike great nations." He
said that in defending the peace, "we face a threat with no precedent."

Bush directed his top national security aides to turn this doctrine
of preemptive action against states and terrorist groups trying to
develop weapons of mass destruction into the foundation of a broad
new national security strategy. His advisers sought to find precedents,
and argued that Bush's approach echoed John F. Kennedy's naval
quarantine of Cuba during the 1962 missile crisis with the Soviet
Union. "It really means early action of some kind," Condoleezza Rice
said. "It means forestalling certain destructive acts against you by an
adversary." There would be times, she said, "when you can't wait to
be attacked to respond."

By the time the new strategy was formally published on September 20, the sweeping breadth of its break with the past would be even
more apparent. Where the Clinton administration, in 1999, had simply said, "We must always be prepared to act alone when that is our
most advantageous course," the Bush Doctrine declared, "We will not
hesitate to act alone, if necessary." Where the Clinton administration
had argued that "arms control and non-proliferation are an essential
element of our national security strategy," the Bush document held
that non-proliferation agreements had failed and Iran, Iraq and North
Korea had obtained weapons of mass destruction anyway. It added:
"We must deter and defend against the threat before it is unleashed."
Where the Clinton strategy said that fighting and winning wars "in
two distant theaters in overlapping time frames" should be the hall-
mark of military preparedness, the Bush policy was much more sweeping in its ambitions: "Our forces will be strong enough to dissuade
potential adversaries from pursuing a military build-up in hopes of
surpassing, or equaling, the power of the United States." That last
point sounded like nothing so much as a reprise of the 1992 draft
preparedness document from Wolfowitz's shop that had been dismissed by the first Bush administration as too bellicose.

Now, ten years later, the new strategy unleashed a fierce debate in policy and political circles. Powell, among others, tried to play down its significance. Preemption had always been an option in the American arsenal, he insisted, and indeed, in the diplomatic and economic realm, forceful preemptive action had long been a major tool of policy, from the Marshall Plan in Europe after World War II to the Clinton administration's threats aimed at forcing North Korea to freeze its nuclear program in the mid-1990s. "We saw it as an important and legitimate arrow in the quiver," said Ashton B. Carter, a former assistant secretary of defense in the Clinton administration. "But when one talks about doctrines and so on, it implies that it's a preferred course." Some old Kennedy hands emphatically rejected comparisons with the Cuban missile crisis. "A preemptive strike is one that he considered," said Theodore C. Sorensen, Kennedy's special counsel. "But he also considered the innocent lives that would be lost, the international laws that would be broken, and the allies and friends around the world who would be disaffected—as any thoughtful president would."

There was little doubt that Iraq would be the first test of the Bush Doctrine, and that, too, prompted worldwide debate about the wisdom of any such effort, and its legitimacy under international law. Senator Joseph R. Biden, a Democrat from Delaware, said, "Constitutionally, the president has the right to act preemptively," but questioned how one could judge whether a country with nuclear, chemical or biological weapons had the intent to use them. "For example," he said, "the Chinese have a capacity. Does the president have the right to preemptively go strike the Chinese, the Communist regime? The answer's no."

Meantime, talks in Vienna aimed at negotiating the return of United Nations weapons inspectors to Iraq for the first time since 1998 broke down in early July. Even the Kurds of northern Iraq, who would have had much to gain from toppling Saddam and would be crucial American allies in any attack, expressed strong reservations. They had not forgotten that they had risen up against Saddam Hussein after his defeat in the 1991 war, with the apparent encouragement of the first President Bush, only to be brutally suppressed by Saddam and his troops. American forces had not intervened as thousands of

Kurds were killed. From their strongholds in the north, where they had enjoyed de facto autonomy for a decade, rival Kurdish leaders who agreed on little else said flatly that they would be reluctant to join any American military operation that put Kurds at risk of any offensive of the kind they had suffered at Saddam's hands.

THERE WAS INTENSE DEBATE MUCH closer to home. On Sunday, August 4, former national security adviser Brent Scowcroft, one of Rice's mentors and a close Bush family friend, appeared on the CBS News program *Face the Nation* to warn that an invasion of Iraq "could turn the whole region into a cauldron, and thus destroy the war on terrorism."

Powell called to thank Scowcroft for taking a stand against rushing into war. Eleven days later, Scowcroft spoke out even more forcefully in an Op-Ed piece in *The Wall Street Journal* headlined "Don't Attack Saddam." While noting that Saddam's desire to dominate the Persian Gulf posed clear threats to U.S. interests, Scowcroft said, "There is scant evidence to tie Saddam to terrorist organizations, and even less to the September 11 attacks. Indeed, Saddam's goals have little in common with the terrorists who threaten us, and there is little incentive for him to make common cause with them." He went on to warn, "There is a virtual consensus in the world against an attack on Iraq at this time. So long as that sentiment persists, it would require the U.S. to pursue a virtual go-it-alone strategy against Iraq, making any military operations correspondingly more difficult and expensive." At a minimum, Scowcroft said, Washington should be pressing the UN Security Council to insist on resuming weapons inspections in Iraq on a no-notice basis—anytime, anywhere, without permission.[4]

With Bush on vacation at his ranch near Crawford, Texas, and senior administration officials largely silent on Iraq, Scowcroft's comments landed like a bombshell in Washington's summer doldrums. Former secretary of state Lawrence Eagleburger, who had also served the elder Bush, issued similar warnings. Even Henry Kissinger, the grand old man of Republican realpolitik, wrote a long, complex article in *The Washington Post,* in which he offered support for Bush's goal of "bringing matters to a head with Iraq" and endorsed the imperative for preemption. But Kissinger also noted that doing so would upend long-settled notions, and he argued that the administration should act carefully to build public, congressional and international support.[5] Powell, who was himself struggling to articulate the case against Iraq in a way that would build maximum international support, could not tell where Kissinger stood, but the two men talked about it at the State Department that week.

For his part, Bush, speaking to reporters at his ranch on August 16, insisted, "I am aware that some very intelligent people are expressing their opinions about Saddam Hussein and Iraq. I listen very carefully to what they have to say."

IN FACT, THE PRESIDENT HAD been listening a lot lately. While the debate was playing out in public, the president and his top national security advisers were engaged in equally intense, secret discussions about what to do next. The sessions were considered so sensitive that the word *Iraq* never even appeared on the private schedules of those attending. Instead, the gatherings were listed under the heading "Regional Strategies Meeting."

After months of largely ceding discussions of Iraq strategy to Rumsfeld and his colleagues at the Pentagon, Colin Powell had decided it was time for him to weigh in. At the beginning of August, on his way back from meetings with Southeast Asian leaders, Powell had begun jotting down notes. Powell took pains, as a former general, not to meddle in military matters, but now he realized that the administration's discussions on Iraq had reached a critical point. The Pentagon was leaking details of possible invasion plans and the president was getting very engaged in those details. But Powell felt that no one had yet taken pains to lay out the whole picture for Bush, to talk about the diplomatic possibilities and pitfalls, as well as the military realities.

So on August 5, the day after Scowcroft's *Face the Nation* appearance, Powell had dinner with Bush and Rice in the White House family dining room. They ate quickly, then adjourned to the president's private office in the residence upstairs. Powell wanted to make sure that Bush understood the implications of action in Iraq—"We'd own a country," he told the president. He also made the case that building international support would be absolutely essential, not only to legitimize any war in the eyes of the world, but also to lay the groundwork for the postwar reconstruction of Iraq. Bush listened closely. What were the alternatives? he asked. Powell told the president it was just possible that Iraq could be induced to comply with the raft of more than a dozen UN resolutions that had been passed since the end of the Persian Gulf war and disarm. Bush said he wanted to think about it.[6]

Nine days later, on August 14, the top national security team, meeting without the president, agreed that it would be a smart move to put pressure on the United Nations to act, to frame the Iraq debate as a failure of the international community to enforce its existing resolutions on disarmament. Even Vice President Cheney, by this point perhaps the most skeptical that war could be avoided, agreed.

Two days later, the same day that Bush told the reporters in Crawford that his ears were open to debate, he and his advisers held a secure videoconference. Powell spoke up. He told his colleagues that he believed they had to take the matter to the United Nations, to build a legal basis for war and to get support from Britain, the one ally that was most willing to help militarily. But Powell warned, "If you take it to the United Nations then you are taking it down a road that will fork. There could be a peaceful solution." Tough new weapons inspections might achieve the goal of Iraqi disarmament, or they might lead to war. The president agreed that he would make his case to the United Nations on his trip to New York the following month to commemorate the first anniversary of the September 11 attacks. It would be a dramatic week, in which the president would turn the nation from the war against the Taliban and the hunt for Osama bin Laden toward his new target.

Powell assumed the question was settled and headed for a brief vacation on Long Island. On August 26, Powell's phone rang. Word came from Washington that Cheney was to make a speech on Iraq that day to the Veterans of Foreign Wars. Rice's office had just got the text. Powell sensed that his day would be spoiled. Hours later, Cheney told the VFW that the world had learned more about Saddam's weapons programs from defectors than it ever had from inspectors. "A return of inspectors would provide no assurance whatsoever of his compliance with UN resolutions," Cheney said. "On the contrary, there is a great danger that it would provide false comfort that Saddam was somehow back in his box."

Powell was stunned. He knew that Cheney's words would send skeptical Arab countries "into the Twilight Zone." Moreover, Bush had already settled on going to the UN and urging the resumption of inspections as a test of Iraq's willingness to comply—and as a test of the world's determination to hold Saddam to account. But the president had so far said nothing in public about that idea. Cheney may have simply been reflecting his own deep skepticism about the usefulness of inspections, but in capitals around the world, the vice president's words seemed certain and dramatic proof that Washington was determined to go to war—alone if necessary.

Cheney's words carried more weight than those of previous vice presidents, because of the unusual stature he brought to the office. Cheney had been a trusted friend and aide of the first President Bush, and his experience at the highest levels of government dated back nearly thirty years, to his days as President Gerald R. Ford's chief of staff in the mid-1970s—a job he had inherited from Donald Rumsfeld. Though just sixty-one in 2002, Cheney was gray and balding and seemed older than his years. In a capital that had become used to the moist confessional politics of the Clinton era, Cheney sometimes seemed a dry and bracing reminder of an earlier time, a never-complain, never-explain politician who reminded many of the younger officials and journalists who came to know him of their fathers.

As a congressman from Wyoming in the 1980s, Cheney had a solid conservative voting record—to the right of the fiery Newt Gingrich, who would later become Speaker of the House—but a manner so low-key and laconic that he seldom seemed threatening to colleagues on either side of the aisle. "What's remarkable is how unremarkable Dick is," Senator Jon Kyl of Arizona, a fellow Republican, once said. "He always comes across as the person in charge. He's so competent, calm and thorough." In 2000, George W. Bush, admiring those qualities, had chosen Cheney to lead the search for a vice presidential nominee—and wound up choosing Cheney himself as his running mate. The vice president had since become a crucial adviser, meeting regularly and privately with Bush, seldom revealing what they talked about. In larger meetings, Cheney tended to keep his own

counsel, so no one could ever be quite sure where he stood. But he—
and his large and active staff—were widely understood to play a central role in reviewing almost every issue.

As a former House Republican whip, or chief vote counter, Cheney
knew Capitol Hill, and could be counted on to lobby his former
colleagues on issues from taxes to domestic security. Since the September 11 attacks, Cheney and Bush had taken special pains to pre-
serve the continuity of government in the event of another surprise
attack, and Cheney had spent a good deal of time working from secret
locations outside the White House. His critics suggested he func-
tioned as a kind of prime minister for the comparatively inexperienced
president, but his champions saw him as a wise and even-keeled counselor—"a combination of both thinker and doer," Rumsfeld called
him. No one underestimated his importance.

Rice reined Cheney in a bit in a lengthy conversation after his
VFW speech, and he made a second, milder speech on the same topic
a couple of days later. But the vice president's skepticism that Saddam
would ever come clean was deep and abiding, and his view of the
threats abounding in the post–September 11 world was dark. From
the moment the planes hit the World Trade Center and the Pentagon,
Cheney had used his special influence to argue forcefully that the
United States would have to do business differently in the world from
now on. In 1991, Cheney had backed the decision to end the Persian
Gulf war without deposing Saddam Hussein, but the fight against
global terrorism was a new kind of struggle that would require new
attitudes from American leaders. Taliban and Al Qaeda fighters who
were captured in Afghanistan would not be traditional prisoners of
war, but "enemy combatants," entitled to fewer legal rights. Cheney
saw Saddam in that same way, as deserving no quarter. If Paul Wolfowitz was the administration's optimistic foreign policy conservative,
firm in his belief about the democratic potential of Iraq, Cheney was
its reigning pessimist, with one simple goal: to stop Saddam once and
for all.

A decade earlier, when Cheney was secretary of defense and Powell
the chairman of the Joint Chiefs, they had tangled—good-naturedly,
but with an edge. Once, when Powell had proposed to deactivate
thousands of small, artillery-fired nuclear weapons in Europe and elsewhere, Cheney told him that not a single top civilian policy aide

favored such a move. In his best-selling memoir, *My American Journey,* Powell recounted that he had replied, jokingly, "That's because they're all right-wing nuts like you!"[7]

Now the two men fought again, this time bitterly, over competing views of the world. Powell believed that the United States had to seek maximum international support for war, and that the president would have to ask the United Nations to pass a new resolution, enforcing its demands on Iraq. Cheney was extremely skeptical. He thought there was nothing wrong with looking out for one's own interests. To him, Bush's image abroad as a cowboy was not all bad: America need not apologize for being a great power, nor hesitate to use its might for right. That fall, the vice president would relish reading *An Autumn of War,* a new book on the meaning of the September 11 attacks by the military historian Victor Davis Hanson, who cited the Greeks to argue that war is "terrible but innate to civilization—and not always unjust or amoral if it is waged for good causes to destroy evil and save the innocent."[8] To Cheney, going it alone was far preferable to simply going along.

Until the moment it was time for Bush to leave for New York, the arguments went on. Powell was not sure of the outcome.[9]

"We cannot know all that lies ahead," Bush said from a windswept Ellis Island on the night of September 11, 2002, the Statue of Liberty aglow behind him in New York Harbor, a towering, silent witness to the changed Lower Manhattan skyline, where Ground Zero still gaped. "Yet, we do know that God has placed us together in this moment, to grieve together, to stand together, to serve each other and our country. And the duty we have been given—defending America and our freedom—is also a privilege we share. We're prepared for this journey. And our prayer tonight is that God will see us through, and keep us worthy."

Chapter 4

RESOLUTION 1441

New York City
Thursday, September 12, 2002

Colin Powell sat in the soaring General Assembly chamber of the United Nations, listening intently to his boss address the world. Artillery fire had destroyed Powell's high-frequency hearing years ago, and he often used translator's earphones to help him understand even English speakers in cavernous halls like this. This morning he was waiting especially to hear a single sentence from George W. Bush: a demand that the United Nations act against Iraq for defying its own resolutions. "The conduct of the Iraqi regime is a threat to the authority of the United Nations and a threat to peace," Bush declared. "Iraq has answered a decade of UN demands with a decade of defiance. All the world now faces a test and the United Nations a difficult and defining moment. Are Security Council resolutions to be honored and enforced, or cast aside without consequence? Will the United Nations serve the purpose of its founding, or will it be irrelevant?"

For Powell, it had been a long, arduous trip to this moment in the American delegate's seat. The president had taken his advice, and was pledging to work with the international community. "My nation will work with the UN Security Council to meet our common challenge," Bush told the listening delegates. "If Iraq's regime defies us again, the world must move deliberately, decisively, to hold Iraq to account." Then Powell's heart stopped. The president's speech had been through so many drafts that the final wording—about a new resolution—did not make it into the prepared text that was unspooling on the teleprompter. Powell could not imagine what had happened. Had Bush decided not to seek a new resolution after all? Had Vice President Cheney changed the president's mind? Then Bush, who realized the wording was missing, ad-libbed: "We will work with the UN Security Council for the necessary resolutions."[1]

Powell was relieved, and the United Nations was all but ecstatic. Only the night before, Secretary-General Kofi Annan was concerned enough about being overshadowed by Bush's planned speech that he took the unusual step of releasing his own text preemptively. "I stand before you today as a multilateralist, by precedent, by principle, by charter and by duty," Annan had said. He warned that "when states decide to use force to deal with broader threats to international peace and security, there is no substitute for the unique legitimacy provided by the United Nations." Now Bush had agreed, and announced in the same breath that the United States would rejoin UNESCO, the United Nations' educational and cultural organization, from which the Reagan administration had withdrawn two decades earlier, on grounds that the group espoused anti-American values. "We knew it was a home run right away," one American official said of the president's speech. "I almost want to use the word *glee* to describe the reaction. The diplomats were saying that we saved the United Nations."

But Bush had also left no illusions about his willingness to go it alone if necessary. "The purposes of the United States should not be doubted," he had warned. "The Security Council resolutions will be enforced. The just demands of peace and security will be met, or action will be unavoidable. And a regime that has lost its legitimacy will also lose its power." His words had a galvanic effect. Within days, the Saudi foreign minister, Prince Saud al-Faisal, indicated that his country would be willing to let Washington use its bases for a United Nations–backed attack on Iraq, an apparent softening of the kingdom's resistance. In a series of weekend meetings and telephone conversations, Arab foreign ministers warned Iraq that it had to let the inspectors return or "you are getting a strike," as one of them put it.

Not everyone was enthusiastic about the American initiative. In Germany, Chancellor Gerhard Schröder was engaged in a reelection campaign in which anti-Americanism had emerged as a prominent theme, and he repeated his opposition to any war in Iraq. "We need more peace, not more war," he said. "And that's why, under my leadership, Germany will not participate." In France, the newly reelected President Jacques Chirac was struggling to reposition his country, America's oldest but often fractious and critical ally, in a new kind of transatlantic partnership in which Paris would seek expanded influence. Chirac's government welcomed Bush's speech to the UN, but strongly favored its own approach, which was to focus first on a new resolution on weapons inspections and only then on a second resolution that would threaten consequences. "We cannot go for two hares at the same time," said the French foreign minister, Dominique de Villepin. "We should look for one and we get one. If we look for two, we won't catch any one."

Behind the scenes, Annan was working with Arab foreign ministers and Iraqi representatives to help draft Iraq's reply. Late on the afternoon of September 16, Annan stepped to the floodlit microphones at the UN to announce that Iraq would accept the return of weapons inspectors "without conditions." Blocks away, in his suite at the Waldorf-Astoria, Powell interrupted a meeting with the Egyptian foreign minister to read the Iraqi offer, which was not as unconditional as Annan had suggested. Iraq did not promise to disarm, or to disclose the state of its weapons programs, or even to allow "unfettered inspections," a term of art that meant "anytime, anyplace, anywhere," including presidential compounds and palaces. "This is a tactical step by Iraq in hopes of avoiding strong UN Security Council action," said a White House spokesman, Scott McClellan. "As such, it is a tactic that will fail."

It was a moment that quickly came to define the differences between Washington and most other members of the Security Council. The Bush administration saw Iraq's offer of conditioned cooperation as the worst kind of trap, one that would cause yet another round of diplomatic wrangling and inconclusive results. The French and others saw the Iraqi offer as a sign of progress, a signal that war might yet be avoided through a new program of inspections and disarmament. The multilateral euphoria had lasted five days.

AS THE EVENTS OF THE autumn began to unfold, Bush had one stalwart ally: Tony Blair. A year earlier, in the immediate aftermath of the September 11 attacks, Blair had helped buttress America's case against Osama bin Laden by releasing an extensive British intelligence dossier. In recent months, his warnings about the dangers of Saddam Hussein had been almost as frequent and vociferous as Bush's. Blair had one big skill that appealed to Americans: force and fluidity in his mother tongue—a fluency that often eluded Bush, who shared his father's fractured impromptu syntax. Asked at an early meeting at Camp David what the two leaders had in common, Bush blurted out, "Well, we both use Colgate toothpaste." This led Blair to quip, "They're going to wonder how you know that, George." But the relationship had blossomed in repeated meetings; Blair's friends said that the prime minister, who had sometimes seemed to chafe as the perpetual junior partner to the larger-than-life, hyper-articulate Bill Clinton, had come to relish a more equal relationship in which he served as an honest broker in articulating European concerns to the American president.

Blair had paid a political price at home for his closeness to Bush. He had long been derided in Britain as an overly slick American-style politico, and the British press had taken to caricaturing the prime minister as "Bush's poodle" for his support of the president's tough stand against Iraq. Polls showed that the British public overwhelmingly disapproved of the prospect of military action against Iraq, but Blair remained unshaken. He knew the importance of the threat of force in getting Iraq to comply with the resolutions, but he also insisted that any military action in Iraq should happen only with UN backing. "He is being very firm about the importance of working through the UN," said Chris Patten, a Briton who was the European Union's commissioner for external relations. "If you go through the UN and you still don't get compliance from Iraq, what are you left with? Writing a letter to the *Times*? Running with a petition up the High Street?"

Ten days after Bush's speech, Blair addressed an emergency session of Parliament. "Our case is simply this," he said. "Not that we take military action come what may. But that the case for Iraqi disarmament is overwhelming." He painted one of the most vivid portraits yet of the Iraqi threat. In a fifty-page report released a few hours before he spoke, Blair's government asserted that Saddam's regime could launch chemical or biological warheads within forty-five minutes of an order to use them, and would be able to acquire a nuclear weapon in one to five years. The report also cited what it said was intelligence information that Iraq was trying to acquire sizable quantities of uranium from unspecified countries in Africa.

In a foreword to the report, Blair said he believed that the compilation of information from Britain's intelligence and security agencies had proved that Saddam threatened the stability of the world and had to be blocked now. "What I believe the assessed intelligence has established beyond doubt is that Saddam has continued to produce chemical and biological weapons, that he continues in his efforts to develop nuclear weapons and that he has been able to extend the range of his ballistic missile program," Blair wrote. "I also believe that as stated in the document, Saddam will now do his utmost to try to conceal his weapons from UN inspectors." The report said Iraq had stored and was continuing to produce chemical and biological agents capable of causing mass casualties, including mustard gas, sarin, anthrax and botulinum toxin.

What Blair did not reveal was that the report's most explosive allegation—that Iraq could deliver germ warheads within forty-five minutes—was based on a single intelligence source, albeit one that his government considered reliable. In at least two speeches in September, George W. Bush would repeat the British claim, though in the months ahead, the assertion would come back to haunt Bush and Blair, as would the allegation about Saddam's quest for uranium from Africa.

No sooner had Blair issued the report than one of Britain's close allies, Germany, reacted dismissively, with a government spokesman saying, "An initial reading of the papers has not found anything yet, but perhaps it lies in the details." The report set off a heated eleven-hour debate in Parliament, as many members, including two ministers from his own cabinet, raised questions about why Blair was willing to support an attack on Iraq if it failed to comply with inspections. In fact, Britain had agreed to sponsor the new UN resolution calling on Iraq to comply. Blair told his colleagues that the measure's introduction was "just days away." That turned out to be too optimistic—by about a month.

FROM THE BEGINNING, THE BUSH team wanted the strongest possible UN resolution, outlining stiff new terms for weapons inspections in Iraq, and threatening unmistakable consequences for noncompliance.

At the same time, Powell and his team did their best to keep diplomatic options open. Though cool to the French idea of two resolutions—one on inspections, to be followed by another on consequences—the Americans did not flatly rule it out. At a dinner for foreign ministers at the Pierre Hotel shortly after Bush's September 12 speech, Powell told de Villepin that France should not vote for a first resolution if it was not also prepared to vote for a second one that would impose penalties. De Villepin agreed, American officials later said. And though Powell initially talked of having draft language on a resolution ready for consideration within days of Bush's speech, it would be six weeks before Britain and the United States formally introduced it, on October 23, for the Security Council's consideration.

The Security Council was by design an unwieldy body, having been established in 1945 not for deliberative efficiency, but to reflect the status of the victorious great powers at the end of World War II—the United States, Britain, France, Russia and China. Besides these five permanent members, each with a veto over any council action, ten other nations sat on the council at any one time, with membership rotating among the United Nations. So from the moment Bush spoke, the real political challenge was to overcome French, Russian and Chinese resistance to the possibility of a new Persian Gulf war and avoid a veto. Other nations, from Mexico to Ireland, would have to be lobbied to build a majority, but those three were crucial.

None would prove more crucial than France. And no Frenchman would play a larger role than Dominique Galouzeau de Villepin, the hyperactive foreign minister who was President Chirac's most trusted aide, almost like a son. De Villepin was the kind of character that perhaps only France could have produced: a marathoner who slept no more than four and a half hours a night and wrote poetry in his spare time. He was tall—six foot three—slim, perpetually tanned and movie-star handsome, with silver hair, a noble profile and a fluency in idiomatic English that obviated any need for translators. One British newspaper described him as "a diplomatic pin-up." He had taken office in the spring of 2002, and in his first ten months on the job he would travel to seventy countries. Asked once about his intensity, he replied, "It is crucial because the urgency is there. The urgency of great international questions. Terrorism, proliferation, the rise of fundamentalism. The multiplicity of crises which have an impact on all of us. Today, you can't put a veil over your face."

If de Villepin had a vision, it was to revive the greatness of France. He had already published the first volume of a biography of Napoleon, *The Hundred Days,* which told the story of the emperor's return from exile, his triumphant march across France and his defeat at Waterloo. De Villepin described Napoleon's philosophy as "Victory or death, but glory whatever happens," and he added, "There is not a day that goes by without me feeling the imperious need to remember so as not to yield in the face of indifference, laughter or gibes," in order to "advance further in the name of a French ambition."

As the fall wore on, de Villepin would establish a close working relationship with Powell, America's own diplomatic pin-up. They did not always agree, but their work would be crucial to the Bush administration's efforts to build international support.

EVEN AS PRESIDENT BUSH PRESSED the United Nations, he also sought support in his own backyard—from Congress, which was then consumed in debate over the proposed new Department of Homeland Security and conscious of the midterm elections just weeks away. On September 19, a week after his speech at the UN, Bush sent a draft resolution to Capitol Hill asking for sweeping authority to use "all means he determines to be appropriate, including force" to disarm Iraq and dislodge Saddam Hussein. "If the United Nations Security Council won't deal with the problem," Bush said, "the United States and some of our friends will."

Senior leaders of both parties expressed general support for Bush's request, but signaled that there would be changes in the wording of the resolution, especially to a clause that would empower Bush to "restore international peace and security in the region." Senator Biden, the chairman of the Foreign Relations Committee, said, "I'm sure the president isn't specifically asking us for unilateral authority to move against Syria or Lebanon if there's not peace on the Lebanese border. So what does it mean?" That same day, at the United Nations, Iraq's foreign minister, Naji Sabri, read a combative letter from Saddam Hussein, insisting that his country had no weapons of mass destruction and attacking the Bush administration for a "cyclone of American accusations and fabricated crises against Iraq."

The next day, the White House formally released its revised National Security Strategy outlining its rationale for preemptive strikes against nations or groups that sought to develop biological, chemical or nuclear weapons, and asserting the unchallenged right of the United States to remain the world's only superpower. That the document had been months in the works did nothing to ease the diplomatic and political damage that its central concept now caused, not only with the French and other European allies but also among wary Democrats in Congress. Bill Graham, the Canadian foreign minister, said, "We are concerned about the signal this might be sending to other parts of the world—that while first strike is a legitimate international law doctrine, I don't believe that is consistent with the United Nations. It is not consistent with the world order we have been trying to build for the last seventy years through the United Nations."

Those tensions exploded into the open on Capitol Hill the following week. Senate Democrats were resisting the homeland security bill's proposal to grant managers in the new department more discretion over employees' traditional labor relations rights, and Bush charged that the Senate was "not interested in the security of the American people" but was instead "more interested in special interests in Washington." The Senate Democratic leader, the usually mild-mannered Tom Daschle of South Dakota, exploded in trembling outrage on the Senate floor. His voice growing raspy, Daschle said, "You tell those who fought in Vietnam and World War II they are not interested in the security of the American people," because they opposed the president's bill. "That is outrageous." Republican leaders promptly lashed out at Daschle, accusing him of taking Bush out of context and criticizing the commander in chief in wartime. The exchange was a revealing harbinger of just how hard it would be for the Democrats to get much political traction by criticizing Bush.

For his part, the president himself kept his outrage focused squarely on Saddam Hussein. At a fund-raiser in Houston that week, he made clear the depth and complexity of his feelings. "There's no doubt his hatred is mainly directed at us," Bush said. "There's no doubt he can't stand us. After all, this is a guy that tried to kill my dad at one time."

By the end of September, the outlines of the proposed Security Council resolution were becoming clear, even if the specific wording had yet to be introduced for formal debate. Under the terms of a draft resolution that was circulated to France, Russia and China in advance of its formal introduction to the council, Iraq would be declared already in violation—the diplomatic legalism was "material breach"— of prior resolutions flowing from the 1991 cease-fire ending the Persian Gulf war. Before weapons inspectors ever set foot in the country, Iraq would be required to provide a detailed account of its programs to develop weapons of mass destruction, and Security Council members would be allowed to send their own inspectors, to supplement the UN's work. Iraq would also have to set aside special accommodations negotiated with Kofi Annan in 1998 that had exempted some presidential palaces and compounds from inspections and allow unrestricted access to all sites. Inspections would be intrusive, possibly with military guards. Saddam would have seven days to accept the resolution and declare his weapons programs, and a month to open up the sites and provide further documentation.

A refusal to comply with the demands, including failure to provide a full and accurate list of weapons, the draft resolution stated, could trigger "all necessary means to restore international peace and security," the strongest diplomatic euphemism for war. The French, Russians and Chinese all balked at this demand, insisting that the paramount goal should be the return of inspectors, with possible consequences to be considered later. The Chinese premier, Zhu Rongji, visiting Europe, was shown on French television saying, "If the weapons inspections did not take place, if we do not have clear proof, and if we do not have the authorization of the Security Council, we cannot launch a military attack on Iraq—otherwise, there would be incalculable consequences." On September 28, Iraq, too, rejected the idea of any new terms for inspections. The Iraqi vice president, Taha Yassin Ramadan, said that his government had agreed to allow the weapons inspectors to return under conditions laid down previously. "The stance on the inspectors has been decided, and any additional procedure that aims at harming Iraq will not be accepted," he said.

• • •

IN THE FACE OF SUCH resistance at home and abroad, the Bush administration now moved aggressively to make the case for the urgency of action against Iraq. Even the president's sharpest critics in Congress and the UN did not dispute that Saddam was a wretched despot, with a long history of misdeeds to his name. But so were any number of other international leaders—and Washington was not threatening to go to war with any of them. Bush and his aides knew that they would have to persuade the American public, and skeptical allies, that the world could no longer risk waiting to confront Saddam. To do so, the president and his top aides unleashed two lines of new and threatening arguments. One was that Iraq had ominous, if still largely unspecified and unproven, ties to Al Qaeda. The other was that Saddam remained determined to build a nuclear weapon that could directly threaten the United States and the world. Both arguments, it would turn out, were hotly debated at the highest levels of the American government, with sharp disagreements over the meaning of the limited intelligence available. The existence of such disagreements was known at the time. But the public—and many politicians—were in the dark about important details as the president and his advisers made their most emphatic arguments in September and October.

For months, since the flap over the disputed reports of a meeting in Prague between the 9/11 hijacker Mohammed Atta and an Iraqi intelligence agent, the Bush administration had largely resisted asserting connections between Al Qaeda and Baghdad. Now a range of top officials, led by Secretary Rumsfeld, began making just such assertions. Rumsfeld and his senior advisers, impatient with other intelligence agencies' efforts to produce information about Iraq's hostile intentions or ties to terrorism, had set up a special Pentagon intelligence unit of their own to review raw information. Using powerful computers and new software, the unit, run by the undersecretary of defense for policy, Douglas J. Feith, sorted and scanned documents and reports from the CIA, the Defense Intelligence Agency and other spy organizations to glean new details that might have been overlooked, or that, when taken together, could produce new theories. "The lens through which you're looking for facts affects what you look for," Paul Wolfowitz said. "The correct process is one that surfaces as many facts as possible."

But some other intelligence officials viewed the new Pentagon effort warily and believed that Rumsfeld and his advisers were intent on politicizing intelligence to fit their hawkish views. In a speech to a Chamber of Commerce luncheon in Atlanta on September 27, Rumsfeld said that American intelligence agencies had, in his words, "bulletproof" evidence of links between Al Qaeda and the Iraqi regime. Earlier that week, Rumsfeld said, "We do have solid evidence of the presence in Iraq of Al Qaeda members, including some that have been in Baghdad. We have what we consider to be very reliable reporting of senior level contacts going back a decade, and of possible chemical- and biological-agent training," although he acknowledged that the report had come from a single source. Rice, too, warned that week that "there are some Al Qaeda personnel who found refuge in Baghdad" after the American air campaign in Afghanistan.

Yet there was ample official skepticism about this new tack, even from some in the president's own party. "To say, 'Yes, I know there is evidence there, but I don't want to tell you any more about it,' that does not encourage any of us," Senator Chuck Hagel, a maverick Republican from Nebraska, told Powell at a hearing of the Foreign Relations Committee. "Nor does it give the American public a heck of a lot of faith that, in fact, what anyone is saying is true." Powell replied mildly that there were confirmed "linkages" between Iraq and Al Qaeda, but added that "perhaps part of the confusion is that we're learning more over time as we get access to more and more" Al Qaeda prisoners and defectors. It was hardly a ringing endorsement of a dangerous link.

The question of Saddam's nuclear capacity was, if anything, more contentious. In September, the weekend before Bush made his speech to the UN, *The New York Times* reported (citing senior administration officials) that over the past fourteen months, Iraq had sought to buy thousands of specially designed aluminum tubes, which the unnamed officials believed were intended as components of centrifuges to make enriched uranium, the central component of a nuclear bomb. The officials said that several efforts to arrange such shipments had been blocked or intercepted—though they would not disclose how—and that the latest attempt had occurred in recent months.

What the initial report did not disclose is that there were disagreements within the American government over Iraq's intended use of the tubes. A secret National Intelligence Estimate—a consensus document representing the collective views of the American intelligence community circulated on October 2—cited Iraq's effort to buy the tubes as "compelling evidence that Saddam is reconstituting a uranium enrichment effort for Baghdad's nuclear weapons program," and was likely to have a bomb by the end of the decade, if not sooner. But the report also noted that technical experts at the Department of Energy and intelligence analysts at the State Department disagreed. They believed the aluminum tubes were intended for use in making artillery rockets, and the State Department concluded that Iraq's known activities did not "add up to a compelling case" that it was pursuing "an integrated and comprehensive approach to acquire nuclear weapons." (The report also flatly declared that "Baghdad has chemical and biological weapons.")

There were also great doubts about whether Iraq was trying to buy uranium on the world market. In his September speech to Parliament, Tony Blair had referred to Iraq's effort to buy uranium from unnamed African countries. Months earlier, Vice President Cheney's office had asked the CIA to look into claims that Iraq had sought to buy yellowcake uranium, a form of lightly processed ore, from Niger. The agency dispatched the veteran diplomat Joseph C. Wilson IV, a former ambassador to Gabon, to investigate. In February, Wilson would conclude that the claims were almost certainly false, given the close oversight of the country's mines, which were run by a consortium of international business interests and monitored by the International Atomic Energy Agency. A top American military commander and the American ambassador to Niger later reported similar conclusions.

For now, the secret National Intelligence Estimate included the report about Niger—and other suggestions that Iraq may have sought uranium ore from Somalia and possibly the Congo—while asserting that it could not confirm their accuracy. Once again, the State Department's intelligence experts offered a dissenting view, calling the claims of Iraq's pursuit of uranium "highly dubious." Virtually none of this was known to the public at the time, however.

One American official who did have an acute sense of the range of the intelligence community's opinions about the Iraqi threat was

Senator Bob Graham, the soft-spoken Florida Democrat who chaired the Senate Intelligence Committee. In that job, he was privy to the government's most secret assessments, and what he knew led him to question the urgency of the case for action in Iraq. He believed that a second Persian Gulf war would be a distraction from what should be the United States' paramount goal: the global campaign against terrorism. Graham did not think that Saddam, vicious as he was, posed an immediate threat to American security. As Congress debated the resolution that would authorize President Bush to use force against Saddam, Senator Graham pressed CIA Director Tenet to declassify some of the National Intelligence Estimate's secret findings. On October 7, Tenet released selected material, including an assessment that "Baghdad for now appears to be drawing a line short of conducting terrorist attacks" against the United States with conventional or chemical or biological weapons. Indeed, Tenet went on to say, "Should Saddam conclude that a U.S.-led attack could no longer be deterred, he probably would become much less constrained in adopting terrorist actions." Finally, Tenet said, "Saddam might decide that the extreme step of assisting Islamist terrorists in conducting a WMD attack against the United States would be his last chance to exact vengeance by taking a large number of victims with him." In other words, the CIA chief seemed to suggest, the greatest short-term risk from Saddam might well lie in provoking him, just as the Bush administration now seemed determined to do. Tenet swiftly insisted that "there is no inconsistency" between the CIA assessment and the president's views, but Graham had made his point.

That same day, in a televised speech from Cincinnati, Bush made his most extensive public remarks yet on how he viewed the Iraqi threat. If his UN address had been aimed at world opinion, this talk was aimed at the American electorate—and their representatives, who were debating the president's request for an authorization to make war if he saw fit. Whatever the nuances and gradations of the existing intelligence, Bush was determined to make a compelling case. Cheney and others had never forgotten that the CIA's best estimates before the 1991 war turned out to have badly underestimated the extent of Iraq's weapons program, and the president and his team were intent on not repeating that mistake.

So in Cincinnati, Bush warned that Saddam could attack the United States "on any given day." He conceded that it was impossible to know with certainty how close Saddam was to developing a nuclear weapon, but said that this did not matter because American intelligence showed Saddam was reconstituting his nuclear weapons program with "a group he calls his nuclear mujahideen, his nuclear holy warriors." He repeated the assertion that Iraq had tried to buy aluminum tubes needed for centrifuges and said that if Iraq could produce, buy or steal an amount of enriched uranium "a little larger than a single softball, it could have a nuclear weapon in less than a year." Significantly, Bush said nothing about Iraqi attempts to purchase uranium from Niger or other African nations. Tenet had prevailed on the deputy national security adviser, Stephen J. Hadley, to remove any such reference.

Taking a page from Powell's diplomatic phrase book, Bush also allowed that if Saddam accepted aggressive inspections and met the rest of a long list of demands, including accounting for Gulf war prisoners, that would "change the nature of the Iraqi regime itself." Bush said that a campaign against Saddam would not distract from the war on terror, but insisted, "To the contrary, confronting the threat posed by Iraq is crucial to winning the war on terror." He quoted John F. Kennedy's warning that doing nothing "is the riskiest of all options," but confirmed that a military option wasn't imminent and that diplomacy still had a chance to work.

Barely three days later, after dropping some of his original broad language and agreeing to report to Congress in the event of war, Bush won strong congressional backing for an authorization to use force, by a vote of 296–133 in the House and 77–23 in the Democratic-controlled Senate. The rift with Tom Daschle had been mended. "It is neither a Democratic resolution nor a Republican resolution," the majority leader said. "It is now a statement of American resolve and values."

SLOWLY, AND DESPITE SEEMINGLY ENDLESS haggling with the French over a new UN resolution, the pressure was bearing fruit in Iraq, too. On October 1, Baghdad agreed that inspectors could return, and the

UN's weapons team agreed to await further instructions from the Security Council before taking up its chores. On October 16, Saddam staged a sham referendum on his tenure, which Iraqi officials claimed he won by a perfect 100 percent of the vote, and he addressed his people the next day. "If Allah Almighty, in his great wisdom and for reasons beyond our comprehension, decides to put you again to the test of fighting on a large scale, then the Almighty, the nation and history will expect you to deliver an effective stand," the dictator said. "Afterward, the enemy will fall on his face, despised, condemned and defeated, while your banner, the banner of 'God is great,' will continue to fly high on its nest, dignified and honorable." Four days later, in an extraordinary move, Saddam ordered a blanket nationwide amnesty that emptied his network of prisons, and a cheering mob swept out to greet families who had not seen them in years. A statement issued in Saddam's name said the gesture was in gratitude for his reelection, but much else suggested that the growing threat of war had spurred his repressive regime to a sudden gesture of magnanimity to rally the populace to his side.

Behind the scenes, debates within the Bush administration wore on. Cheney and Rumsfeld insisted that only a single UN resolution, threatening unmistakable penalties for noncompliance, would be acceptable. Senior administration officials let it be known that they were already sketching visions for a postwar occupation that could govern Iraq after Saddam fell. As the full Security Council held an unusual open debate, Bush warned other Middle Eastern and European states that time was running out, and that "those who choose to live in denial may eventually be forced to live in fear." On October 23, the United States and Britain formally presented their revised resolution, Number 1441, to the Security Council. Gone was the warlike language about "all necessary means," and the demand that Washington be allowed to send its own inspectors. But the resolution still stipulated that Iraq was already in "material breach" of its obligations under past resolutions, and that new infractions, even minor ones like inconsistencies in its weapons inventory, would compound the violation. The measure concluded by noting that the council had in the past warned Iraq that it would "face serious consequences as a result of its continued violations of its obligations."

For the Americans, this was enough to argue that any subsequent war would have a legal underpinning, because the U.S. believed that any nation on the council was empowered by the UN charter to take action, including military force, to compel compliance by any country in material breach of its resolutions. This became the basis for two more frantic weeks of negotiations, especially with the French, who remained concerned about what they called the potential "automaticity" of any military response. On October 26, Chirac's government announced it might even offer its own competing resolution.

It was Powell who broke the logjam in a marathon series of negotiations with his counterpart de Villepin. On the night of Saturday, November 2, the secretary was in frantic telephone talks with the foreign minister over what precisely would trigger "material breach," just twenty minutes before walking his daughter Anne down the aisle at her wedding. The final compromise amounted to a two-part test, and a two-part process. Iraq would be in further material breach of its obligations if it made false statements or omissions in its weapons declaration (now due in thirty days) *and* if it failed to "cooperate fully" with inspectors. Any future breach by Iraq would have to be reported to the Security Council for its assessment. The result was deliberate ambiguity, *necessary* ambiguity, Powell would later say.

Each side could claim victory. The French took comfort in the belief that they had won their right to a second round of debate over use of force, and they focused on the requirement that the weapons inspectors would have to report back to the Security Council. The Americans focused on the strict standards for compliance—that a failure by Iraq to cooperate would trigger "material breach." Bush had preserved his ability to go it alone if he saw fit.

With Bush surrounded by skeptics like Cheney and Rumsfeld, Powell argued that, at the end of the process, the French would recognize the futility of inspections, and agree to war. Rice, the president's trusted sounding board and foreign policy tutor, was the decisive voice. "Condi was the tipping factor," one administration official said. "Powell convinced her that the French would be with us."

In the end, the vote in the Security Council on November 8 was unanimous, 15–0. Even Syria, a nonpermanent member and a longtime ally of Saddam and his circle, voted yes. Three days earlier, in the midterm elections, Republicans had swept into scores of offices around the nation and had regained control of the Senate. Bush's party now held the presidency and both houses of Congress for the first time in a half century, and the president was riding high. At a Rose Garden appearance hailing the Security Council's vote, the president pointedly turned to Powell and praised his "leadership, his good work and his determination."

But there were already signs of disagreement about what had just been agreed to. One senior administration official said that, as inspections got under way, Washington would look for "a pattern of non-compliance," insisting that the United States was "not poised looking for the first comma out of place." But another official said, "The United States believes that after all Saddam has done, we have to have a zero-tolerance view." And still another warned, "We're not going to sit back and wait until we see day after day, week after week of violations."

Chapter 5

THE FAILURE OF DIPLOMACY

Washington, D.C.
Saturday, December 21, 2002

Four days before Christmas, the Bush White House was bedecked with poinsettias, pomegranate topiaries and a 150-pound model of itself in frosted gingerbread. But it remained so battened down against potential terrorists that the usual public tours of the decorations had been suspended in favor of an online tour of the mansion on the White House website, recorded by the president's Scottish terrier, Barney, with a lipstick-sized video camera on his collar. In the Oval Office, the president huddled with Condoleezza Rice and George Tenet, listening to freshly intercepted recordings of Arabic-speaking voices.

"Captain Ibrahim?" a colonel in Iraq's Second Republican Guard Corps asked a fellow officer on the scratchy radio conversation.

"I am with you, sir," the captain replied, as if taking dictation.

> COLONEL: Remove.
> CAPTAIN: Remove.
> COLONEL: The expression.
> CAPTAIN: The expression.
> COLONEL: Nerve agents.
> CAPTAIN: Nerve agents.
> COLONEL: Wherever it comes up.
> CAPTAIN: Wherever it comes up.
> COLONEL: In the wireless instructions.
> CAPTAIN: In the instructions.
> COLONEL: Wireless.
> CAPTAIN: Wireless.
> COLONEL: O.K., buddy.
> CAPTAIN: Done, sir.

The exchange was terse, even cryptic. Yet to the president and his aides, the meaning seemed clear—and ominous. Iraqi officials were trying to cover up evidence that they possessed deadly nerve agents, and were concerned that they might be overheard discussing the subject.

Barely four weeks earlier, United Nations inspectors had arrived in Baghdad for the first time in four years, to take up their duties under Security Council Resolution 1441. After initially balking at the inspectors' return, Saddam's regime had agreed to accept them, despite the resolution's "bad contents." Led by Hans Blix, a mild-mannered Swedish lawyer who was the chief inspector for chemical and biological weapons, and Mohamed ElBaradei, the director general of the International Atomic Energy Agency, the inspectors operated with utmost discretion. Fearful of Iraqi electronic surveillance, their team talked strategy on walks in the garden of their headquarters in a converted Baghdad hotel. Sometimes they would slip one another notes or use sign language. And when they took off in the mornings in quest of hidden weapons or missiles that could carry them beyond the borders of Iraq, they did so by weaving through early morning rush-hour traffic at speeds of up to ninety miles an hour, trying to shake their Iraqi followers. They seemed to face an impossible task. One senior official summed up his feelings: "Do the Americans want us to succeed? How would I know?" And the Iraqis? "Basically, they sit across the table from us and tell us, 'We have zero, zero, zero.' And, of course, 'zero, zero, zero' is a red flag to our bull." Still, the inspectors worked around the clock, their Toyota Land Cruisers equipped with radiation detectors and advanced scanners to detect microbes. And unlike the former inspections regime, Blix and his colleagues operated boldly. At 8:55 on the morning of December 3, two teams of inspectors stepped out of the fog in front of Saddam's Al Sajoud presidential palace, one of at least twenty the dictator kept, and demanded that its imposing iron gates be rolled open. Seven minutes later, Saddam's guards stepped back, and even the Iraqi minders assigned to monitor Western reporters who witnessed the scene seemed to acknowledge, if only by facial expressions, that something fundamental had changed in their country.

Just how much had changed depended on one's point of view. On

December 7, in compliance with the requirements of Resolution 1441, Iraq released 12,000 pages of files that purported to account for the state of its weapons programs. The documents arrived at UN headquarters in New York at about 8:30 the following evening, having been ferried by the inspectors through Cyprus and Frankfurt, and were swiftly translated and scrutinized for any possibly dangerous disclosures, like bomb-making instructions. Within days, American intelligence agencies concluded that the bundles of paper failed to account for the chemical and biological elements that had been missing when UN inspectors left Iraq in 1998, while the declaration on Iraq's nuclear program left many open questions. One American official complained that there were "omissions big enough to drive a tank through." Another person, who worked closely with the White House, described the situation as "a tinpot dictator was mocking the president," adding that within the administration the Iraqi documents "provoked a sense of anger."[1]

By December 19, Powell declared that Iraq had failed to disclose the required information about its weapons programs, and hence was once again in "material breach" of Security Council resolutions and "well on its way to losing this last chance." At the UN, Blix said "an opportunity was missed" for Baghdad to come clean, and told the Security Council in a closed briefing that there were "inaccuracies" in Iraq's claim that it had destroyed a huge stockpile of anthrax it had built up from 1988 to 1991. It was the first time the new inspectors suggested that Iraq had lied. The next day, Bush said he found the report "not encouraging," and added, "We expect Mr. Saddam Hussein to disarm."

The problem for Bush was that, even as they pronounced the report inadequate, Blix and his colleagues said that Iraq was "cooperating well" in providing access to inspectors. Days later, in what the Americans interpreted as a grandstanding gesture, Baghdad invited the CIA to come find any prohibited weapons, and by New Year's Eve, the inspectors once again repeated that they had thus far been unable to find any evidence of prohibited weapons. All this was enough to convince the French, the Russians and other skeptics that the inspections were working and needed more time. The Russian ambassador to the UN, Sergey Lavrov, argued that the Bush administration had overstepped by characterizing any flaws in Iraq's weapons declaration as amounting to "material breach," insisting that only the Security Council was empowered to make such determinations, not the intelligence agencies of individual members. "The work of inspectors is at a very early stage," he said. The consensus of early November was fraying by the day.

THE SECURITY COUNCIL MEETING ON Monday, January 20, 2003, was called not to discuss Iraq, for a change, but global terrorism. France held the rotating presidency of the council for the month, and de Villepin had summoned his fellow foreign ministers for what seemed like a routine session. Instead, Joschka Fischer, the foreign minister of Germany, which had taken a rotating seat on the council at the first of the year, brought up the subject of Iraq, stating that Baghdad was fully complying with "all relevant resolutions" and arguing that inspectors should have "all the time which is needed."

Powell seemed taken aback, setting aside his prepared remarks to warn the council, "We cannot be shocked into impotence because we're afraid of the difficult choices that are ahead of us." Speaking to reporters after the session (and after Powell had left the building), de Villepin dropped another bomb. Accusing Washington of "impatience" with Baghdad, de Villepin declared, "We believe that nothing today justifies envisaging military action." He then threatened to use France's veto if the United States pressed the council to authorize military action. French officials would later insist that de Villepin had not meant to sandbag Powell, merely to express his own views. But Powell felt betrayed. De Villepin's remarks had undermined Powell's own position with the more hawkish members of Bush's cabinet and crystallized the growing gulf between the United States and Britain and much of the rest of the world. Increasingly, other nations seemed willing to wait, while Washington seemed ready and even eager for war. Only the week before, the UN inspectors had found eleven empty chemical warheads at an ammunition storage dump in southern Iraq. The Bush administration immediately saw this as a sign that Iraq had failed to disclose its weapons; others saw it as a sign that the inspectors were making progress.

The search for a diplomatic solution was now complicated by the steady buildup of American and British forces headed toward the

Persian Gulf: the negotiating at the UN was getting out of sync with the increasingly obvious display of American manpower and firepower on the ground. The day of de Villepin's threat, Britain announced it was preparing 30,000 troops for possible action, its biggest step so far. For its part, the Pentagon had called up more than 78,000 National Guard troops and reservists. More than 50,000 American troops were already in the region, and the Pentagon let it be known that three times that many could be in place and ready for an attack on the president's orders by mid-February. In late December, General Richard B. Myers, the chairman of the Joint Chiefs of Staff, had toured the temporary structures that had been set up outside Doha, Qatar, to serve as a high-tech command center for a possible war. Since the passage of Resolution 1441, there had also been stepped-up exchanges between American and British planes patrolling the no-fly zones and Iraqi antiaircraft batteries, and senior Bush administration officials had been feverishly negotiating with the government of Turkey, Iraq's northern neighbor, for the right to base troops and planes there. Saudi Arabia had given senior American officials private assurances that the kingdom would make its airspace and bases available to American planes. Saddam, too, had taken a bellicose tone, warning early in January that he was ready for war and accusing the inspectors of spying. But Tony Blair told the British Parliament that a "massive amount" of new intelligence suggested that the buildup of forces was unnerving Saddam and undermining his grip on Iraq.

Just two days after the French veto threat, Rumsfeld lashed out at the French and Germans when asked by foreign journalists about the apparent lack of European support for the war. "You're thinking of Europe as Germany and France," Rumsfeld said. "I don't. I think that's old Europe." Dismissing those countries as "problems," he added, "You look at vast numbers of other countries in Europe. They're not with France and Germany on this. They're with the United States." Fischer, the German foreign minister, countered, "Our position is not a problem; it is a constructive contribution." In fact, the French and German resistance was causing huge problems for Powell and was driving him closer to Rumsfeld and the other administration hawks. "The Europeans have this idea that they can empower Powell," one administration official said. "They haven't empowered him. They have undercut him." It was far from clear just what Powell's private misgivings about a potential war might be, but in public he pressed on. On January 26, at the World Economic Forum in Davos, Switzerland, a gathering of deep thinkers and deep pockets, Powell acknowledged the strains with the French. "One or two of our friends, we have been in marriage counseling with for over 225 years nonstop," he said. Powell was unyielding on Iraq, however, all but dismissing the expected findings of Blix and ElBaradei's first report on their inspections, which was due at the UN the next day. "We're in no great rush to judgment tomorrow or the day after," he said, "but clearly time is running out."

When Blix and ElBaradei appeared before the Security Council on January 27, they offered a mixed assessment of Iraq's cooperation. "Iraq appears not to have come to genuine acceptance—not even today—of the disarmament, which was demanded of it and which it needs to carry out to win the confidence of the world and to live in peace," Blix said, summing up a grim, fifteen-page catalog of Iraq's chemical and biological programs that provided ample evidence of the ways in which Saddam had failed to prove that he had given up illegal weapons. ElBaradei was more upbeat, declaring that his team had so far found no evidence that Iraq had tried to revive its nuclear arms program, and beseeching the Security Council for "a few more months" to finish his job. The American ambassador to the UN, John D. Negroponte, was blunt. "There is nothing in either presentation," he said, "that would give us hope that Iraq has ever intended to fully comply."

The next night, Bush used his State of the Union Message to enumerate Saddam's offenses and make an implicit case for war, even without further UN approval. "Trusting in the sanity and restraint of Saddam Hussein is not a strategy, and it is not an option," the president said. "We will consult. But let there be no misunderstanding: If Saddam Hussein does not fully disarm, for the safety of our people and for the peace of the world, we will lead a coalition to disarm him."

Inexplicably, and despite the warnings from the CIA, Bush's speechwriters included in his catalog of indictments against Saddam the dubious charge about Iraq's efforts to buy yellowcake uranium from Niger, attributing it to British intelligence. In sixteen words that would later cause the president and his aides considerable political grief, Bush declared: "The British government has learned that Saddam Hussein recently sought significant quantities of uranium from Africa." But the British were facing their own problems with their intelligence. A week after Bush's speech, Tony Blair's government was forced to acknowledge that a recently published report listing Iraq's offenses, depicted as an up-to-date assessment by British intelligence services, had in fact been cobbled together from various public sources, including a paper by a graduate student in California. Sometimes the lifting was so extensive as to amount to plagiarism. This report would come to be known in the British press as the "dodgy dossier," but Blair's spokesman nevertheless defended its contents as "solid" and "accurate."

THE UNITED NATIONS CALLS THE Security Council chamber the emergency room of diplomacy, and in more than fifty years, there has often been the equivalent of blood on its floor. But the decor, a gift from Norway, is full of optimistic symbols, with blue-and-gold silk tapestries depicting the anchor of faith, the growing wheat of hope and the heart of charity. On the morning of Wednesday, February 5, it was packed to overflowing for what was expected to be the most dramatic meeting since John F. Kennedy's ambassador, Adlai E. Stevenson, confronted the Soviet Union over missiles in Cuba in October 1962. Now, to counter the flood of international resistance to the use of American force, and to rebut Blix and ElBaradei's careful, cautious reports, President Bush had decided to roll out his biggest diplomatic gun: Colin Powell.

In a meeting in the Oval Office in mid-January, Bush had said he needed to use Powell's unique credibility. "We're going to put our case down," the president had said. "I want you to do it. I have confidence in your ability and people will listen when you speak." A working group of the National Security Council, including Vice President Cheney's key aides, had been preparing a possible indictment against Iraq. There were several options. Should the administration focus on Saddam's weapons of mass destruction? On possible ties to terrorism? On Iraq's abysmal human rights record? On all three, or some combination? Some administration aides wanted Powell to make a three-day presentation, one day on each subject. He promptly vetoed that as impossible. The world's foreign ministers would not sit still for a graduate seminar; it had to be one tight presentation of less than two hours.

On January 29, Powell got the first draft from the working group. It contained everything but the kitchen sink, an untidy mix of allegations and unsubstantiated intelligence tips thrown together. Powell knew the presentation had to be in plain English. It had to flow. And above all, it had to be factual, and as airtight as Powell could make it. So the secretary detailed a group of senior aides to go over everything with a fine-toothed comb. For four nights in George Tenet's conference room at CIA headquarters in Langley, Virginia, this group of thirty people vetted the voluminous material. On the second day, Powell joined them. Tenet was there, too, and, toward the end, Condoleezza Rice. Powell believed that he had to make absolutely sure he did not say anything that could be disputed. He knew the Iraqis would "bust their ass to see what they can put up to contradict whatever I say." Powell insisted that virtually every item in the presentation be double-sourced. And he kept working on the style. He had made a small fortune as a public speaker and he thought some of the material the White House had produced was hopelessly turgid, and far too long. "I can't read this!" he said at one point.

Powell threw out the Niger allegations. He rejected advice to hold up a photo of an aluminum tube, and instead decided to acknowledge—tersely—the debate over whether Iraq wanted them to build centrifuges or artillery rockets. At one point, the CIA showed Powell a photograph that supposedly pictured Saddam and his nuclear advisers.

"Now tell me who those guys are," Powell said.

"Oh, we're quite sure this is the nuclear crowd," came the response.

"How do you know?" Powell pressed. "Prove it. Who are they?" No one could. Out it went. "There were a lot of cigars lit," Powell recalled later. "I didn't want anything going off in my face or the president's face."

On Tuesday afternoon, February 4, Powell and his aides went to New York, to practice the presentation at the U.S. mission to the

United Nations, across First Avenue from the headquarters, where the top-floor conference room had been set up to resemble the Security Council chamber. They went over the whole speech, then took a dinner break and did it again.

Powell had insisted that Tenet—a fellow New Yorker and frequent ally in administration debates—accompany him to the UN, and he was so determined that they be photographed together that he picked up the CIA director at his hotel room that morning. When Powell had to have a brief meeting before the Security Council session, he arranged for Tenet to be waiting in a small anteroom off the chamber floor, so that they could stroll in together. Tenet's sober face would be visible in virtually every frame of film and video that day, just behind Powell's.

Now, in front of the council, Powell pulled out all the stops. He held up a small vial of white powder, declaring that "less than a teaspoon of dry anthrax, about this amount," had shut down the U.S. Senate in the fall of 2001. Then, without a pause, he said that Iraq had declared past possession of 8,500 liters of anthrax but that the UN inspectors in the 1990s had estimated he could have produced 25,000 liters. On two big screens, Powell showed satellite photographs of what he said were chemical and biological plants, and drawings, based on witnesses' descriptions, of trucks and railroad cars that had been converted into mobile labs. He played recordings of intercepted conversations like the one the president had heard weeks before in the Oval Office. The translations of the scratchy Arabic echoed in the tense room: "We evacuated everything." "Remove." "Forbidden ammo." "Nerve agents." Powell played one tape from November 26, the day before the UN teams resumed their inspections in Baghdad, in which a colonel and a brigadier general in the Republican Guard discuss how to handle ElBaradei's inspectors.

"We have this modified vehicle," the colonel said.

"Yeah," the general replied.

"What do we say if one of them sees it?" the colonel demanded.

"You didn't get a modified—you don't have a modified—" the general said, before the colonel cut him off: "By God, I have one."

"They acknowledge that our colleague Mohamed ElBaradei is coming," Powell told the council, spinning out the tale. "And they know what he's coming for. And they know he's coming the next day. He's coming to look for things that are prohibited. He is expecting these gentlemen to cooperate with him, and not hide things. But they're worried."

Powell was worried, too. "Leaving Saddam Hussein in possession of weapons of mass destruction for a few more months or years is not an option, not in a post–September 11 world," he declared. To make his case, Powell gave an extraordinary public glimpse of the CIA's secret tools: defectors, informants, intercepts, procurement records and testimony from detainees seized in Afghanistan and elsewhere. Many times, he said, information from one source confirmed tips from another. For example, he said, "We have firsthand descriptions of biological weapons factories on wheels and on rails," confirmation of which did not come until later when "the source was an eyewitness, an Iraqi chemical engineer who supervised one of these facilities."

Powell was careful not to overstate the case for possible links between Iraq and Al Qaeda, but he left strongly menacing impressions. He said that "colleagues" of a known Al Qaeda leader, Abu Musab al-Zarqawi, had been identified as coming and going from Baghdad, and he went out of his way to note that Al Qaeda operatives had been working in France, Germany, Britain, Spain, Italy and Russia—trying to persuade skeptical Europeans that they, too, were at risk.

Powell's language was careful and nuanced. His case was legalistic. But the overall impression he left was one of threatening urgency. His fellow diplomats reacted respectfully. Yet it was not enough to turn the tide of sentiment on the council. France, Russia and China all said that the evidence reinforced their view that the inspectors needed more time to do their work, without deadlines, and that Iraq should be pressed to cooperate.

The next day, the Bush administration ordered the 101st Airborne Division, the military's largest air assault unit, to send more than 15,000 troops and 300 combat helicopters to the Persian Gulf. At the end of the week, Blix and ElBaradei gave mildly positive reports on the progress of their inspections, and Blix pointedly questioned some of the evidence Powell had presented. He took issue with the American intelligence assessment of certain trucks identified as working on chemical decontamination, saying that their movements "could just as easily have been a routine activity." The only strong phrase of support Blix offered Powell came when he said the time needed for Iraqi disarmament "could still be short" if full cooperation "were to be forthcoming." Later in the day, de Villepin drew a rare burst of applause from the council gallery with an impassioned speech. "In this temple of the United Nations, we are the guardians of an ideal, the guardians of a conscience," he said, proposing a new meeting of council foreign ministers for March 14, to take stock of the situation. "This onerous responsibility and immense honor we have must lead us to give priority to disarmament through peace." Powell again set aside his prepared remarks to respond. "My friends, we cannot allow this process to be endlessly strung out as Iraq is trying to do right now," he insisted. "My friends, they cannot be allowed to get away with it again."

American annoyance at the French bubbled over into a populist rechristening of French fries as "freedom fries," and threatened boycotts of French wine and cheese. The comedian Dennis Miller cracked that the only way Washington could persuade France to help invade Iraq "is if we tell them we found truffles in there." Peter T. King, a genial, outspoken Republican congressman from Long Island, summed up attitudes toward the European resistance, telling the BBC, "France is no longer a world power," and "Germany started two world wars."

But that weekend, worldwide frustration at United States policy sparked massive, mostly peaceful protests that drew millions into the streets of the world's major cities, in the largest demonstrations since the Vietnam war. In New York, at least 100,000 people, and perhaps several times that, poured onto First Avenue north of the UN headquarters building, barred from marching by a court order. "The World Says No to War," a huge banner proclaimed. There were similar, if smaller, outpourings in Philadelphia, Seattle, San Diego, Sacramento, Miami, Detroit, Milwaukee and other American cities, as speakers denounced what they called Bush's rush to war, while offering no sympathy for Saddam Hussein. In London, an estimated 750,000 people rallied in Hyde Park, while 200,000 gathered at the Brandenburg Gate in Berlin and hundreds of thousands more demonstrated in Paris, Amsterdam, Brussels, Barcelona, Rome, Melbourne, Cape Town, Johannesburg, Auckland, Seoul, Tokyo and Manila. A recurring theme was that America's interest in Iraq had more to do with oil than with dangerous weapons and tyranny. In all, there were protests in some 350 cities around the world. The police in Athens fired tear gas and clashed with demonstrators who threw a gasoline bomb, but most of the marches were peaceful. There were college students, middle-aged couples, older people who had marched for civil rights in the 1960s, along with groups representing labor, the environment and religious, business and civic organizations. Mary Baxter, a thirty-one-year-old software company worker from Cambridge, Massachusetts, seemed typical in her quiet solemnity. "I came to go to the rally and be a part of a global voice against going to war in Iraq again," she said in Manhattan. "I feel the current administration has been escalating and destabilizing things. I'm disappointed that Colin Powell is going along with Bush, Cheney and the rest of them."

Angela Tsang, a twenty-one-year-old Barnard College student, said she believed an attack on Iraq would achieve nothing but death and injustice. "We don't believe Bush's rhetoric," she said. "I think he's not acting in the best interest of the American people. We're risking the lives of hundreds of American soldiers and an untold number of lives in the Middle East, and a war will not solve the problem of terrorism. It disgusts me. I can't accept that."

Such a mass expression of public sentiment posed further challenges for the diplomats at the UN. The Catholic Bishops of the United States were also on record as opposing war, while Pope John Paul II had said war was "always a defeat for humanity" and had met with the deputy Iraqi prime minister, Tariq Aziz, in Rome. But polls showed that overall public opinion remained generally supportive of the president's course, and even Bill Clinton, in a speech at the University of Texas, declared, "President Bush, I think, deserves a lot of credit for saying we can't just ignore this forever, it's time to deal with it."

Bush himself insisted that the mass marches would have no effect on his decision making. "Size of protest—it's like deciding, well, I'm going to decide policy based upon a focus group," he told reporters at the White House several days later. "The role of a leader is to decide policy based upon the security, in this case, the security of the people." He referred scornfully to the idea of giving Saddam "another, 'nother, 'nother, last chance."

• • •

ON MONDAY, FEBRUARY 24, THE Bush administration was ready to declare that Iraq's last chance had come and gone. Together with Britain and a new partner, Spain, Washington offered a terse new Security Council resolution, which fit on a single page. Its operative sentence: a declaration that "Iraq has failed to take the final opportunity afforded it in Resolution 1441." The decision to pursue a new resolution came after a weekend summit at Bush's Texas ranch with Prime Minister Jose María Aznar of Spain, which had taken a rotating seat on the Security Council at the new year. Bush and Aznar had telephoned Blair and Prime Minister Silvio Berlusconi of Italy to map out the final strategy.

There were still deep doubts—in the White House and elsewhere—about whether a second resolution was a wise idea. In a twist, France, which had initially been the most ardent advocate of a second resolution, now argued against one. On February 21, Jean-David Levitte, the French ambassador in Washington, went to the White House to see Rice's deputy, Stephen Hadley. If the United States was bent on war, Levitte said, it should proceed under Resolution 1441, which was ambiguous enough to provide legal cover, and France would not make a fuss. Demanding a new resolution would risk a French veto and a splintered alliance. But now it was Bush—initially so skeptical about a second resolution—who was determined to press for one, almost entirely as a favor to Tony Blair, who was facing increasing domestic political pressure and the threatened resignation of some of his cabinet ministers.

One complication that Powell had been facing for weeks was the changed composition of the Security Council itself. On January 1, five nations—Colombia, Ireland, Norway, Singapore and Mauritius—which, except for Mauritius, had been mostly supportive of the American position, rotated off the council in favor of Angola, Chile, Germany, Pakistan and Spain, which, on balance, were more problematic. Bulgaria, Cameroon, Guinea, Mexico and Syria had retained their nonpermanent seats on the council, but Mexico, which could have been a key American ally, was instead balking. Mexico's president, Vicente Fox, had initially formed a close bond with Bush after their respective elections in 2000, as the two leaders envisioned relaxing immigration regulations on their common border. After the September 11 attacks, however, that initiative died and a distinct chill and resentment had descended over the relationship. So Powell was facing another uphill fight at the UN. The same day the Americans introduced their new resolution, France, Germany and Russia offered a "memorandum" of their own that argued that conditions for resorting to force had not yet been met and that "the military option should only be a last resort." At the White House, Rice dismissed the French approach as "the worst of both worlds." She said it was tantamount to an admission that Saddam was not fully complying with the resolution ordering him to disarm, while allowing him to "alter and play with" the resolution's requirements. "It's time to deal with this problem," she said.

Foreign Minister Tang Jiaxuan of China told Powell secretly in mid-February that Beijing would not stand in the way with a veto. But with the threat of French and Russian vetoes hovering in the air, the American strategy in the final round of diplomacy gradually began to shift toward building a nine-vote majority on the council, to make a statement of international support for war, even if a second resolution could not be passed. And there was still some hope that Paris would come around by at least abstaining.

France, for its part, was just as determined to build a council majority against war. Ambassador Levitte was privately warning the Chirac government that an outright French veto would be considered a devastating blow to Franco-American relations. On the other hand, if France could build a council majority in opposition to the Americans, then it could simply abstain—a move that would amount to a "no," of course, but without the sting of a veto, Levitte said. But the only way to persuade wavering Security Council members that France remained unyielding in its opposition to war was to hold out the explicit and credible threat that France would use its veto if needed.[2]

On March 6, Bush held his first prime-time news conference in eighteen months, and only the second of his presidency, in the gold-and-ivory East Room of the White House. Bush said that only days remained for a diplomatic solution, but vowed to press on for a new resolution, even if it appeared he could not muster a majority or avoid a French and Russian veto. "You bet," Bush said. "It's time for people to show their cards."

Even as Bush spoke, de Villepin was preparing to show his. At the Waldorf-Astoria in Manhattan, Powell and his fellow foreign ministers had gathered in anticipation of a Security Council meeting the next morning. In an upstairs suite, Powell's and de Villepin's aides watched Bush on television together in subdued silence. Just after the president finished, de Villepin went into Powell's separate suite, alone. The two men knew each other well by now. There was no anger. De Villepin was matter-of-fact, straightforward, as he told Powell that he did not want there to be any confusion or surprise. He passed the definitive word: France would veto any resolution authorizing war. Just as calmly, Powell replied: There were no circumstances under which France could block Washington's way.[3]

Diplomacy had failed.

Chapter 6

THE WEEK OF WAITING

Baghdad
Tuesday, March 18, 2003

It was 4 A.M. when the two men arrived in the empty darkness of downtown. They carried a letter from the president, bearing his signature and authorizing a large transaction. They gave no reason. They did not have to. No questions were asked. Soon enough, Qusay Saddam Hussein, the president's second son, and Abid Hamid Mahmoud al-Tikriti, Saddam's cousin and top personal aide, were overseeing the loading of 236 boxes into three tractor-trailers outside Iraq's Central Bank. A team of workers took two hours to finish the job. The bank employees were meticulous, good bureaucrats to the end. They kept records of every batch of bills, then placed a packing slip enumerating the contents into each box before it was sealed. Over the years, Saddam and his family would sometimes demand cash from Iraqi banks. "Small amounts, maybe $5 million," one official said.

This withdrawal was something else again. The total haul: almost $1 billion. There was roughly $900 million in $100 bills and perhaps $100 million worth of euros, about a quarter of the country's hard-currency reserves, enough to rank as one of the largest bank robberies in history. Then again, Saddam's power was so absolute that this seizure might have broken no laws. What was the money for? Where was it going? No one may ever know. But on that early spring morning, Saddam Hussein, president-for-life of the Republic of Iraq, chairman of the Revolutionary Command Council, Central Leader of the Baath Party and Great Uncle to the fearful populace he had ruled for almost a quarter century, surely knew this: Far away in Washington, the president of the United States had given him and his sons just forty-eight hours to surrender power and leave their country—or face war.

Later that Tuesday, Saddam appeared on television, wearing his olive drab field marshal's uniform for the first time since the Persian Gulf war. With a pistol holstered at his right hip, he railed at the "American, English and Zionist invading aggressors," and warned that they faced defeat. Surrounded by the handpicked political and military cronies of his inner circle in an undisclosed location, he denounced Bush's ultimatum as "debased and baseless," and said it represented "a sick hope" that "he can win the war without having to fight." Echoing his prediction that the 1991 war would be the "Mother of All Battles," Saddam declared, "This will be Iraq's last great battle with the malicious tyrant in our time, and America's last great war of aggression, too." As he spoke, his advisers laughed when he laughed, and leaned forward to take notes when he turned serious. Throughout the day, the government organized demonstrations of loyalty, beginning with a predawn rally in which men of all ages volunteered to serve as fedayeen, or soldiers ready to sacrifice themselves to God and Saddam. "Saddam, Saddam, we pledge our blood and soul to you," crowds shouted. "Whatever we are able, we will do," said a twenty-year-old plumber named Haki Ismail. "We are not afraid of this war, and it does not matter if it is short or long. Hopefully, America will not dare to invade our land. But if they do, we will not let them in here in Baghdad."[1]

Most of Baghdad, a normally bustling city of nearly five million people, was eerily empty. Only days earlier, thoroughbreds still ran at the Amiriya racetrack, and 5,000 people turned out to watch the Friday meet, on the Muslim day of rest. Now shops were closed, their doors locked, their windows taped against expected bombs. There had been a run on water-storage tanks, kerosene lamps, electrical generators, flashlights and batteries, and canned food. At major government buildings, including one headquarters for the secret police, workers loaded computers and filing cabinets onto trucks, to allow work to go on in the event of war, officials said—perhaps in the vast network of underground tunnels and bunkers that Saddam had built with German and other Western help. The expressway westward to Jordan, a haven about 350 miles away, had been thick with families who bribed officials for exit visas, and huge lines had formed to buy gasoline, at 2 cents a liter one of the few material privileges left in Iraq. The government had announced that Qusay Hussein, considered his father's heir apparent, would take personal charge of the defense of the Baghdad military district. The few remaining Westerners left in the city debated what would happen next. Would they be arrested? Deployed around the country as human shields, as Saddam had done with scores of Western business executives before the 1991 war?

Twenty-four hours earlier, in northern Iraq, Kurdish civilians began fleeing cities or safeguarding their homes along the front lines with the Iraqi army where the Kurdish-controlled zone met the rest of the country. They crowded into taxis and buses, rode in trailers behind tractors, or simply piled into cars, forming long lines on the highways seeking what they hoped would be safety from chemical or conventional attack. "We are afraid of chemical weapons, we are afraid of the tanks, we are afraid of the artillery," said Faizulla Karim Rahman, a retired policeman who was moving ten family members from Chamchamal. "We are going to a village away from here." Infida Hussein, a schoolteacher, was searching for plastic, to seal her house against a chemical attack. "We will use the plastic and stay in our home," she said. "Fear is everywhere."

At a suburban school outside Baghdad, fourteen-year-old boys were ordered to dig a series of trenches, about ten feet long by five feet deep. As they worked, they chanted. "This may look like trench, but it's not," they said. "It's George W. Bush's grave."

THE PREVIOUS TEN DAYS HAD seen one last frantic attempt at resuscitating the diplomacy that had effectively died with de Villepin's blunt warning to Powell that France would veto any UN resolution authorizing war. On March 7, the morning after that message was delivered at the Waldorf, Blix and ElBaradei reported to the Security Council that, under threat of force, Iraq's cooperation with the weapons inspectors was increasing. "One can hardly avoid the impression that after a period of somewhat reluctant cooperation, there has been an acceleration of initiatives from the Iraqi side since the end of January," Blix said. On January 30, Bush had insisted that he would only wait "weeks, not months" for proof of disarmament. Now, in a twist on the president's words, Blix said the job would "not take years, nor weeks, but months." ElBaradei had more bad news for the Americans, completely demolishing the allegations that Iraq had tried to buy uranium from Niger: He said that the claim was based on patently forged documents. It was a black eye for the Bush administration.

But Powell had had enough. Responding to Blix's assessment of Iraq's growing cooperation—over the past week, Iraq had destroyed thirty-two Al Samoud 2 missiles—the secretary of state said, "I don't know if we should call these things initiatives." The Americans and British said they would press for a vote on a second resolution that would give Iraq just ten days to disarm, until Monday, March 17.

De Villepin was scornful. "By imposing a deadline of a few days, would we merely be seeking a pretext for war?" he demanded. "I will say it again, as a permanent member of the Security Council: France will not allow a resolution to pass that authorizes the automatic use of force." The Russian and Chinese foreign ministers followed suit. In the face of threatened vetoes by the permanent members, the only hope left for the Americans, British and Spaniards was to get a simple majority of the fifteen council members—eight, or preferably nine, votes—as a kind of moral imprimatur for the use of force. "Part of the strategy was to get 9 or 9.5 or 10, or 11 votes, and push the French into a corner," one American diplomat said. Blair was facing a vote in Parliament on the use of force and needed all the backing he could get. So did Prime Minister John Howard of Australia, who had volunteered about 2,000 troops, fighter planes and three ships. The Americans had hoped they could isolate the French, and argue that its veto should not thwart the will of the council. Instead, a senior administration official would recall, "The dynamics of the French veto threat had a different effect. It made people scramble for some kind of other solution, because the French were hell-bent on their veto."

What followed was a kind of Keystone Kops ballet, in which the rival camps courted members of the Security Council and foreign ministers floated various proposals, however unlikely, in an effort to keep diplomacy going. One such proposal was for the council to set some concrete disarmament "benchmarks" for Iraq to meet, perhaps by the end of March. Too long, the Americans said. Seventy-two hours would be more like it. Other ideas never surfaced openly. On Sunday, March 9, Luis Ernesto Derbez, the Mexican foreign minister, proposed to Powell the idea of sending 50,000 blue-helmeted United Nations peacekeeping troops to back up and enforce a coercive inspections regime. The notion went nowhere. The scrambling put terrible pressure on some of the less prominent Security Council members. President Pervez Musharraf of Pakistan had told Powell in February, "I am with you." He had been a staunch ally in the campaign against the Taliban and Al Qaeda, but he was the military leader of an Islamic country deeply wary of war with Iraq. Now he called with another message: It's very difficult. Confusion was rampant. Powell and Bush burned up the international telephone lines, calling their counterparts.

Over the weekend of March 8–9, de Villepin flew to Angola, Cameroon and Guinea to lobby the African members of the Security Council to vote against Washington. It was an extraordinary step: France was not simply opposing the United States itself, but trying to rally other nations into opposition as well. But the French diplomats saw the effort as necessary to their broader strategy of blocking a new resolution without having to resort to a veto. And they rejected American complaints that their campaign was somehow unfair. After all, Washington itself was leaning on undecided members to vote its way. "It's a strange argument to say we can campaign but you can't campaign," one French diplomat said.

On Monday, March 10, President Chirac said in an interview on French television that his country would use its veto, "whatever the circumstances." The French later insisted that Chirac had only been referring to the specific resolution under consideration, because it would allow an immediate resort to war if Iraq did not comply by March 17. They said that France would have been willing to support a resolution that gave the inspectors more time to do their work. But by then, the Bush administration had no patience left.

At the State Department, diplomats watched in a mix of irritation and amusement as de Villepin courted votes. They were confident they had the Africans' support. On Tuesday, March 11, François Fall, the foreign minister of Guinea, called Powell to say he had a green light to support the American resolution. The next day, an urgent cable came from Guinea saying that the country's president, Lansana Conté, was ill and at home in his ancestral village, and that his local medical adviser had told him not to vote for the American resolution. The next day, after some consultation, Powell's aides reported that Guinea was back to "yes."

Despite Bush's vow to press for a vote no matter the likely outcome, Powell had growing doubts. To take a vote and lose might well be worse than to take no vote at all—and simply insist that Resolution 1441, passed by a vote of 15 to 0 in November, gave sufficient grounds for war. Powell talked with his British counterpart, Jack Straw, and Foreign Minister Ana Palacio of Spain. They agreed that if they could not be sure of nine votes, it would be better not to go ahead. Powell talked to the president about the possibility of pulling the resolution. The White House allowed that Bush would accept a short extension of the March 17 deadline, but by only perhaps three days to a week.

In London, Blair was facing open debate about his political future. "I don't think it is possible to exaggerate the degree of concern about the illegality of what is proposed," said Tam Dalyell, a longtime maverick legislator from Blair's Labour Party. "If there is no UN mandate and if there is not a vote in the Commons before the commitment of British troops, then we ask the Prime Minister to consider his position as leader of the party." At the Pentagon, the ever-diplomatic Rumsfeld compounded Blair's predicament by telling reporters that he and British officials were reviewing the extent of British participation in any military campaign, suggesting that the United States might proceed without the British, taking go-it-aloneism to its furthest extension. After frantic transatlantic phone calls of protest, Rumsfeld backed away from this statement, explaining that his remarks were intended only to note that obtaining a second UN resolution "is important to the United Kingdom," and adding, "In the event a decision to use force is made, we have every reason to believe there will be a significant military contribution from the United Kingdom." That same day, Rumsfeld and General Myers met with the president at the White House. No one would reveal what they talked about, but Myers said later at the Pentagon that the United States now had more than 225,000 soldiers, sailors, airmen and marines in the Persian Gulf region. "If this president makes the decision to do so," the general said, "they stand ready to disarm Iraq."

• • •

By MID-MARCH, THE BUILDUP of troops and equipment in the Kuwaiti desert was massive. At night, a full moon illuminated an array of American and British ground forces across 5,000 square miles of flat, open terrain just across the border from Iraq. There were giant M1A1 Abrams tanks, armored vehicles of every description, hulking Humvees and humble troop transports, many of them still short of spare tires and equipment as quartermasters struggled to catch up. In front of the formations, engineering battalions wheeled bulldozers and heavy equipment into position, to practice breaching the ditches and earthen berms that marked the border. Troops cut away large sections of the chain-link fence that had marked the border since 1991. One night, the sky over northern Kuwait was so thick with assault and transport helicopters that meteorologists trying to track an approaching sandstorm were barred from launching weather balloons. Hundreds of chopper pilots ran last-minute training drills to master blind descents through the clouds of sand kicked up by their churning rotors. All that equipment had to be funneled in through a single port in Kuwait City, and some had been delayed by high winds and some was still arriving. Other units were scheduled to flow into the region once the conflict began. But there was a big unknown: Three dozen ships carrying tanks and heavy equipment for the Army's Fourth Infantry Division waited off the coast of Turkey, because of a continuing standoff over whether Turkey would allow American forces to mount a northern front from its soil.

Of the 130,000 Americans on the ground in Kuwait, roughly 16,500 were from the Army's Third Infantry Division, with a like number from the 101st Airborne, the famous "Screaming Eagles," whose seventy-two Apache attack helicopters were ready to leapfrog into enemy territory. The Third Infantry had about 250 tanks and a formidable array of other weapons, and was the heir to the 24th Mechanized Division, which had swept into the Euphrates Valley in the 1991 war. There were 64,000 marines deployed as well, prepared to stretch far beyond their usual amphibious operations on the long land route to Baghdad. About 25,000 British troops were also on the ground in Kuwait, along with the shadow soldiers no one much talked about—several thousand Special Operations forces, who would sneak across the border even before hostilities commenced.

The Iraqi army that these forces were preparing to face was a shadow of its 1991 strength and readiness. But the American force was also less than half what it had been in 1991, when the Powell Doctrine called for the application of overwhelming force. Rumsfeld was out to get more firepower from fewer troops, and already some former top commanders were warning that the demands of a long land advance to Baghdad, the surrender of prisoners and the need to secure supply lines, plus the inevitable surprises of battle, would leave the quarter-million allied troops in the region stretched thin. "The key to success is rapid victory on the ground, and bringing stability as quickly as you can," said one former senior officer who had commanded land forces during the Gulf war. "Based on what I know about the forces in the region, or flowing in, I am concerned they don't have enough to give high assurance they can do this quickly. It's strange for most of us. If we did it so well last time, using the Powell Doctrine, why would you do anything less than that now? Why take that risk?"

THE FIGHTING FORCE THAT WAS waiting in the Kuwaiti desert represented a broad slice of American society, but by no means all of it. Since the draft had ended in 1973, the United States armed forces were increasingly made up of a professional warrior caste, which often perpetuated itself from father or uncle to son or niece, whose political and social attitudes tended to represent a particular slice of civilian society. Political conservatism was ascendant in the officer corps, and reading scores for enlisted personnel were a full grade higher than for their civilian counterparts. Whites accounted for three out of five soldiers in the 1.4-million-strong active-duty military, but the armed services had become a powerful career magnet for blacks, who were represented in greater numbers than their proportion of the civilian population. Both the wealthy and the underclass were essentially absent. More than anything, it was a self-selecting group, a volunteer force that was bearing an increasing burden as troops deployed from Afghanistan to the Persian Gulf. "As it stands right now, the country is riding on the soldiers who volunteer," said Sergeant Barry Perkins, a thirty-nine-year-old career military policeman at Fort Benning, Georgia. "Everybody else is taking a free ride."

A good number of the soldiers training in Kuwait had served in the 1991 war, and were now back for a second crack at Saddam. One of them was Lieutenant Colonel Eric Schwartz, commander of Task Force 1-64, a battalion-sized armored combat team of the Third Infantry's 2nd Brigade. Although his father and grandfather had served in the military, Rick Schwartz did not start out on this path. At Lynchburg College in Virginia he had majored in elementary education, joined the Reserve Officer Training Corps (ROTC) and then spent a year teaching second and third graders before enlisting. In the last war, he had been a captain and a tank company commander in the 24th Mechanized Division under General Barry McCaffrey, one of the most aggressive commanders in that conflict. Schwartz had won a Bronze Star for action at Jalibah Airfield in Iraq, and now he was back, at age forty, in charge of a combat team that had known from the beginning that it would be among the units heading to Baghdad.

The men of Task Force 1-64 called themselves the "Desert Rogues," and Schwartz had pushed them hard. "We make things so difficult out here, that when we actually do it, it doesn't seem that difficult," he had said in December. At the same time, he had warned his men against worrying too much about the Iraqis' power. "We can overestimate the enemy to the point we can tie our own hands," he said.[2] Days before the war began, Schwartz summed up his battalion's view. "The soldiers are saying it looks like we're going to have to go through Baghdad before we go home," he said. "So let's go."[3]

Indeed, for the forces bivouacked in the tent cities, savoring their last showers and last hot meals for who knew how long, the waiting was becoming a grind.

"Let's get on with it," Sergeant Jose Roscoe from New York City said at Camp New Jersey. "Let's get it done. Let's go home." Rosaries were in short supply. "Everyone's nervous, it's natural to be nervous," said Sergeant Major Ray Lane of the 22nd Signal Brigade. "If you're not nervous you're a cowboy—and this is no time for cowboys."

In northwestern Kuwait, where the Third Infantry waited under the relentless sun of a washed-out sky, Corporal Benjamin R. Richardson cut hair. Captain Michael T. O'Neill did laundry, the guy ropes of his tent festooned with damp fatigues, shirts and socks. "I haven't done it since I got here," he said.

At a pier in the port of Kuwait, Major General David H. Petraeus, fifty years old with a Ph.D. in international relations from Princeton, was forehead to forehead with Jonathan Aleshire, a nineteen-year-old private. Petraeus, five-foot-nine and 150 pounds, commanded the 101st Airborne, and was touring the port when a good-natured jibe from one of the enlisted men sparked a sudden push-up contest.

"Stay with me," the general said to the private, face down on the pier.

"Sir!" the private said.

"Just stay with me," Petraeus replied.

At push-up number 24, a little gasp emerged from Private Aleshire's mouth. Petraeus, who had lost part of a lung in a range accident and had broken his pelvis skydiving, never blinked. After number 26, Aleshire was through. The general pumped on for another twenty or so. When he stood, the only sign of exertion was a throbbing vein on his neck.

"You can write that off on your income taxes as an educational expense!" he told the private.

On the USS *Abraham Lincoln,* a 97,000-ton nuclear-powered aircraft carrier in the Persian Gulf that was weathering the longest naval deployment since the 1991 war, Captain Scott Swift, deputy commander of the ship's air wing, summed up the mood. "All the machismo, all the talk about what the future will bring," he said. "Well, reality is here."

As the last days of diplomacy wore on, the American public increasingly saw war as a foregone conclusion. Polls showed that citizens were impatient with the United Nations, and that slightly more than half—55 percent—would support American military action, even without Security Council backing. President Bush increasingly set his sights on a post-Saddam Iraq, approving plans for the creation of an interim Iraqi authority to help form a new government after any war. The administration refused to offer any public assessment of what war and reconstruction might cost. There were reasonable guesses, however, and they were sobering. A blue-ribbon panel headed by James R. Schlesinger, a former defense secretary, estimated that rebuilding Iraq would take at least $20 billion a year and require

75,000 to 200,000 troops stationed in the country to keep order. In February, the Army's chief of staff, General Eric K. Shinseki, had warned that several hundred thousand American troops might be needed in Iraq after the war, but was swiftly slapped down by Wolfowitz and Rumsfeld, who called the estimate far off the mark.

The government warned of possible terrorist reprisals in event of war, and the FBI alerted local police about possible "sleeper agents" with ties to Iraqi intelligence. Cities around the country announced stepped-up security plans and candlelight vigils.

And in a sign that war was drawing closer, the Air Force dispatched one of the last major components of its plan for huge air assaults: Four B-2 stealth bombers, to be based on the island of Diego Garcia in the Indian Ocean. Powell told a House appropriations subcommittee that he had not entirely given up hope at the Security Council. "We are still talking to the members of the Council to see what is possible with respect to coalescing around a position that wouldn't draw a veto, but the options remain: go for a vote and see what members say, or not go for a vote." The effect of his comments was to leave wavering Security Council members unwilling to take the domestic political risk of backing Washington if Bush might decide to abandon a vote altogether.

Meanwhile, the pressure on Tony Blair had become excruciating. On Friday, March 14, as a favor to the prime minister, Bush reversed his previous policy of inaction on the Israeli-Palestinian conflict, and promised to soon unveil the so-called road map toward a peace settlement, which had been worked out with European allies over the preceding months. It was an important issue for Blair—and for Europe more broadly. Much of Western Europe, grappling with its own legacy of Middle East colonialism and the waves of Arab immigrants who had settled in European countries in recent years, tended to see Washington's strong support for Israel as an impediment to a peaceful solution of the Israeli-Palestinian struggle. Only by resolving that conflict, the Europeans believed, could there be stability in the Middle East and quietude in their own sometimes disaffected Arab populations. Only a week earlier, Bush had said he would not turn his attention to that issue until after the war. Now, he announced that he was prepared to publicly detail the long-deferred plan as soon as the Palestinians elected a new prime minister to take power from Yasir Arafat, which could happen any day. In London, Blair promptly said that Bush's announcement showed "the obligation of even-handedness" on the eve of a possible war in the heart of the Arab world.

That same day, Bush and Blair announced that they would meet on Sunday, March 16, with Prime Minister Aznar of Spain in the Azores, in the eastern Atlantic, in a last-ditch effort to see if there was any hope of bringing the UN together in support of an ultimatum to Saddam. But the wavering Security Council members were not invited, and the session had the hallmarks of an elaborate shadow play. The U.S. had written off France, the one player with real power to change the situation. "This has gone on long enough," Condoleezza Rice told the Arab-language television network Al Jazeera. Back in Washington, Dick Cheney made the startling claim that the administration believed that Saddam "has, in fact, reconstituted nuclear weapons."

As Bush and his allies gathered for their hour-long meeting, they declined to say directly whether they would seek a vote at the UN. In their eyes, the next day's deadline still stood. "Tomorrow is the day that we will determine whether diplomacy can work," Bush said, his voice rising and his jaw clenched as he punched the air with his fist before flying home to Washington late that night. Aboard Air Force One were the president's two main speechwriters—Michael Gerson, whose eloquent prose had informed some of Bush's best rhetorical moments, and Karen Hughes, his trusted media counselor who had left the White House staff but still showed up at times of crisis. As war drew nearer, Bush knew he would need their services.

By 9:00 the next morning, Bush had his answer. At a meeting of the National Security Council in the White House situation room, Powell told the president the result of a half-dozen telephone calls he had made to his counterparts around the world overnight: Nothing had changed. Bush, too, said that he had reached the same conclusion in his own early-morning calls with Blair and Aznar. The leaders instructed their UN envoys to withdraw the resolution, and the White House announced that Bush would address the nation that evening.

At UN headquarters in New York, Kofi Annan sounded a mournful note. "I have made it very clear that in my judgment, if the Council were to be able to manage this process successfully and

muster the collective will to handle this operation, its own reputation and credibility would have been enhanced," he said. "If this
action is to take place without the support of the Council, its legitimacy will be questioned, and the support for it will be diminished."
In Britain, Robin Cook, a former foreign minister and leader of the
Commons, resigned from Blair's cabinet in protest. "In principle, I
believe it is wrong to embark on military action without broad
international support," he said. "In practice, I believe it is against
Britain's interest to create a precedent for unilateral military action."
In France, Dominique de Villepin declared, "We are advancing to
war even though today it is possible to disarm in peace. Is war
today really necessary? It is not, because the inspections are going
ahead on the ground."

In Washington, Senator Daschle, the Democratic leader, told a
gathering of labor union members, "I am saddened, saddened that
this president failed so miserably at diplomacy that we're now
forced to war. Saddened that we have to give up one life, because
this president couldn't create the kind of diplomatic effort that was
so critical for our country." He was swiftly denounced by Republicans for criticizing his commander in chief on the eve of war. But
the stock markets rallied strongly after months of uncertainty, and
by day's end, all the major indices had gained slightly more than 3
percent. Jay Garner, the retired American general designated by the
Pentagon to be the point man in supervising Iraq in the immediate
aftermath of war, arrived in Kuwait, where a staff of veteran diplomats and military officers was already at work, laying the groundwork for an occupation.

Bush himself kept to his schedule, a disciplined creature of routine as always. He practiced his speech with Gerson and Hughes. He
met for a half hour on battle plans with Rumsfeld and Wolfowitz.
He threw a ball on the South Lawn with his dogs, Barney and Spot.
He took a midday workout in the exercise room in the family quarters. As darkness fell, he summoned congressional leaders for a
preview of his speech. Then, at just after 8 o'clock, he strode to a lectern in the columned White House Cross Hall, the elegant red-
carpeted first-floor gallery that links the east and west sides of the old
house. He faced the television camera, and the world. "All the

decades of deceit and cruelty have now reached an end," Bush said. "Saddam Hussein and his sons must leave Iraq within forty-eight hours. Their refusal to do so will result in military conflict, commenced at a time of our choosing."

In downtown Baghdad, three trucks pulled up to the bank.

PART TWO

AMERICA'S WAR

Chapter 7

BEST-LAID PLANS

In the southern Iraqi desert
Tuesday, March 18, 2003

The three MH-53 helicopters swept low and fast across the darkened sand. At almost ninety feet long and twenty-five feet high, they were the Air Force's largest, with the streamlined, bulb-nosed look of flying locomotives. Their official name was Pave Lows, but they were still widely known by the Vietnam-era nickname of the craft they had succeeded: Super Jolly Green Giants. Wrapped in armor plating and able to hug the ground to avoid being detected by radar, they were custom-made for long-distance covert missions on nights like this. With midair refueling, they could fly almost indefinitely, with a top speed of 196 miles per hour. On this night, their mission was top secret and the cargo in their big bellies precious: Toyota pickup trucks full of Army Special Operations soldiers, the unconventional vanguard of an invasion that had yet to begin.

As the giant choppers approached a landing zone in the open desert, one of them clipped a rock outcropping as it tried to land in the swirling dust. Suddenly unbalanced, it whipped and roared like a bucking bronco before crashing sideways in a screech of twisting metal, with the truck inside flipped on top of a soldier. "Chopper down!" rang out in one of the other aircraft, and a soldier aboard assumed they had lost a third of their team. "We're done," he thought to himself. "We'll have to go home." At an air base in Kuwait, commanders watched in horror as the scene played out in real-time video, transmitted from an unmanned Predator drone circling the site.

But the crew and commandos walked away from the crash without serious injuries. The soldiers crowded into the remaining two trucks and raced into the darkness toward their final destination, the strategic crossroads city of Nasiriya, some 200 miles south of Baghdad on the Euphrates River. Over the next seventy-two hours, dozens more twelve-member teams from Special Operations made less dramatic landings throughout southern and western Iraq. Their jobs: to hunt for Scud missiles, pinpoint bombing targets, seize oil terminals. Once viewed as mavericks and cowboys needing to be kept separate from conventional troops, these special soldiers had been a key element of the Pentagon's planning from day one. Fresh from their starring role in Afghanistan, where Army Green Berets and Navy SEALs led the fighting, Special Ops were now set to play a key role in a far larger, more conventional war.

The Special Operations forces called themselves "the quiet professionals," and they relished the aura of mystery in which their missions were wrapped. "Even my wife doesn't know what I do," one team sergeant said. They were all part of a new kind of American warfare— and a new kind of war plan that had taken shape over the past months in an intense dialectic between Donald Rumsfeld (and his civilian Pentagon planners) and Tommy Ray Franks, the blunt-spoken four-star general in charge of the war.

FROM THE OUTSET, RUMSFELD WAS determined that this war with Iraq would not look like the last one, and the war plan that finally emerged as "1003 Victor" did not. Flush with the swift success of the Afghan campaign, Rumsfeld believed that American forces could be far lighter and more flexible and still succeed. In the twenty-first-century conflicts to come, the defense secretary liked to say, "Business as usual won't do it."

In the 1991 Gulf war, the United States amassed nearly 550,000 troops in the theater over six months, and had pounded Iraqi forces from the air for almost six weeks before beginning the short and decisive land attack to oust Iraqi troops from Kuwait. It was a pattern that the historian Russell Weigley called "the American way of war" (summed up in his 1973 book of the same name), a strategy of using sheer numbers of troops to wear down an enemy and bring him to his knees through attrition and sheer destructive capacity. This had been the favored approach of American generals from Ulysses S. Grant to Dwight Eisenhower to Colin Powell. Within days of Saddam Hussein's invasion of Kuwait on August 2, 1990, American forces had arrived in the region, and within months, the American-led coalition had amassed several hundred thousand troops in Saudi Arabia and neighboring countries. In November 1990, the United Nations passed a resolution authorizing the use of "all necessary means" to remove Iraqi forces from Kuwait by January 15, 1991, and when that deadline passed, the United States and its partners unleashed a barrage of air and missile attacks on Baghdad. On February 21, Secretary of Defense Dick Cheney was threatening "one of the largest land assaults of modern times," and two days later the ground war began. On February 26, as Iraqi troops began withdrawing from Kuwait, allied planes killed thousands of them on the "Highway of Death" leading back to Iraq. One hundred hours after the ground campaign began, allied forces entered Kuwait City—and the first President Bush suspended the fight, announcing that the objective of removing Iraqi troops from Kuwait had been achieved.

Now, twelve years later, the goal was far more ambitious, not just to repulse Saddam's invasion of a small neighboring country but to crush him on his own turf. Yet Rumsfeld envisioned an entirely different type of war: one relying on a few divisions, backed by precision bombing from an arsenal of warplanes and missiles, steered by a constellation of sensors in the sky that could give commanders a round-the-clock look at the battlefield below them. The lighter, more mobile approach fit perfectly with Rumsfeld's larger goal of transforming the military from a lumbering industrial behemoth trained to fight a fixed enemy like the Soviet Union to a nimble, information-age force able to move quickly to engage a range of potential threats around the world.

The Pentagon's top generals—especially those in the Army—had deep misgivings about Rumsfeld's ideas. Franks, the commander in chief of the U.S. Central Command, was an old artilleryman who had won three Purple Hearts in Vietnam, and he had his doubts, too. In the summer of 2002, Franks had presented a planning document, titled "Centcom Courses of Action." It was broadly conceptual, and called for tens of thousands of soldiers and marines to invade Iraq from Kuwait—along with air-, land- and sea-based forces to attack from the north, west and south. Special Operations forces or covert CIA operatives would strike at suspected chemical or biological weapons labs and storage depots. The document was far short of a full war plan, but Rumsfeld and his Pentagon planners found it insufficiently creative and all but dismissed it. Indeed, at every turn, Rumsfeld challenged his generals to think in new ways. Franks's plan called for about 250,000 troops—including three divisions of heavy armored forces—but Rumsfeld asked if the attacking force could be far smaller, perhaps fewer than 100,000 troops.

Part of Rumsfeld's argument was technological: New developments now allowed greater precision in bombing, and greater coordination between air and ground forces, meaning that fewer boots on the ground would be needed. The technical innovations in the decade since the first Gulf war were real enough. There was the Joint Tactical Ground Station, a sophisticated new ground-based early-warning system, which could alert commanders to hostile missile launchings, using data from satellites. The single greatest loss of American lives in the Gulf war had come when an Iraqi Scud missile hit a barracks in Dhahran, Saudi Arabia, killing twenty-eight and wounding about a hundred others. Defense officials believed that the new ground system, combined with other air defenses, would give them more time to warn troops of an enemy missile strike, and then fire off a quicker and more accurate counterattack. The new PAC-3 model of the Patriot missile was also an advance over its Gulf war predecessor, designed to hit its target head-on, instead of just exploding nearby. The Patriot system had initially been much lauded in 1991 but turned out to be far less effective than promised.

The military had also developed a new arsenal of electronic and psychological weapons that moved well beyond the traditional dropping of propaganda leaflets. Radio transmitters hauled aloft by Air Force Special Operations EC-130E planes were prepared to broadcast directly to the Iraqi public, in Arabic, with messages like "Do not let Saddam tarnish the reputation of soldiers any longer. Saddam uses the military to persecute those who don't agree with his unjust agenda. Make the decision." American commanders were talking of super-secret weapons that could be used to flash millions of watts of electricity to cripple Iraqi computers and literally turn off the lights in Baghdad in the case of full-fledged combat. And they were taking great pains to avoid either large-scale destruction of civilian infrastructure or block-to-block urban combat that could inflict heavy casualties on both sides.

There was another basic assumption—promoted by Deputy Secretary Paul Wolfowitz and others—that also seemed to argue in favor of a smaller force: that the Iraqi army, perhaps only a third of its size before the 1991 war, would fold quickly in combat. According to this line of thought, the Shiite areas in the south of the country, grateful for deliverance from decades of Saddam's repression, would welcome the advancing Americans with cheers and flowers. The advance to Baghdad would then be swift and largely unopposed. American troops would not have to enter or besiege the southern population centers, but could simply bypass them on their way to the capital. It was in Baghdad that Saddam's loyalists were expected to make their last stand, so the American goal was to get there as quickly as possible, isolate the city, then take control gradually by seizing or destroying key targets of Saddam's power. "If we have to fight a pitched battle in Baghdad," one senior officer said, "it means we screwed up somewhere along the way."

Franks held his ground on the need for more troops than Rumsfeld wanted. But, in an ongoing dialogue over the summer and fall of 2002, new ideas came and went, and the plan incorporated more fully the idea of attacking swiftly from multiple directions, with more reliance on unconventional forces. Franks won approval for a key element: There would be a northern front, with a heavy armored division, to put a pincer move on Baghdad, in combination with the main thrust from the south. That would mean getting permission from Turkey, a NATO ally and one of Washington's most reliable partners in the Middle East, to move American forces across its soil. It should have been comparatively easy to arrange. It was not.

FROM THE BEGINNING OF THE war planning, Washington considered the use of Turkey's air bases to be crucial for any new campaign against Iraq, Turkey's immediate neighbor to the southeast. Yet almost from the outset, the American attempts to secure basing rights were complicated by Turkey's economic troubles, by vocal opposition from its overwhelmingly Muslim population—which was suspicious of American intentions—by internal political problems, and by concerns that a war in Iraq would embolden the Kurds in northern Iraq to assert nationalistic demands that could spill over into Turkey's own large Kurdish population, with destabilizing effects. Turkey had allowed the United States access to its territory for the 1991 war, and for patrolling the no-fly zones since, and had contributed peacekeeping troops in Afghanistan after the fall of the Taliban. But it had suffered severe financial hardships as a result of the 1991 war—hardships that many Turks felt could have been mitigated by the United States, but were not. The prospect of convincing the Turkish public to accept participation in a new, full-scale conflict was daunting.

In the fall of 2002, the Bush administration began an aggressive campaign to win Turkey's approval to use its bases. In December, Wolfowitz went to Ankara to make the case, offering the incentive of American support for Turkey's much-desired entry into the European Union. The Turkish government made it clear that it would want any war to proceed with United Nations backing, and that it would also expect a significant American financial incentive in exchange for its support. Turkey's internal politics were also unsettled, which added a further complication to the negotiations. The Justice and Development Party had come to power in parliamentary elections in November; its leader, Recep Tayip Erdogan, had been barred from serving in the government after a jail term for sedition in 1998, and he was eager to shore up his own political standing and to press for Turkey's admission into the European Union. Bush invited him to the White House on December 10 for a pep talk, but Turkish public opinion remained opposed to joining a war against Iraq. On December 20, Prime Minister Abdullah Gul, who was essentially Erdogan's placeholder, declared, "Turkey is a democratic country. We have to convince our people, we have to convince our parliament. Whether we fully cooperate or do nothing, we are going to suffer." Under Turkish law, parliament would have to approve the stationing of any foreign troops on Turkish soil.

By January, the Bush administration had grown increasingly frustrated with Turkey's indecision, and in the middle of that month, General Myers, the chairman of the Joint Chiefs, made an inconclusive lobbying trip of his own. Meantime, a parallel crisis was emerging. The United States had asked NATO to send defensive weaponry, including AWACS radar planes, Patriot missiles and anti–chemical weapons gear to Turkey, to help it protect itself in the event of war.

But France, Germany and Belgium, key members of the NATO alliance, remained so adamantly opposed to an American-led war against Iraq that they blocked a measure to send the weapons. NATO debated the question in a series of emergency talks, while Washington threatened to take its own steps to defend Turkey, no matter what. By mid-February, NATO's defense planning committee finally agreed to send the weapons, but not before one more damaging and divisive wedge had been driven into the Atlantic alliance.

Even as NATO approved the dispatch of the AWACS radar planes and other assistance, Turkish officials postponed a planned parliamentary vote on Washington's request for basing rights, and continued haggling over a package of American economic assistance that was rumored to be as much as $15 billion in outright grants and loan guarantees. Skeptics of the Bush administration's policy cracked that the "coalition of the willing"—its name for the nations volunteering support for a war against Iraq—was becoming a "coalition of the billing." On March 1, in a stunning blow, the Turkish parliament rejected the proposal to allow American troops to operate from Turkish bases. The vote was 264 in favor to 251 against, with 19 abstentions, but under the parliament's rules, a majority of members present—or 268 votes—was required for passage. In Washington, Secretary Powell said that the American military would be "flexible enough" to proceed without Turkish help, while General Myers said, "It'll be tougher without Turkey, but nevertheless, it'll happen."

On March 9, Erdogan, his eligibility to hold office restored, at last won his expected seat in the Turkish parliament (with 85 percent of the vote), and his assumption of the prime minister's post revived American hopes for a deal. Vice President Cheney spoke with Erdogan on March 13, but one administration official said, "The message was clear that by the time Turkey got its act together, it would be too late to do us any good."

In hindsight, a number of American miscalculations clearly contributed to the Bush administration's failure to win Turkey's support. Wolfowitz had asserted that Turkey's eventual support was assured, which may have come across not as optimism, but as arrogance. Secretary Powell himself never made a personal lobbying trip to Ankara to sway wavering Turkish legislators or influence Turkish public opinion. Powell's aides contended that he was hamstrung, because he could not be seen as seeking support for a military campaign at the very time he was still pursuing diplomacy at the United Nations aimed at avoiding a war.

So now, on the eve of war, there would be no northern front. The 16,500 members of the Army's Fourth Infantry Division—its most technologically advanced tank troops—were still waiting for the order to leave their bases in Texas and Colorado. Long ago, they had loaded 14,000 pieces of gear onto ships headed for Turkey. Still, General Franks, determined to hold out hope and keep psychological pressure on Iraq until the last possible moment, had ordered those three dozen ships to remain floating in the Mediterranean with their tanks and heavy equipment. The war would have to begin without them.

OVER THE TENSE MONTHS FROM July 2002 to February 2003, General Franks's war plan went through nearly two dozen revisions, before finally winning approval from Secretary Rumsfeld and President Bush. Franks had first learned to work with Rumsfeld in the heat of the Afghan campaign, in 2001. Neither man was shy about speaking his mind. Their final plan combined some of Franks's old Army ideas with many of Rumsfeld's new ones. The war would begin with stealth, with teams of several hundred Special Operations forces sneaking into Iraq under cover of darkness to secure oil facilities, take out Iraqi missile sites and hunt for chemical or biological weapons. Forty-eight hours later, there would be a short, intense version of the air campaign that heralded the start of the 1991 war. Its goal would be to "shock and awe" the Iraqi regime with its suddenness and destructive power. The plan called for unleashing 3,000 precision-guided bombs and missiles from five aircraft carriers and land bases over three days, in an attempt to stagger the Iraqi forces and pave the way for an equally swift ground attack to follow. The initial bombardment would use ten times the number of precision-guided weapons fired in the first two days of the 1991 war, and the targets would be air defenses, political and military headquarters, communications facilities and suspected chemical and biological delivery systems.

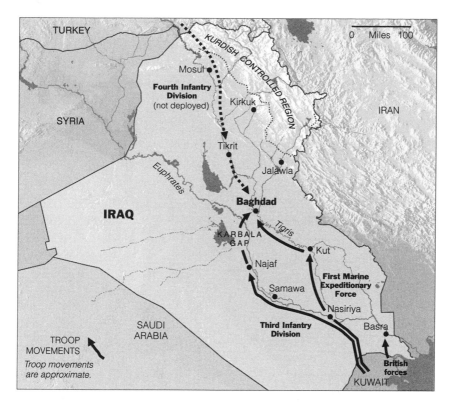

In a sharp departure from past military doctrine, the plan envisioned a rolling start to the invasion, which could be launched even as troops and equipment were still arriving in the region. Rather than waiting months to mass the kind of heavy forces that had been used twelve years earlier, commanders would begin the battle with fewer troops, while deployment orders went out to assure that forces would continue to flow into the region if needed. Without doubt, it was a bold plan, if not a risky one. Troops would be stretched thin, with long supply lines, and limited rear-area security. Because of Turkey's refusal to allow an invasion from the north, the American force would be even lighter than Franks's compromise plan. It was now even more critical that American troops encounter only limited resistance in the south and receive the cooperation of Iraqi civilians.

So as the hours ticked down toward the expiration of President Bush's forty-eight-hour ultimatum to Saddam, this is how the American and British forces in the region stacked up: There were more than

225,000 American troops in the Persian Gulf, with more than 130,000 on the ground in Kuwait, together with about 25,000 British ground troops. (On March 18, the day after Bush delivered his ultimatum, Tony Blair staved off opposition from members of his own Labour Party and at last won the support of the House of Commons to disarm Iraq by "all means necessary," thus assuring Britain's military participation in the war.) The basic plan was for two long columns of American forces to roll north from Kuwait more than 300 miles to Baghdad, with the Army moving swiftly through open desert on the west side of the Euphrates River, and the Marines taking a parallel route to the east, in the valley between the Euphrates and Tigris Rivers. The two American columns would reach north through the country like a giant pair of outstretched arms, with their hands and fingers ready to meet and close in an interlocking vise around Baghdad itself. The British would secure the second largest Iraqi city, Basra, in the south not far from the Persian Gulf, and would protect the Americans' right flank as they advanced on the capital. American Special Operations troops in the north and west would supplement the efforts of the main invading forces, and deal with special threats, like suspected chemical and biological weapons sites.

Emblematic of the unusual nature of the war plan, the largest American ground contingent would not be the Army at all, but the First Marine Expeditionary Force, about 50,000 strong, under the command of Lieutenant General James T. Conway. Its advance toward Baghdad, in amphibious assault vehicles more often used for beach landings, would be the longest Marine land attack since 1805, when Lieutenant Presley O'Bannon marched 600 miles from Alexandria, Egypt, to Derna, Tripoli, in seven weeks during the war with the Barbary pirates that inspired the words of the Marine Hymn ("From the halls of Montezuma to the shores of Tripoli . . ."). For the Marines, a key objective on the road to Baghdad would be a strategic pair of bridges in Nasiriya that would allow them to cross the Euphrates about 200 miles south of the capital. The extended march would be a stretch. "It is a long way from the sea, no question about that," General Conway conceded.

The Army's attack would be led by Lieutenant General William Wallace, commander of the V Corps, Colin Powell's old command, based in Heidelberg, Germany. His main fighting force when the war began would be the Third Infantry Division, with roughly 16,500 troops with heavy tanks and armored vehicles, organized in three brigades. The division had been training for months in the Kuwaiti desert and now its job would be to roll up the west side of the Euphrates, before making a dangerous dash across a narrow strip of desert outside the city of Karbala on its final push to Baghdad. The Karbala Gap was a perilous area; American commanders feared that if Saddam Hussein chose to use chemical or biological weapons, this might be the spot. The Third Infantry would be supplemented by long convoys of fuel and supply trucks in its rear, and by a fleet of attack helicopters from the 11th Aviation Regiment. The Army would also be able to call on elements of the 82nd Airborne Division, already in Kuwait and available for special missions, and on the venerable 101st Airborne Division, whose forces were just arriving on the eve of the war, preparing to play the key role of leapfrogging the ground units to provide more manpower for the advance into Baghdad.

Like all military plans, this one had almost infinite alternative options, a flow-chart system of "root-and-branch" contingencies that could change as needed. But some of those options would depend, uncharacteristically for the U.S. military, on forces that had not yet arrived in the region. In a military culture long renowned for belt-and-suspenders redundancy, this force had an undeniable seat-of-the-pants feel.

THE SPECIAL OPERATIONS FORCES WHO had almost crashed in the Iraqi desert were well on their way to their secret missions, linking up with friendly Iraqis on the ground who had been prescreened by the CIA, setting up reconnaissance and picking out targets for American bombs. Early on Wednesday morning, March 19, the mood in the White House situation room, the secure basement command post down a back stairway under the West Wing, was sober. The president's ultimatum to Saddam and his sons to get out of Iraq was due to expire at 8 P.M. Washington time. Now Bush polled his National Security Council—Rice, Rumsfeld, Powell and the rest—for any last-minute reservations, any lingering doubts, any un-dotted i's. He heard none. From a command post in Saudi Arabia, Franks's weathered face appeared on the flickering screen of a secure videoconference call with Bush and his commanders. "This force is ready to go," Franks said.[1]

President Bush gave the command: Execute. More Special Operations teams would go into Iraq that night. The massive air campaign intended to shock Saddam's regime into submission would begin on Friday, and the ground invasion on Saturday. Franks saluted back, and the videoconference call ended.

No one knew how long a war might last. Three days? Three weeks? Three months? "You could have heard a pin drop in that room," recalled one official. "It was silent for a couple of minutes." Then Powell, whose experience of battle and all its risks so far exceeded anything that Bush could imagine, made a wordless gesture of support: He reached out to touch the president's hand. A few minutes later, Bush went outside and walked around the White House grounds, to get some air and collect his thoughts.[2] The meeting broke up, and Rumsfeld and some military aides stayed behind to go over battle plans.

Bush met later that day with his secretary of homeland security, Tom Ridge, and with Mayor Michael R. Bloomberg of New York, to discuss domestic security plans and costs. He also made a round of phone calls to let world leaders know that he was ready to act. In a seven-page message to Congress—required by the resolution authorizing war—the president declared that the only way to "adequately protect the national security of the Untied States" was to topple the Iraqi regime by force, as a "vital part" of a broader war against terrorism. Senator Robert C. Byrd, the West Virginia Democrat and country orator who had been among the handful of members to argue vociferously against war, made no secret of his gloom. "Today, I weep for my country," he said, adding: "No more is the image of America one of strong, yet benevolent peacekeeper. The image of America has changed. Around the globe, our friends mistrust us, our word is disputed, our intentions are questioned."

Washington was eerily quiet, with the whole area around the White House sealed off by police. "I thought I was pretty well through with the day," Bush would recall.[3] In fact, he was just beginning.

Chapter 8

THE ELEMENT OF SURPRISE

Washington, D.C.
Wednesday, March 19, 2003

The war plan that President Bush approved that Wednesday morning lasted for about six hours. Just before 3 P.M. at CIA headquarters in Langley, Virginia, Director George Tenet got an extraordinary tip: He might know where Saddam would be that night. For months, intelligence officers had been struggling to get inside Saddam's inner circle of secrecy, to find some turncoat who could help them pinpoint the comings and goings of the tyrant who would never stay—or even sleep—in one place for very long. Past efforts aimed at sparking a coup or destabilizing Saddam had always bumped up against the hard reality of his impenetrable cone of security, and the loyal cadre that kept him in power. Now, Tenet suddenly had a spymaster's dream: a man in Saddam's orbit who was telling the CIA where Saddam, and probably his two sons, would be this very night. The location was a concrete underground bunker about 100 feet away from a nondescript house in a residential sector of Baghdad known as Dora Farms. It was already nearly 11 P.M. in Iraq, and there was no time to waste.

Tenet raced in his car along the Potomac to the Pentagon, where Rumsfeld and Wolfowitz were in the middle of a meeting. They summoned General Myers and headed for the White House. In the Oval Office, they met with Bush, Powell, Rice, Cheney and Andrew Card, the chief of staff, along with a few CIA agents Bush had never met before. Rumsfeld and Tenet wanted permission to launch an air strike that night. The war planning had long envisioned a possible option of striking first at Baghdad itself, aiming at key targets in hopes of forcing a quick disintegration of Saddam's regime. The approach, nicknamed "inside-out," was explicit in its goal of killing or isolating Saddam, and preventing him from launching chemical or biological attacks. Some senior civilian officials at the Pentagon had pushed hard for this idea, and now there was a chance to try it. Rumsfeld had often remarked that a war plan was like a family budget: something someone sets down, then never lives with. This sudden opportunity was proof.

But Bush was hesitant. "I was worried," he later recalled, "that the first pictures coming out of Iraq would be a wounded grandchild of Saddam Hussein" and that Saddam, "who was not there at the time we started making the decision, would never show up—that the first images of the American attack would be death to young children." For hours, the group talked through the possibilities. How would a sudden strike affect the rest of the war plan? What if the information was wrong? What were the propaganda risks? "You know—that the Iraqis might do the baby-milk thing again," one participant said, in reference to the famous moment in the 1991 war when reporters were taken to see bomb damage at what the Iraqis said was a civilian milk plant but that the Americans contended was a biological weapons lab. Rice reminded the group that the Iraqis "love to propagandize and lie about what's just taken place." Tenet insisted that the intelligence was solid, and as afternoon turned into evening, it "got richer and richer," Bush recalled. "The guy on the ground was calling into Centcom headquarters, who was immediately calling in to the White House more and more information. As the intelligence got richer, I got more confident with the notion that Saddam would, in fact, be there."[1] From his headquarters, Franks ordered two F-117A Nighthawk stealth aircraft aloft, just in case the president ordered a strike.

At 7:12 P.M. Washington time, three minutes before what Franks said was his deadline for making a decision, Bush decided it was worth the risk. "Let's go," he told his team. It was just after 3 A.M. in Baghdad. But there were some concerns. Franks had about forty cruise missiles standing at the ready on ships and submarines in the Red Sea and the Persian Gulf. But they would not be able to penetrate a concrete and steel-reinforced bunker, so the bombers would have to go in first, armed with their 2,000-pound EGBU-27s, the so-called bunker-busters, followed by the missiles, which would have to be quickly reprogrammed. Moreover, the moon was full over Baghdad, and the bat-winged, jet-black planes might well be visible. "It was," Bush said, "a dramatic several hours."[2]

THE DRAMA IN THE OVAL Office was nothing compared to the one unfolding in the cockpit of Lieutenant Colonel David Toomey's Nighthawk high over Iraq. It was more than an hour after Bush had ordered the secret strike, and dawn was fast approaching. Suddenly, Toomey realized he had a big problem: An indicator light on the satellite guidance system for one of his plane's bombs had gone dead. Without the target's coordinates locked in, Toomey could drop only one of his two bombs, reducing the mission's chances of success. His problem was compounded by the fact that the new bomb—guided by laser beam, or by satellites if clouds obscured a target, as they did tonight—had never been used in combat. Toomey and two dozen other Nighthawk pilots had never even seen one until a few hours earlier at their base in Qatar.

Nothing was easy about this night. A typical stealth fighter mission requires about six hours of meticulous planning, reviewing high-resolution photographs of the intended targets and coordinating refueling and radar-jamming planes to help protect the Nighthawks, which fly at subsonic speeds, have marginal maneuverability and carry no onboard defensive countermeasures. Missions are planned to the second, and shortly after a plane takes off, a computer flies it according to a detailed flight plan, leaving the pilot to worry about locating and hitting the target. Toomey's planning time this night had been only about two hours. Already, a supervising officer in Saudi Arabia had nearly canceled the flight, fearing it would take too long to coordinate with the ships and submarines that were firing the Tomahawk cruise missiles at the same bunker. A Qatari air traffic controller almost blocked Toomey and his wingman, Major Mark Hoehn, from taking off until Air Force officials intervened. By sheer coincidence, when the new bombs had arrived at the base the previous day, weapons handlers had loaded two onto Toomey's jet for practice. That had saved thirty precious minutes tonight.

Short and balding, Toomey looked more like an accountant or a middle manager than a fighter jock. But he and his fellow pilots in the 8th Fighter Squadron, the "Black Sheep," based at Holloman Air Force Base in southern New Mexico, knew their stuff. In the cockpit, his radio was crackling. His plane's lethal enemy—the sun—was coming up. He had support from two F-16 jets, which could attack Iraqi antiaircraft defenses, and three Prowler aircraft, to jam radar, but he did not want to be seen. He was just trying to stay focused. With the target minutes away, Toomey quickly glanced at the troubleshooting guide prepared by his squadron. He got the faulty guidance system working again in time to drop both bombs. Major Hoehn dropped both of his as well. "I didn't have time to have doubts until it was all over," Toomey said.

It was just after 5:30 A.M. Baghdad time on Thursday morning, March 20. The streetlights were still on.

Suddenly, air-raid sirens squealed out. In the distance around the city, antiaircraft fire broke the morning stillness; heavy bursts erupted from at least half a dozen locations, bursts of red and yellow tracer fire flying into the air. Now there were loud explosions: bombs, including one that threw a great cloud of dust into the air in central Baghdad. The Tomahawk cruise missiles rained down. The first drivers of the day raced down the city's highways in the haze of dawn, apparently fleeing the attack.

Fifteen minutes later, in Washington, where it was 9:45 P.M. Wednesday night, the White House press secretary, Ari Fleischer, stepped quickly to the lectern in the blue-curtained briefing room. He had practiced for this moment, recalling the words that his predecessor Marlin Fitzwater had uttered at the beginning of the Persian Gulf war twelve years earlier: "The liberation of Kuwait has begun." Now Fleischer put his own twist on that phrase: "The opening stages of the disarmament of the Iraqi regime have begun. The president will address the nation at 10:15."

BUSH HAD BEEN PLANNING A speech—but for later, at noon Friday, when the air campaign was scheduled to begin. That timetable had been overtaken by events. After giving Franks the order to strike, the president summoned his speechwriter Mike Gerson to the Oval Office. Then Bush walked over to the White House residence for a dinner of chicken pot pie with his wife, Laura. A little after 8 P.M., Andrew Card officially informed the president that the forty-eight-hour deadline for Saddam to leave Iraq had come and gone without compliance.

A little more than two hours later, after he received confirmation that Toomey and Hoehn had carried out their mission, Bush addressed the nation and the world. "On my orders," he said, "coalition forces have begun striking selected targets of military importance to undermine Saddam's ability to wage war. These are the opening stages of what will be a broad and concerted campaign." To the men and women of the American armed forces in the Persian Gulf, Bush said, "The peace of a troubled world and the hopes of an oppressed people now depend on you." He vowed to make every effort to spare innocent civilians from harm, but he also issued a somber warning, in contrast to the optimistic public assessments of the preceding weeks. "A campaign on the harsh terrain of a nation as large as California could be longer and more difficult than some predict," he said. "And helping Iraqis achieve a united, stable and free country will require our sustained commitment." He declared: "Now that conflict has come, the only way to limit its duration is to apply decisive force, and I assure you this will not be a campaign of half-measures and we will accept no outcome but victory."

Within minutes, Iraqi officials began telling journalists in Baghdad that Saddam would soon make a statement of his own, and three hours later, a bespectacled, mustachioed man who certainly looked like Saddam began speaking on Iraqi television, referring to the date in local time: March 20. He spoke contemptuously of "the criminal, junior Bush," and told his people, "Go, use a sword." After a series of rambling denunciations of "criminal Zionists and those who have agendas," he concluded, "God is great and let the losers lose. Let Iraq live. Long live jihad and long live Palestine."

By 10:40 P.M. Washington time, the president was back in the White House residence, watching the television news with his wife. At one point, a crawl line crept across the screen on one of the cable news channels, informing viewers that the president and first lady had gone to sleep.

"Whoops," Laura Bush said. "We'd better go to bed."

• • •

HOURS LATER AMERICAN TROOPS WERE pouring across the Iraqi border from Kuwait in Abrams tanks so large and lumbering that it took five gallons of gasoline just to start them. The troops of the United States Army's Third Infantry Division had practiced this crossing for weeks, using heavy armored bulldozers to punch lanes across deep ditches and twelve-foot sand berms. Now, in the silver, sand-screened moonlight of the open desert, they were finally moving—about thirty-six hours ahead of schedule, because of President Bush's decision to launch the surprise strike against Saddam. In response to the sudden air attack, the Iraqis had set fires at a handful of the 1,000 oil wells in the southern part of the country, and General Franks was unwilling to take any chances that the rich Rumaila oil fields might go up in flames, so he sped up his plan. The waiting had been tense, but the risks of combat were real. Already this Thursday, American troops waiting in the northern Kuwaiti desert had hustled in and out of their "Mission Oriented Protective Posture," the heavy, charcoal-lined nylon suits and stifling vinyl boots and gloves designed to protect them from chemical or biological attack. No one knew what might be lurking across the narrow no-man's-land that had divided Iraq and Kuwait since the 1991 war.

The Third Infantry's attack began with a barrage of ATACMS missiles. They rose through the darkened sky like white comets, prompting whoops from the soldiers waiting in the endless armored columns. At 6:15 P.M., the troops began moving through the severed chain-link fences and electrified razor wire into enemy territory. "It hit me when I saw the missiles," said Second Lieutenant Peter A. Ricci of San Diego, who had graduated from West Point the previous June and found himself in combat far more quickly than he had imagined. "Man, it's the real deal. If you don't have fears, you're not human."

The columns plowed through billowing clouds of their own dust, passing the broken hulks of tanks and trucks half buried in the sand from the last war on this ground. The boneyard, they called it. Engineers cleared a passage through a minefield. Earlier in the day, the Iraqis had fired missiles toward American and British troops camped in northern Kuwait, and one Seersucker cruise missile exploded within

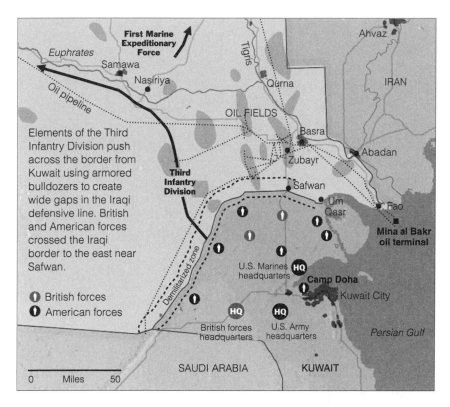

First Marine Expeditionary Force

Euphrates

Samawa

Nasiriya

Tigris

Ahvaz

Qurna

IRAN

Oil pipeline

OIL FIELDS

Basra

Elements of the Third Infantry Division push across the border from Kuwait using armored bulldozers to create wide gaps in the Iraqi defensive line. British and American forces crossed the Iraqi border to the east near Safwan.

Third Infantry Division

Zubayr

Safwan

Abadan

Um Qasr

Fao

Mina al Bakr oil terminal

🄞 British forces

🄞 American forces

Demilitarized zone

U.S. Marines headquarters

Camp Doha

HQ

Kuwait City

HQ British forces headquarters

HQ U.S. Army headquarters

Persian Gulf

SAUDI ARABIA

KUWAIT

0 Miles 50

600 yards of Camp Commando, the headquarters of the First Marine Expeditionary Force, leaving a two-foot-deep crater in the desert. At Camp Doha, the headquarters of the allied ground forces commander, Lieutenant General David McKiernan, the camp's "Giant Voice" loud-speaker system had warned of two other incoming missiles: "This is not a drill." Staff members put on their chemical protective suits and masks and kept working. An American PAC-3 Patriot missile struck the incoming missile just five miles from the camp, the first time the new model had been used in combat.

But now resistance was light. Through night-vision goggles, troops scoured the open horizon. The only things moving were other American vehicles, and the occasional herd of wild camels. But already, destruction from this new war was becoming apparent. Two Iraqi border posts lay in twisted ruins, and an American tank platoon encountered and destroyed two Iraqi T-72 tanks. "Honestly, I never thought I'd be back," said Major Michael D. Oliver, the operations officer of the 3rd Battalion, 69th Armored, who fought in the 1991 war and whose companies led the breach this night.

Even as the Army forces broke across the border, the First Marine Division crossed into Iraq at a number of points to the east, following the battle plan that called for the Marines to thrust toward Baghdad via the valley between the Tigris and Euphrates Rivers, while the Army would strike out for the capital across the open desert to the west. Dozens of Super Cobra helicopter gunships rattled off toward their targets. The Marines launched a barrage of withering artillery fire at Safwan Hill, the 444-foot site of an Iraqi observation post near the border town that had been the scene of the cease-fire agreement twelve years earlier. At the same time, British and American forces began moving toward the southern objectives of Basra and Um Qasr, Iraq's only real port. The strategy was swift and daring, and far riskier than anything allied troops had attempted in the 1991 war. Franks had counted on the element of surprise in formulating the advance. The overnight cruise missile and bomb attacks in Baghdad had removed one element of that surprise, so now Franks used the stepped-up advance to offer up another.

At the same time, as a waning moon popped out intermittently from high cirrus clouds over Baghdad, a second wave of American air strikes rained down on the capital. At about 9:15 P.M., a huge blast rang out on the western bank of the Tigris, and several of Saddam's ministries and palace compounds erupted in dense smoke and flames. One was the home and office complex of Iraq's deputy prime minister, Tariq Aziz. Other missiles appeared to hit Republican Guard strongholds on the outskirts of the capital. The Iraqi information minister, Muhammad Said al-Sahhaf, was defiant. Hours earlier, he had scoffed at a Western reporter's suggestion that there was little Iraq could do to counter the American onslaught. "Our reaction has not started yet, you'll see," he said. "In 1991 we saw a much larger scale of military action than we have seen now. We can absorb all military threats."

IN WASHINGTON, TOP OFFICIALS OF the Bush administration were consumed with what one of them called "one of the great mysteries of the first day of the war." Had they hit anyone in the sudden "decapitation strike" on the Baghdad bunker, and if so, was it Saddam? Almost from the beginning, there was uncertainty. Some analysts watching the videotape of the man in heavy-rimmed glasses who appeared on Iraqi television after the attack believed it was Saddam speaking. But the man seemed shaken and aged, and Saddam did not usually wear glasses in public, so others were not sure. Intelligence agencies monitoring Iraqi communications detected a sharp falloff in chatter that morning. Had the leadership gone underground? Had "their phones melted," as one official wondered? "We have not reached a conclusion on whether it is him," one intelligence official said. Another added, "It may take days to sift through it all." Soon, reports surfaced that a man looking like Saddam had been carried out of the bunker, unable to speak. The CIA operative who had given the initial tip "felt like we got Saddam," Bush would later say. George Tenet became convinced they had. It would eventually turn out that there was no bunker on the Dora Farms site, and officials would debate the evidence for months. But on this morning after, no one really knew.

At the Pentagon, Donald Rumsfeld knew one thing: It was only a matter of time before the Iraqi regime fell. "There's no question that the people of Iraq and the people of the region have to know that his days are numbered—he's not going to be there," the defense secretary said. "We are in communication with still more people who are officials of the military at various levels, the regular army, the Republican Guard, the Special Republican Guard—who are increasingly aware that it's going to happen, he's going to be gone. We continue to feel that there's no need for a broader conflict if Iraqi leaders act to save themselves, and to prevent such further conflicts." He said Washington was reaching out to Iraqi civilian leaders and military officers with "every conceivable mode and method." He gave his most specific warnings to Iraqi civilians to remain at home, avoid their workplaces and stay away from military targets, while warning officials not to use chemical or biological weapons, destroy dams or flood villages. Some commanders would later complain that Franks's decision to begin the ground war ahead of schedule effectively short-circuited the efforts by Special Operations forces and CIA operatives

to negotiate a possible surrender with Iraqi commanders whose cellphone numbers they were busy dialing. It is an intriguing question,
but the answer may never be known.[3]

By midday Washington time, American television audiences were
witnessing warfare in a way that home-front civilians never had in
history. The pictures on their television screens were not grainy news-
reel footage, as in World War II, or two- or three-day-old color film
of firefights, as in Vietnam. They were not video of bombing runs, or
pictures of air raids taken from fixed camera posts, as in the 1991
Persian Gulf war. Instead, some of the most familiar faces in television
news were perched atop Humvees, tanks and armored personnel carriers, speeding across the desert in real time, beaming back live, clear,
satellite pictures of frontline invading troops.

But as the campaign edged toward its second day, much of the
action was still invisible to a watching world. Late that Thursday
night, on a darkened pier in Kuwait, teams of Navy SEALs stood
ready to board four quiet high-speed jet boats for a secret mission.
Their leader, Lieutenant Jake Heller, a twenty-six-year-old Harvard
graduate, pumped them up. "We're going to change the world
tonight," Heller said. "Let's do it right." Their destination: two offshore Iraqi oil terminals. In the 1991 war, Saddam had opened the
terminals' spigots into the Persian Gulf, releasing five million barrels
of crude oil that blackened beaches for hundreds of miles and fouled
marine habitats for years. Now the fear was that he might do this
again, or set the platforms ablaze. Wearing green jumpsuits and body
armor packed with ammunition, one team of SEALs sped out about
twenty-five miles offshore to the Mina al-Bakr terminal, while another
landed moments later at Khawr al-Amaya, five miles to the north.
They found the Mina al-Bakr terminal wired with explosives, but it
seemed to have been a halfhearted effort, and the Iraqis manning the
terminal were preparing for bed. The commandos used shotguns and
crowbars to break through metal doors, and they took more than forty
prisoners. The Iraqi men were living in fetid squalor and put up no
resistance when the SEALs broke in shouting, "Hands up!" American
commanders monitored the raid in real time via a grainy video feed

beamed back to the *Valley Forge*, a Ticonderoga-class missile cruiser five miles away.

Other American forces were a lot less lucky. Hours later, a CH-46 Sea Knight helicopter full of marines was on its way back to Kuwait after its own first-night mission. Among those on board was Captain Ryan Anthony Beaupre, a former high school track star from St. Anne, Illinois, a farming town of 1,300 people sixty-five miles south of Chicago. He had given up an accounting job to seek more adventure in a career in the Marine Corps. His relatives were watching television late Thursday when word came that a CH-46 had crashed. "You kind of get that sick feeling in the pit of your stomach when you know that's what your loved one flies," said Ryan's older sister, Alyse. A few hours later, three marines knocked at the Beaupres' door with the worst kind of news: Ryan, three other Americans and eight British troops had all died, the first allied casualties of the war.

Still, the bulk of the early going was good for American and British forces. On Friday morning, March 21, 4,000 British Royal Marines seized the Fao Peninsula, on the southeastern tip of Iraq, and hours later, after bucking sometimes stiff resistance, American marines, the first American troops to operate under a British commander since World War II, seized control of Um Qasr, at the head of the Persian Gulf. Sporadic fighting continued. A marine briefly raised an American flag, only to quickly haul it down after commanders warned against any signs of triumphalism.

Over and over, American commanders reported that most Iraqi regular forces simply fell apart and gave way as they came over the border, stripping off their uniforms and disappearing into the civilian population. In the dusty border town of Safwan, residents' joy at the arrival of American forces was tempered by crushing and bitter memories of all they had endured under Saddam's regime. Zahra Khafi, an elderly mother of five, cried out to a group of American and British visitors who came into the town after the Iraqi forces disappeared, "Peace be upon you, peace be upon you. . . . I'm not afraid of Saddam anymore." But then she started to tell the story of her son Massoud, who had been killed by Saddam's henchmen for a crime no greater than his being Shiite rather than Sunni, and suddenly she began to weep. "Should I be afraid?" she asked. "Is Saddam coming back?" In

this part of the country, memories of the aftermath of the Gulf war—
when the Shiites rose up against Saddam only to be crushed by him
because of a lack of American support—were still fresh. Najah Neema,
a member of the Iraqi army, openly trembled. He had torn off his
uniform, thrown down his gun and run away as the American columns
approached, but now he had a new fear. "There, there are Saddam's
men," he said. "And if you leave me, they will kill me right now." A
panicked woman waved her arms and wailed as the pickup truck in
which she was riding pulled up, two dead Iraqi men in the back. "It
came from the foreign helicopter," she cried out. "It came right into
the house."[4]

INSIDE THE COMBINED ALLIED LAND headquarters at Camp Doha in
Kuwait that Friday, anticipation was high. The punishing air strike
that had been publicly promised by the Pentagon for weeks to "shock
and awe" Iraqi resistance was set to begin. In the camp's war room,
the targets in Baghdad were marked with glowing red triangles on a
classified laptop computer. The whole area on the west side of the
capital, near Saddam's main presidential palace compound and other
leadership targets, was a blaze of red. "That's a bad neighborhood to
be in tonight," a senior commander said. An armada of planes converged on the capital: B-2 Spirit bombers, F-117A Nighthawks,
B-52 bombers with air-launched cruise missiles, plus Tomahawks
launched from ships in the Gulf. There were twenty-nine flights from
the deck of the USS *Abraham Lincoln*. At 9 P.M., the skies above
Baghdad were once again alive with a ferocious display, fifty strikes
in one ten-minute interval, at least a hundred devastating explosions.
After the earsplitting explosions, a cauldron of fireballs and drifting
smoke rose as one building after another erupted into tongues of flame
and smashed granite, marble and steel. The raid ground on for nine
hours overnight in a city that seemed to be running on vestigial fear
more than under any organized regime. By Saturday morning, at least
fifteen of the city's most important buildings, including Saddam's
Republican Palace and a huge new palace named for his wife, Sajida,
had been hit, with some appearing so damaged as to be uninhabitable
and perhaps irreparable. From a distance, the Sajida, a huge domed

structure with four thirty-foot bronze busts of Saddam dressed as the ancient warrior Saladin, could no longer be seen on the horizon. By dusk Saturday, huge trenches of heavy oil burned all around Baghdad, lit as a smokescreen to mask the city from American air strikes and casting a black and hazy pall.

Back in Washington, Bush had gone to Camp David for the weekend, just as his father had done on the first weekend of the 1991 war. The president warned in his weekly radio address against easy euphoria and restated, as he had on Wednesday night, that the conflict "could be longer and more difficult than some have predicted." White House aides went out of their way to say that Bush was not following the war developments minute by minute, but an old college friend of the president, Roland W. Betts, told a different story. Betts spent the weekend at Camp David and for hours that Saturday he and Bush walked the trails, worked out in its gym, watched the battle news on television and talked of little else. "He is just totally immersed," Betts said.

For the first time, White House aides quietly let it be known that on Monday the president would ask Congress for close to $80 billion to pay for the initial cost of the war. And even as the fighting began on the battlefield, the public political battles over the wisdom of the war continued around the world. From New York to Helsinki, from Chicago to London, another round of worldwide war protests played out. More than 100,000 people marched in Manhattan, with signs bearing slogans like PLEASE STOP THE KILLING and NEW YORKERS REMEMBER OUR OWN SHOCK AND AWE. On the Alexanderplatz in Berlin, demonstrators also waved signs: DRESDEN 1945, BAGHDAD 2003. In Rome, Pope John Paul II said the war "threatens the fate of humanity," and declared, "Violence and weapons can never resolve the problems of man."

By nightfall in Iraq that Saturday, the forward elements of the Third Infantry had pierced 150 miles into the country, almost halfway to Baghdad, bypassing potential trouble spots in cities. American and British forces were closing on Basra and clashed through the day with Iraqi forces, capturing an airport on the city's western outskirts. But they had yet to push inside. From his headquarters in Qatar, Tommy Franks held his first media briefing of the war, projecting crisp optimism from an elaborate stage designed for this purpose, created by a

Hollywood designer to convey American authority and high-tech efficiency. The general said that 1,000 to 2,000 Iraqi troops were in allied custody and that thousands more had laid down their weapons and simply gone home. "This will be a campaign unlike any other in history," Franks said, one "characterized by shock, by surprise, by flexibility and by the employment of precise munitions on a scale never before seen, and by the application of overwhelming force." It was a bold claim. It was also close to the mark.

Chapter 9

SHOCK AND AWE

In the skies over Baghdad
Saturday, March 22, 2003

On the third day of the war, a mysterious flying object lingered high over Baghdad for hours on end, evading a withering barrage of Iraqi missile and artillery fire. It looked for all the world like something out of *Popular Mechanics* or *Boys' Life*, an overgrown rubber-band airplane with the white silhouette of an upside-down spoon. In fact, it was something much more sophisticated: an RQ-1 Predator drone, a twenty-seven-foot-long unmanned surveillance and attack aircraft and one of the war's most effective weapons. With a range of 450 miles and a cruising speed of about eighty miles per hour, this propeller-driven robot could take on some of the war's riskiest missions, without putting American lives in jeopardy. Operators flew the plane from control stations on the ground, using satellite links and remote-controlled color video cameras. Its 1,500-millimeter zoom lens was so precise that analysts watching the pictures back on the ground could distinguish uniformed soldiers from plainclothes civilians from more than three miles away. Fifteen Predators were operating in Iraq—almost one-third of the total fleet—and the Air Force considered them such an important asset that it had recently changed regulations to make every hour spent guiding a Predator count as flight time when determining pilots' pay raises and promotions. How better to lure jet jocks who would rather pierce the skies at Mach speeds than sit in a trailer with a joystick and video screen? One of the most respected Predator pilots of the Afghanistan campaign had been so concerned that her tour with the remote-controlled planes could limit her career that the Air Force arranged meetings with top Pentagon officials, including Wolfowitz, who personally thanked her. The pilot had become so good at the controls that she was chosen to fly the super-secret CIA missions in which a version of the Predator armed with Hellfire missiles tracked and attacked Taliban and Al Qaeda leaders.

The goal of this mission over Baghdad was simple: Flush out the city's air defenses so they could be pinpointed, targeted and attacked later by American fighter-bombers. When its thirty-three-hour flight was over, the plane, stripped down on purpose to serve as cannon fodder, landed in a lake—seventy-five miles from Baghdad.

Not all of the allied air war was so secret, but most of it was just as invisible. Months after the major combat ended, many details remained publicly unknown about one of the war's most important strategic elements: the steady, relentless destruction from the air of much of what was left of Iraq's military infrastructure and fighting capacity. The dramatic nighttime bombings of Baghdad and Saddam's palaces and government buildings amounted to only the most obvious part of the effort. Missions like the Predator's flight over Baghdad were among the most secret operations of the campaign. In between were thousands of missions—between 1,000 and 2,000 flights a day at the peak—that pounded Iraqi tanks, artillery and antiaircraft positions to pave the way for the American forces advancing so swiftly on the ground. For the first three weeks of the war, there were never fewer than 200 planes aloft. Even when blinding sandstorms slowed troops and grounded other reconnaissance planes, the high-flying Global Hawk drone tracked the movements of Iraqi forces from 60,000 feet up, using special cloud-piercing radar. It performed the functions of a U-2 spy plane, without risking a pilot's life, and the information it gathered was beamed back to American commanders within minutes, providing all-weather, day-or-night pictures over an area the size of Illinois.

In the 1991 Gulf war, coalition forces conducted a thirty-eight-day air campaign against Iraqi forces from Kuwait to Baghdad before beginning a ground war that lasted just four days. Almost since the dawn of military flight, debates had raged about the relative effectiveness of air power and ground troops, and about the limits of air power alone to topple an enemy. As this unusual new war began with the sudden strikes on Baghdad, and the relatively light American ground force began racing across the open desert, there was considerable debate about the wisdom of the Pentagon's plan.

In fact, an active—and partly secret—American and British air campaign against Iraq had been under way for weeks before President Bush ordered the formal beginning of the war, both in terms of stepped-up patrols over Iraq's northern and southern no-fly zones and selective strikes at other targets. Known as "Southern Focus," the operation called for attacks on the network of fiber-optic cable that the Iraqi government used to transmit military communications, as well as strikes on command centers, radars and other military assets. From the beginning, the plan was intended to defang Iraqi defenses and destroy Saddam's capacity to control his government and armed forces, while leaving intact as much civilian infrastructure as possible—including much of the electrical grid—to speed postwar reconstruction. "At the end of this, we want to have an Iraq that is a viable country to build up," General McKiernan, the commander of combined allied land forces, had said before the war began.

On February 11 and 12, American air strikes hit two Iraqi Ababil-100 missile systems in the southern city of Basra, which American commanders said had the range to hit American troops and equipment in Kuwait, where forces were massing for an invasion. The CIA believed that the truck-mounted Ababils exceeded the ninety-three-mile range that the United Nations permitted for Iraqi missiles, and the great fear was that they could be outfitted to deliver chemical or biological warheads. On February 18, American planes carried out another strike against an Ababil system in the Basra area. On February 25, allied planes bombed an Iraqi Astros 2 multiple rocket launcher in the south of the country, while in the north, allied bombers attacked three Frog rocket systems, a Soviet-designed short-range weapons system deployed south of the city of Mosul.

At the time, the American and British forces who carried out the raids justified them as a means of enforcing not only the no-fly zones but also the UN resolutions that were intended to keep Iraq from building up its offensive capacity and threatening its neighbors. Before the war, American commanders said the strikes were necessary because the Iraqis had stiffened their air defenses and were shooting more often at allied patrols. After the war, Lieutenant General T. Michael Moseley, the chief allied air commander, acknowledged that the reality was more of a chicken-and-egg question. "We became a little more aggressive based on them shooting more at us, which allowed us to respond more," he said. "Then the question is whether they were shooting at

us because we were up there more." Whatever the truth, the raids did
their work: 606 bombs were dropped on 391 carefully chosen targets
before the war ever began.

"I don't think the potential adversary has any idea what's coming,"
said Colonel Gary Crowder, chief of strategy at the Air Combat Command, which was responsible for all Air Force warplanes, as the war
started.[1]

IT MAY HAVE BEEN THE most overused phrase of the war. But the
concept of "shock and awe" was as old as combat itself. In 1996, a
former Navy commander named Harlan K. Ullman helped write a
paper for the National Defense University in Washington called
"Shock and Awe: Achieving Rapid Dominance," in which he and his
coauthors aimed to go beyond traditional defense doctrines (summed
up by phrases like "overwhelming force") to conjure up something
more all-encompassing, a concept that could reflect the intangible,
psychological effects of warfare, as well as physical destruction. They
were guided in their thinking by the writings of Sun Tzu, the great
Chinese military strategist of the sixth century B.C.; by Pizarro's defeat
of the Incas; by the German blitzkrieg of World War II and even by
the atomic bombing of Japan in 1945. "Since before Sun Tzu," they
wrote, "generals have been tantalized and confounded by the elusive
goal of destroying the adversary's will to resist before, during and after
battle." Ullman worried that the American military had come to rely
too much on "the slow destruction of enemy forces," and he argued
instead, "We want them to quit, not to fight." With their high-tech
gear and superior surveillance capacity, the concept went, the U.S.
forces could have near-total awareness of the shape of the battlefield
and should use that edge to press the enemy.

The notion had been incorporated into Franks's and Rumsfeld's
planning for a new kind of war. Rumsfeld, the old Navy pilot, was
certain that air power could be an important component of military
transformation, and he intended Iraq to be a major laboratory.

But air power alone was never likely to be enough. That was why,
as the drone flew over Baghdad on the first Saturday of the war, the
Army's Third Infantry Division was racing through the open desert

toward Baghdad as fast as it could, and the Marines were headed toward Nasiriya to cross the Euphrates and make their parallel advance. British forces, with support from American marines, were likewise moving on Basra, in an effort to gain a swift foothold there and show that Saddam's days were numbered. The whole idea was to make air and ground power work together, like a "hammer and anvil," in the words of Robert A. Pape, an expert on air power at the University of Chicago.

Despite the claims of air power's strongest advocates, Pape contended, the experience of the modern era showed that when it was used alone, it either failed or backfired, beginning in 1986, when the U.S. forces bombed Muammar el-Qaddafi's tent in Libya, missing him but killing his young daughter and most likely precipitating the Libyan bombing of Pan Am Flight 103 over Lockerbie, Scotland, two years later. As recently as the fall of 2001, weeks of precision air strikes aimed at killing Mullah Muhammad Omar and other Taliban leaders in Afghanistan had had relatively little effect. It was only when air power was used to hit Taliban forces in conjunction with ground assaults by Special Operations forces and the Northern Alliance that the tide turned.

In the 1991 Gulf war, despite the drama of television pictures showing precision bombs hitting targets in Baghdad, the truth was that the steady bombing of Iraqi forces in Kuwait had the greater effect. Iraq had some 336,000 troops and thousands of tanks and artillery defending its occupation of Kuwait, but after more than five weeks of allied bombing, some 100,000 Iraqi troops had deserted and 20 percent of their heavy equipment had been destroyed.

From the new war's first night, the hammer and anvil doctrine was in play. The surprise strike on Saddam in the war's opening moments was aimed above all at paralyzing the Iraqi regime's ability to resist—essentially a bid to end the war before it could even truly begin. Then the swift land advance, accompanied by the punishing barrage of air strikes on Baghdad, was intended to have a similar effect, by disrupting the Iraqis' ability to command their far-flung ground forces, and thus help the allied ground invasion. "What this does is open up opportunities to exploit your offensive maneuver," said Major General J. D. Thurman, the chief operations officer at the allied ground forces command. "That allows you to maintain the tempo of the operation. There are resistance pockets all over. This continues to weaken their command and control."

The air campaign was not hitch-free. Just as important as what it managed to do initially was what it did not. In the opening days of the war, commanders avoided bombing as many as three dozen high-priority targets—including the Ministry of Defense and television and communication facilities—for fear of civilian casualties. "It would be highly desirable to have completely, totally ended any ability on their ability to communicate," Rumsfeld said in the war's early days. "They have put their communications systems in downtown Baghdad, and commingled civil action, civil activities, with military activities. And they have done it in very close proximity to large numbers of innocent men, women and children."

Still, in the twelve years since the last Gulf war, technological improvements had revolutionized almost all aspects of military operations, perhaps none more than air operations. In 1991, it would take hours for commanders to compile and distribute daily air-tasking orders. First the comprehensive flight schedule for all the aircraft in the theater would have to be printed out—and it was the size of a telephone book—then ferried by plane to the carriers. Now everything could be sent in a ten-megabyte e-mail file.[2] No less an authority than retired general H. Norman Schwarzkopf, the commander of Operation Desert Storm, would declare that air power in 2003 was "far more devastating than anything we had a capability to do."[3] This war would show the extent of those capabilities—and also the limits.

ON THE NIGHT OF SUNDAY, March 23, thirty-two Army AH-64 Apache Longbow attack helicopters gathered at a secret assembly point near Najaf, about eighty miles south of Baghdad. These machines were the most lethal, deployable, survivable attack helicopters in the world. They had the bug-eyed look of big, olive-drab insects, and were armed with radar and target-acquisition systems that could track as many as 128 separate targets, identify the sixteen most dangerous and share the information with other Apaches and planes. Each one cost about $22 million. Part of the V Corps' 11th Attack Helicopter Regiment, the Apaches had flown up that afternoon from Kuwait with a secret objective: to pave the way for the advancing ground forces by starting the American attack on the 2nd Armored Brigade of the Medina Division of Saddam's Republican Guard. This unit was blocking the approach to Baghdad from the southwest, controlling multiple highways and rail lines and crossings over the Euphrates River. No goal was more important. The American forces had to take Baghdad.

This Sunday night, military intelligence suggested that the Iraqi forces were deeply dug in, with some ninety T-72 tanks, perhaps thirty armored personnel carriers and some artillery pieces. To set the stage for the assault, the Americans had hammered Iraqi radar and tried to suppress the enemy's surface-to-air missiles. Now the choppers would go to work.

The crews flew north in the darkness, past the town of Hilla and east of Karbala. All seemed well enough. But as the choppers neared their targets, all the lights on the ground below flashed off for about three seconds, and then came back on. Suddenly, the American pilots found themselves in a wild hailstorm of lead and colored tracer fire, a Fourth of July barrage aimed straight at them. The choppers had flown into a hornet's nest, with small-arms fire coming from everywhere, including houses. "Man, don't fly through that!" Chief Warrant Officer Ronald D. Young, Jr., told his copilot, Chief Warrant Officer David S. Williams.

"I'm not going to fly through that," Williams answered, just as the first bullets hit. A round came through the chopper and split open the top of Williams's left boot, nicking his big toe and leaving stinging powder burns. It was like the wildest laser show Young had ever seen in his life, unbelievably intense. Bullets whizzed within an inch of Young's head, and he suddenly realized he wasn't breathing; he had to tell himself to start again. "Holy crap!" he thought to himself. "I can't believe this!" His weapons system was knocked out and he could not return fire. By then, Williams realized he was missing an engine and running out of options. "We're going down!" Williams called out.

"Try to keep flying," Young answered. "Try to keep flying!" They could hear the rounds of bullets hitting the sides and seats of the chopper, and smoke was everywhere. Before they knew it, they were on the ground, so dazed they barely felt the impact, and scrambling out of the cockpit.

Young radioed that he and Williams were on foot, but the other pilots were in tough fights of their own, and no help came. So the two crewmen began running through the weeds, just trying to get away from their downed craft. Suddenly Young noticed that Williams still had his tiny yellow "lip light," a miniature flashlight, attached to his helmet, and it was sending a sharp beam of light that made them easy targets for the Iraqis they could hear converging on them. Young tackled his copilot and tried to rip the light off. Then Williams looked at Young and realized his light was on, too! They threw down both helmets and ran on, clutching their 9-millimeter sidearms. When they came to an irrigation ditch, they crept in and swam a quarter mile, quietly, like alligators, their noses barely breaking the surface. At first, they were flushed and sweaty from their hard landing and the run, their adrenaline pumping. Then the water got cold, so cold they could barely move. They could hear Iraqi voices coming closer. "What do you want to do?" Young whispered. Williams could hear his heart beating as he prayed silently: *Please, just walk by.* Then a group of three Iraqis converged on them, soon joined by others, shouting in Arabic. The two Americans sat on the ground with their arms stretched out. The Iraqis kept yelling.

Thinking he ought to get up on his knees, Young rose with his hands behind his head. A shot rang out, and the bullet flew past his ear. Both pilots dove to the ground. Now Williams prayed out loud to God: "Please don't kill me, please don't kill me, please let me survive this."[4] An Iraqi hit Williams in the lower back with a stick, and Young in the back of the head. Another kicked Young in the ribs. Their captors dragged the two Americans to a police station in nearby Karbala, taking their watches, rings, money, identification cards, survival supplies—everything but their flight suits and boots. Soon the world would know their fate, but for now all their colleagues knew was that one helicopter was missing.

The raid had been a disaster: virtually all of the thirty-two choppers had been struck by fire, most of them many times. "Every single one of the Apaches that went out on the mission took between ten and twenty hits from antiaircraft fire, rocket-propelled grenades and surface-to-air missiles," said Colonel Daniel Ball, the unit's commander.[5] The three-hour American attack managed to destroy only ten to fifteen Iraqi armored vehicles and the pilots came back subdued and shaken by what, for many, was their first real combat experience. Only seven of the helicopters remained battle-worthy. The Apaches "did not meet the objectives that I had set for that attack," the V Corps commander, General Wallace, said with some understatement.

It had been an ambush.

The Americans later learned that the Apaches' supposedly secret departure from the assembly area was spotted by an Iraqi observer, thought to be a general somewhere in Najaf. He used a cellphone to speed-dial a number of Iraqi air defenders, giving them enough time to prepare an effective defense, using mostly small arms. The Iraqis had used the power outage on the ground as a signal to their gunners to begin the attack. For the rest of the war, Apaches would be used mostly for armed reconnaissance and close-air support, not as the vanguard of the advancing forces. "We learned from our mistakes," Wallace said. "We adjusted and adapted based on what we learned."[6]

For their part, the Iraqis had yet to put a single airplane aloft. The best prewar intelligence estimates suggested that Saddam still had about 300 combat aircraft, most of them aging Soviet-era MiGs, and Sukhois and older French Mirage jet fighters, but many were thought to be unflyable. Inexplicably, the Iraqis had completely buried some planes in the desert. The UN weapons embargoes had prevented Iraq from importing spare parts, and Iraqi pilots had received little training since the Gulf war. Some experts suggested that the Iraqis might be saving the last of their air force in reserve for a final defense of Baghdad. But for the moment, the allied forces had "a total dominance of the air," Rumsfeld said.[7]

The absence of Iraqi planes from the skies did not mean that American air-defense batteries sat on their haunches. In fact, on the same day as the failed Apache attack, the Americans made a nightmarish mistake. Jets flying in certain ways can appear on Patriot radar systems as incoming missiles, and an American Patriot battery close to the Kuwait border shot down a Royal Air Force Tornado GR4 as it returned from a nighttime mission over Iraq. Both members of the British crew were killed.

●　　●　　●

THE 11TH ATTACK HELICOPTER REGIMENT'S mission against the Medina Division was just one small example of the kind of offensives the American battle plan envisioned. The 101st Airborne, with its fleet of seventy Apaches, more than a hundred Blackhawk troop carriers and forty Chinooks, was to be in the thick of the leapfrogging advance toward Baghdad. The division's nickname was the "Screaming Eagles," and it was a legendary unit. When it was formed in World War II, its first commander, Major General William C. Lee, echoed Franklin D. Roosevelt's famous phrase by saying, "The 101st has no history, but it has a rendezvous with destiny." And so it did. Only one in three men passed the initial selection criteria—which included a 140-mile march in three days—to serve in an outfit whose members could survive a parachute drop behind enemy lines and then begin fighting. The 101st landed in Normandy on D-day, and fought on through the Battle of the Bulge and Bastogne—all the way to Hitler's Bavarian mountain retreat at Berchtesgaden. During the Vietnam war, Bob Hope greeted troops of the 101st by cracking, "These guys have seen more action than a Swedish movie director."

But on that Sunday, March 23, many of the division's 18,000 troops in the region were still in Kuwait, getting organized and setting up equipment that had just arrived. Because of the war plan's reliance on a rolling flow of forces into the region, the 101st would not be fully deployed and ready to fight for another few days at least. Commanders were counting on its combat punch to play a major role in the advance to Baghdad. "In the right circumstances, the attack helicopters are absolutely deadly," said the division's commander, General Petraeus, the push-up king of the Kuwait docks. "And we'll try to put them in the right circumstances. They give you tactical and operational mobility, but the logistics have to catch up with you." The distances in Iraq would be a formidable challenge. The 300-plus miles from Kuwait to Baghdad was twice as far as the division liked to fly its helicopters, which would mean making elaborate provisions for refueling inside Iraq. Petraeus knew the challenges he faced. His doctoral dissertation had studied how the use of military force after the Vietnam war had been shaped by what were assumed to be the lessons of that conflict. "You learn that a certain degree of intellectual humility is a good thing," he said. "There aren't always a helluva lot of absolutely right answers out there."

On this day, Petraeus had more immediate worries. At Camp Pennsylvania in Kuwait, the headquarters of the 1st Brigade of the 101st Airborne, the post-midnight quiet was suddenly interrupted by a power failure and the bang of successive explosions. At 1:21 A.M., someone rolled three grenades into three tents in the heart of the command. When the stunned occupants rushed out, a gunman sprayed them with an assault rifle. One soldier was killed on the spot, and fifteen more were wounded, one of whom would later die as well. At first, commanders were concerned that this was a terrorist attack. They seized two Kuwaiti men who worked as contractors at the camp. Then they found the real culprit, an American sergeant attached to an engineering unit, who had been missing during a head count after the attack. It was fratricide, horrifying and inexplicable. The sergeant was a convert to Islam named Asan Akbar, the sole Muslim in a sea of American soldiers. He thought his fellow soldiers were prejudiced and had been deeply disturbed by their joking threats to rape and kill Iraqi Muslims. In camp, Akbar's platoon leader, Sergeant First Class Daniel Kumm, had received complaints from other soldiers that Akbar was "scatterbrained" and "incompetent," not ready for combat. Kumm had raised their concerns with his superiors but was told, "You will take him. We need the numbers. We need to take full strength into Iraq."

The attack was a bad omen. Much worse was soon to come.

Chapter 10

A TURN FOR THE WORSE

Outside Nasiriya, Iraq
Sunday, March 23, 2003

The sun was just coming up as the exhausted soldiers of the 507th Maintenance Company drew near to Nasiriya, a crossroads market town where southern Iraqi farmers came to sell their dates. The straggling convoy of soldiers in eighteen trucks and Humvees had traveled all the way from Kuwait, at the tail end of a 600-vehicle column that was snaking across the open desert toward Baghdad. The soft sand had been hard on the 507th's heavy trucks, and vehicles had gotten stuck repeatedly. Others had run out of gas. By dawn this Sunday morning, the forward elements of the invading American army were 130 miles ahead of the 507th, and by nightfall, the 7th Cavalry Regiment would press north of Najaf, putting it less than eighty miles south of Baghdad.

The Third Infantry's seventy-two-hour trek was the longest mass movement of armor since World War II, and one of the swiftest in history—"the cannonball run," one of the division's officers, Captain Adam J. Morrison, called it. Allied forces were on the march all over: British troops were encircling Basra; the 101st Airborne was leapfrogging in helicopters to a forward base near Najaf; Special Operations forces were busy securing targets in the western deserts; the fleet of cargo ships that had waited off the Turkish coast for weeks had been ordered through the Suez Canal to unload the Fourth Infantry Division's equipment in Kuwait, and on Saturday, the vanguard of American marines had crossed the Euphrates here in Nasiriya to begin their march up the center of the country.

But these thirty-one soldiers from the 507th, and two others from the 3rd Forward Support Battalion of the Third Infantry, were struggling hard to keep up. The 507th was based at Fort Bliss, in El Paso, Texas, and was on its way to help set up Patriot antimissile batteries for the Army's V Corps forward bases near Najaf. These soldiers were not combat forces. They were maintenance workers, support staff for the troops far ahead of them. They carried weapons, and knew how to use them, but they had been trained as mechanics, supply clerks, cooks, computer technicians—so none expected to see frontline action.

Nothing about their trip so far had been easy. They were as much as twelve hours behind the main convoy. None of the soldiers had had more than a few hours' sleep since Thursday. The batteries in their radios had died. They fought to stay awake. Their leader, Captain Troy Kent King, had already sent another thirty-two soldiers from the 507th, whose trucks were having less trouble, ahead with the main convoy, and was now bringing up the rear along Highway 8, a major north-south artery. Captain King knew his route lay north, toward Baghdad. But he was not supposed to drive into Nasiriya, which was far from secure and had been the scene of frightening firefights only hours earlier. In fact, he was not supposed to cross the Euphrates at all, but was instead supposed to take a left turn on the southern outskirts of the city, and head west along Highway 1, circling around Nasiriya before rejoining Highway 8 on the far side of town. Captain King had a pocket Global Positioning System (GPS) device—a satellite-driven directional aid the size of a cellphone—and an annotated map. But he had highlighted only the path along Highway 8, and not the left turn onto Highway 1. By the time his little convoy actually got to the intersection of the two highways, the traffic control officer who had been on duty to guide the advancing convoys was long gone. The American troops present simply confirmed that Highway 8 led north.

So now, in the rising light of dawn, Captain King plunged ahead, straight into town. Once again, he missed a turn, this time another left that would have kept him on Highway 8, and on the west bank of the Euphrates. Instead, the convoy drove straight on, across the river, and then across a second bridge over the Saddam Hussein Canal. It was so early on Sunday morning that hardly any residents were up and about. The few Iraqis that the Americans saw simply waved. There was no sign of hostility.

But by now, it was clear that the group had lost its way. King

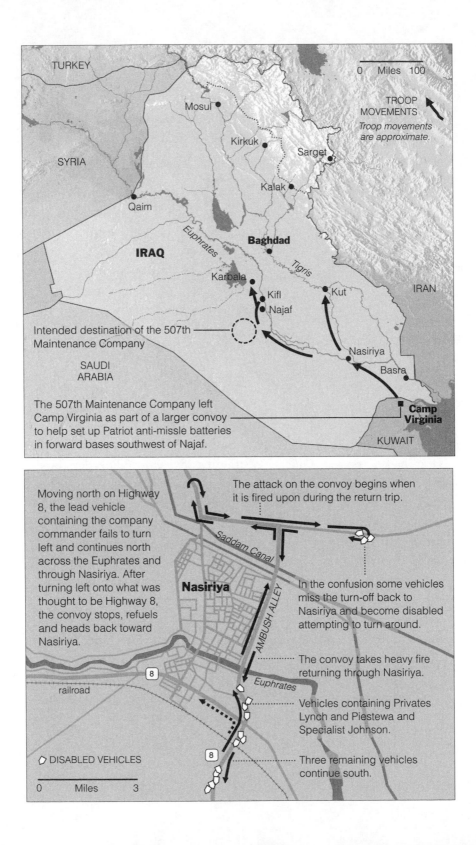

TURKEY

SYRIA

0 Miles 100

TROOP MOVEMENTS
Troop movements are approximate.

Mosul

Kirkuk

Sarget

Kalak

Qaim

Euphrates

IRAQ

Baghdad

Tigris

Karbala

Kifl

Kut

Najaf

IRAN

Intended destination of the 507th Maintenance Company

Nasiriya

Basra

SAUDI ARABIA

The 507th Maintenance Company left Camp Virginia as part of a larger convoy to help set up Patriot anti-missile batteries in forward bases southwest of Najaf.

Camp Virginia

KUWAIT

Moving north on Highway 8, the lead vehicle containing the company commander fails to turn left and continues north across the Euphrates and through Nasiriya. After turning left onto what was thought to be Highway 8, the convoy stops, refuels and heads back toward Nasiriya.

The attack on the convoy begins when it is fired upon during the return trip.

Saddam Canal

Nasiriya

AMBUSH ALLEY

In the confusion some vehicles miss the turn-off back to Nasiriya and become disabled attempting to turn around.

The convoy takes heavy fire returning through Nasiriya.

Euphrates

8

railroad

Vehicles containing Privates Lynch and Piestewa and Specialist Johnson.

8

◇ DISABLED VEHICLES

0 Miles 3

Three remaining vehicles continue south.

ordered the line of trucks to turn around and they doubled back, retracing their route through town. The captain told the soldiers to lock and load their weapons, and keep a sharp eye out for trouble. More Iraqis were beginning to appear on the streets.

Suddenly, there was gunfire, out of nowhere, then seemingly from everywhere. The convoy broke apart, as heavier vehicles fell behind the lighter Humvees. Racing back through town, they again missed a turn, a right that would have taken them south, back toward Highway 8. Again, some trucks broke down. Again, the group doubled back. There was dust and confusion and small-arms fire. There were pickup trucks filled with fedayeen irregulars, militia loyalists of Saddam in civilian clothes or their trademark black ninja masks. They chased the Americans back through town, along a stretch of highway with wide aprons. The Iraqis were firing AK-47s, machine guns and rocket-propelled grenades, and they were lobbing hand grenades. It was an ambush, and not a small one. "It was a whole city, and we were shot from front, rear, left," Sergeant James Riley remembered. "It was like being in the middle of a parking lot and everyone is shooting at you."

About 7:20, a five-ton tractor-trailer driven by Specialist Edgar Hernandez came under heavy fire. He tried to avoid hitting an Iraqi truck blocking the road in front of him, and lost control of his rig, veering off the right-hand side of the road. Behind him, a speeding American Humvee approached and was suddenly hit by a rocket-propelled grenade. Its driver, Private First Class Lori Piestewa, lost control and slammed into Hernandez's tractor-trailer, where he and the other occupant, Specialist Shoshana Johnson, were still sitting. The crash was awful. First Sergeant Joseph Dowdy, sitting in the front passenger seat of the soft-topped Humvee, was killed instantly. Piestewa was badly injured. And so was a slender, blond nineteen-year-old private first class from West Virginia named Jessica Lynch, whose arms and legs were crushed by the impact.[1]

Other members of the 507th tried to return fire. But the long trip across the desert had filled their guns with sand and dirt, and weapon after weapon jammed and failed to fire. Specialist Johnson, a thirty-year-old single mother who had joined the Army in hopes of becoming a chef, dove under her truck, but was hit in the ankles.

Near her were Sergeant Riley, Specialist Hernandez, who was wounded in the right arm, and Specialist Joseph Hudson, who had been shot in the buttocks and side. The rest of the convoy was spread out and separated, "all over hell and creation," Riley said. Iraqis came out of their houses brandishing weapons, and the Americans were overwhelmed, like Custer, Riley thought. They could not even make a bayonet charge. Now they were prisoners, surrounded and scared, and their captors poked at some of them. But when the Iraqis opened Johnson's chemical weapons suit and saw she was a woman, they left her alone.[2]

THE ATTACK HAD LASTED MORE than an hour. Eleven Americans died, some in the crash, some presumably in combat. In the immediate aftermath, senior American officials suggested that some of the soldiers might have been summarily executed, and months later, the Army was still investigating the incident for possible Iraqi war crimes. The convoy should not have made the wrong turn, of course. But accidents happen in war, and perhaps the unit should not have been stretched so thin in the first place. Perhaps overconfidence played a part. The official Pentagon report would eventually conclude that fatigue, stress and the surprising nature of the guerrilla attack all contributed to the ambush. It would find that the weary soldiers had all done their duty. It would blame no one.

On that Sunday morning, the ambush of the 507th suddenly came to seem like a metaphor for a war that was not going quite as smoothly as planned. While it was true that the U.S. Army and the Marines were advancing swiftly toward Baghdad, and the punishing air campaign was well under way, the unexpectedly stiff fighting in Nasiriya showed the downside of the lighter invasion force, with its long, unsecured supply lines. The strategy of simply bypassing southern Iraqi cities—where Wolfowitz and others had argued that American troops would be greeted as heroes—was proving more complicated than expected.

The vanguard of the Third Infantry's troops had passed around Nasiriya, a city of about 300,000 near the ruins of Ur, the birthplace of the biblical patriarch Abraham, on Saturday. Nasiriya was important to the Americans for two reasons: the bridges that spanned the

Euphrates River and the Saddam Hussein Canal, and Tallil Air Base southwest of town. The bridges would be a key ground supply link for the Marines on the road north to Baghdad, and the airport would allow American cargo and support planes to land and keep the forward troops resupplied. American marines had claimed and crossed the bridges on Saturday, and the Third Infantry had captured the airport. But the town was hardly under American control. At first, no one thought it would have to be. This was, after all, a Shiite city, whose residents had long been among those most repressed by Saddam's Sunni regime. At the very least, the war planners thought pockets of resistance in places like this could be safely bypassed—and dealt with in due course—as the American advance pressed on toward the objective that mattered most: Baghdad itself. This approach was at the very heart of the war plan, the concept that would let American forces forge ahead so fast. But because the Turks had refused permission for a northern front, there was not as much American pressure on Saddam as Franks and Rumsfeld had hoped. Militia and regular forces had been sent south to challenge the American advance.

Since Friday, there had been unexpected resistance in the port of Um Qasr, and the British troops ringing Basra had yet to enter the city because of determined resistance there. The resistance in Nasiriya was all too clear to Staff Sergeant Jamie Villafane and Gunnery Sergeant Charles Horgan on Saturday afternoon, when they were sent to check out reports of unruly Iraqi civilians near a bridge south of the city. As they drove up in their unarmored Humvee, the first thing Horgan noticed was a group of Iraqis in Bedouin robes running away. There was something wrong with them, he thought. They were jumpy, edgy. The next thing Horgan saw from his machine-gun turret was a wire-guided missile whistling toward his truck. "Oh, my God," he thought. "I am going to die."

He was blown off the truck, and found himself dazed and bloody on the ground. Though the Army had briefed them that this sort of thing might happen, Villafane and Horgan took it for granted that their problems would be with soldiers, not civilians. Now this sudden attack had left Villafane's forearm bleeding from a gaping shrapnel wound and his ring finger shattered. Horgan's boot was blown open and he thought his foot was gone. In fact, part of the right heel had been blown off. He tried to stand but kept falling, so he thought to himself, *I'd better crawl.* Despite their injuries, the two managed to capture four Iraqis who dropped their rifles and surrendered. When the Iraqis took off their robes, they were wearing military uniforms underneath. A cache of weapons was stashed in a nearby mud hut. "I could see they were all terrified," Villafane said.

Days later, in a military hospital in Germany, Villafane was still seething at the idea of Iraqi soldiers passing as civilians. "It was disgusting," he said. But he understood why the Iraqis resorted to such methods. "They do," he said, "whatever they can do."

THE AMBUSH OF THE 507TH was barely over when American marines came into Nasiriya in support, trying to secure the bridges and retrieve wounded soldiers reported to have been stranded after their colleagues were killed or captured. Tank and light armor units crept forward into town, 100 yards at a time, taking fire from pockets of Iraqi infantry and bands of fedayeen guerrillas. Some of the Iraqis were apparently soldiers from the 11th Mechanized Infantry Division, whose leadership the marines believed had surrendered to American Army forces the day before. Now here they were, still fighting, firing from machine-gun nests on the outskirts of the city. From the center of town, Iraqi mortar fire sounded. American radar detected the location of the mortars and Marine cannons returned fire, but it was impossible to tell what had been hit. Mortars were easily hidden, and a shooter could fire his weapon, then drag it around a corner and inside a doorway before the Americans could find it.

For most of the morning, a Marine infantry unit code-named Timber Wolf and its forward artillery observers were pinned down. Finally, shortly before noon, they advanced, meeting machine-gun fire and fighting that would not let up. Cobra helicopters flew low, barely above the oversized balloons launched by the artillery to test the wind. South of town, at an impromptu command center code-named Nightmare—evocative of the heat and flies that permeated the air at midday—officers struggled to work their lunchbox-sized portable phones, and to be heard above the din. The voices on the other end of the phones, crackling back from forward positions, sounded frantic, shouting above the machine-gun fire that could be heard in the distance. Colonel Glenn Starnes's artillery battalion often held its fire, worried about hitting fellow marines inside the city. He and Major Phillip Boggs were also concerned about the enemy. "We're suppressing him, probably, but we're not killing him," Boggs said. Another worry grew out of the fact that the Iraqis' own mortar and artillery fire was missing the American positions by large distances, prompting Starnes to suspect that the enemy was simply trying to uncover the Americans' location. "I'm afraid he's trying to unmask me," he said. Lieutenant Michael Slawsky spoke up in frustration. "It would be really nice to have some forward observer out there to tell us 'left' or 'right' or whatever, and what we hit," he said.

The worst blow came in the afternoon. A group of Iraqi men displayed a white flag as if to surrender, but when a group of marines approached in an amphibious vehicle, the enemy opened fire, slamming a rocket-propelled grenade into the vehicle, killing the marines inside. The six-hour battle ended only after the Marines called in air support from F/A-18 Hornets, AV-8 Harriers, A-10 Thunderbolts and AH-1 Cobra attack helicopters. The Americans reported destroying ten Soviet-era T-55 tanks, as well as an artillery battery and an anti-aircraft gun.[3] That afternoon, at a temporary base south of town, helicopters landed with the casualties. Sergeant First Class Carey Clay stuck his head inside one to see if he could help unload the wounded but was waved off by the crew. "It was just bodies everywhere," Clay said. "Just an unbelievable sight. There was blood everywhere. A lot of blood on the floor. I was in Desert Storm, but I've never seen that. I only saw the enemy like that."[4] Commanders first said that nearly ten marines had died; in fact, the total number would turn out to be nearly twice that: eighteen. Some fifty others were wounded. By the end of the day, Major Boggs declared: "The bridge is considered secured."

"It is," Colonel Starnes replied tightly, "but I wouldn't want to drive on it."

And by nightfall, the stretch of road between the two bridges in Nasiriya had a new name. The Americans called it "Ambush Alley."

AT 6:30 P.M. local time, Iraqi television began airing raw and grisly footage of several dead American bodies. Their shirts were pulled up and their trousers lowered, almost obscenely. At least two seemed to have been shot in the head, execution-style. There was also video of five American captives, soldiers from the 507th Maintenance Company. Some were obviously wounded. Others were bruised. All looked shaken—and frightened.

It was 10:30 A.M. in Washington, right in the middle of the Sunday morning talk shows, and one of them, CBS's *Face the Nation,* broke in with some of the images. Later, after the Pentagon protested that the prisoners' families had not yet been notified, most American networks showed only snippets. But television viewers around much of the rest of the world saw a grim parade. Specialist Hernandez lay on a sofa, his face covered in blood. He had obvious wounds to his side and arm and seemed to be gasping for breath. But the Iraqi interviewer lifted his head and pulled it toward the microphone, asking his name. "Edgar," he said. "My name is Edgar." Specialist Johnson had no boots and a bloody, bandaged ankle. Her eyes darted back and forth like a frightened fawn's. She said her name and hometown. Sergeant Riley sat on a chair, pale and shaking, his hands clamped between his knees. Specialist Hudson said impassively, "I follow orders." The interviewer demanded to know why Private First Class Patrick Miller had come to Iraq. "I was told to come here," Miller answered. "I come to shoot only if I am shot at." He added, "I come to fix broke stuff. I don't want to kill anybody." At one point, the Iraqi commentator said, "These are the ones trying to invade Iraq, but they were faced with our courageous troops," adding, "Here they are, shamed and defeated."

In Washington, Secretary Rumsfeld swiftly declared that Iraq's broadcast of the video was a violation of the Geneva Conventions, which bars public humiliation of prisoners of war. At the American command in Qatar, Franks's deputy, Lieutenant General John Abizaid, called the broadcast "absolutely unacceptable." But elsewhere in the world, especially in the Muslim nations, the Americans' protests rang hollow. Only months before, it was recalled, the Bush administration had refused to accord the full formal protections of the Geneva Conventions to the Taliban and Al Qaeda fighters who had been captured in Afghanistan and had allowed photographs to be taken of them in detention at the U.S. naval base at Guantánamo Bay, Cuba.

President Bush, spending the weekend at Camp David, had been

awakened in his cabin early that morning with news of the ambush
and captures, including the information that at least one of the prisoners, Specialist Johnson, was a woman. Upon his return to Washington, he stopped to make brief, sober remarks outside the White
House, clearly concerned. "This is just the beginning of a tough fight,"
he said. "It's going to take a while to achieve our objective. But we're
on course, we're determined and we're making good progress." He
added, "We ask God's comfort for those who mourn today." Rumsfeld,
as usual, was blunter. "A war is a war," he said on NBC's *Meet the
Press* that morning. "It's a brutal thing."

In fact, that Sunday would stand as the single worst day of the
war for the Americans. The Iraqi information minister, al-Sahhaf, said
that American troops had been "taught a lesson they will never forget:
We have placed them in a quagmire from which they can never
emerge except dead." In Qatar, General Abizaid acknowledged, "It's
the toughest day of resistance that we've had thus far."

But the broader picture was much more encouraging. The Third
Infantry's 7th Cavalry—General George Armstrong Custer's onetime
command—had moved north of Najaf and was headed toward Baghdad. The ambush in Nasiriya had been tragic, but it had not stopped
the American advance. The Marines were still fighting in the city,
but they did control the bridges, and with them the Euphrates
crossing. The resistance in the south would obviously now have to be
dealt with, and it would be. American commanders insisted their plan
was on track.

The big picture was scant comfort to the handful of American
families most in the dark that night: Those whose relatives were members of the 507th but who had not been seen on videotape or confirmed dead, and whose whereabouts remained a mystery. At their
home in Palestine, West Virginia, Gregory and Deadra Lynch learned
on television that afternoon that an Army maintenance unit was in
trouble. They grew fearful, because they knew their daughter Jessica
was in the 507th. She had joined the military, in part, because she
feared that her job prospects in West Virginia were so slim. Worried
about the reports, Gregory Lynch called the Red Cross and waited to
hear back. At 10 P.M., he told his wife, "No news is good news," and
they went to bed. An hour later, a West Virginia state trooper and

an official from the National Guard arrived at their door to tell them that Jessica was missing. They didn't sleep the rest of the night. They sat up crying—and praying.

ON MONDAY MORNING, THE FIGHTING in Nasiriya ground on. Iraqi fighters leapt out of buses and taxis to shoot at the 5,000 marines of Task Force Tarawa, who were charged with securing the city. From above, American helicopter gunships fired into the city. It was just the sort of catch-as-catch-can urban combat that the Americans had sought to avoid and now they were in the middle of it. As many as 400 Iraqi fighters remained inside the city, and for the Marines, it was a mess. "It's not pretty. It's not surgical," said Chief Warrant Officer Pat Woellhof. "You try to limit collateral damage, but they want to fight. Now it's just smash-mouth football."

No one may ever know how many Iraqi civilians were killed that day, but plenty of Nasiriyans did not see the Americans as liberators. "No Iraqi will support what the Americans are doing here," said one resident named Nawaf, who stood at an American checkpoint that Monday. "If they want to go to Baghdad, that's one thing, but now they have come into our cities, and all Iraqis will fight them." Mustafa Ali, a medical assistant at the Saddam Hospital, spent much of that morning hauling dead and wounded civilians out of bombed buildings. He had been inclined to support the Americans, but not now. "I saw how the Americans bombed our civilians with my own eyes," he said. "You want to overthrow Saddam Hussein's regime? Go to Baghdad. What are you doing here?" A farmer named Mohsen Ali agreed, saying, "Of course these people will fight. They will fight against the invaders." Fedayeen troops in their black masks and head scarves swarmed around the town. Some residents said their commander was Ali Hassan al-Majid, the infamous Saddam henchman known as "Chemical Ali," for his use of chemical weapons against the Kurds in the 1980s. Iraqi regulars, even those who wanted to give up, reported being coerced into fighting. Hussein Habbas, who had fled Nasiriya on Sunday, said, "You can't run away from the unit. If you try to take off your uniform, they will kill you."

That same day, Iraqi television broadcast more pictures of POWs, this time of Chief Warrant Officers Young and Williams, the Apache helicopter pilots who had been forced down in the ill-fated raid near Karbala in the wee hours that morning. Watching the silent pictures at her home near Atlanta, Young's mother, Kaye, recognized her son in his khaki pilot's coveralls and felt like the top of her head was going to come off. In Orlando, Florida, Williams's father, David Sr., at least thought his son seemed in good spirits.

In Baghdad, a figure identified as Saddam Hussein appeared on television for the first time since the first night of the war. In a twenty-five-minute speech aimed at stiffening Iraqi defenses, he told the groups of paramilitary fighters who were striking in the south, "Hold against them. Hit them hard. Hit them with all force and accuracy." He mentioned by name several officers who had led resistance in Um Qasr, lending credence to the notion that he was really Saddam, and still alive. He added, "These are your decisive days. Hit now. According to what? According to what God has ordered you to do: 'Cut their throats and be patient.' "

Chapter 11

THE BRITISH IN BASRA

Basra, Iraq
Monday, March 24, 2003

The Third Infantry had raced to Najaf and paused for rest, refueling and resupply. The vanguard of American marines had crossed the Euphrates at Nasiriya and moved north, while other units faced dogged fighting to secure the town. Now the British—the other major component of the allied invading force—were outside the southern Iraqi city of Basra, fighting to contain an unknown number of Iraqi forces inside.

Basra, a once-elegant commercial center of 1.5 million people, had been a gateway to the Persian Gulf for 1,400 years. Its population was overwhelmingly Shiite, and it had been a center of the uprisings against Saddam after the 1991 war. American and British commanders had expected its residents would greet the advancing allied troops with open arms. The British knew the city; they had occupied it in World War I and used its port, and wound up remaining until 1930, as the British-backed Iraqi monarchy took shape. So Franks had assigned British forces the task of securing Basra and protecting his right flank as the American troops moved north.

Basra sat seventy-five miles from the mouth of the Gulf, on the Shatt al Arab waterway, near the country's rich southern oil fields, which had been developed starting in the late 1940s. The city was no stranger to armed conflict—the Persians and Turks had fought over it centuries ago—and because of its proximity to the oil fields, it was hit hard in the Iran-Iraq war of the 1980s, and bombed again during the Persian Gulf war. Now, however, it was seen not so much as a significant military target as a place where American and British troops could begin their march with upbeat images of civilians welcoming them as liberators. If Basra could be quickly pacified, it would send an ominous signal to Saddam and his loyalists in Baghdad that their control over the country—and their only access to the Persian Gulf—was slipping away. It was to be another page in the "shock and awe" playbook, a swift way to demonstrate the allies' determination to seize control of as much Iraqi territory as quickly as they could. But Basra was not turning out as planned, because Iraqi renegades were "not playing by the rules," as Major Charlie Lambert, second in command of the Royal Scots Dragoon Guards battle group, put it after three days of engagements around the city. Lambert's colleague Sergeant Mark Smith agreed, observing, "It's not the Iraqi army we have to worry about; it's the person with the Kalashnikov in the back garden. The Iraqis are smiling assassins. They wave at you as you go past, then shoot you in the back."[1]

The British had reached the outskirts of the city on Friday, the second day of the war. American marines captured the international airport, on the west side of town, the following day, before moving on north and leaving the British in control. But the expected quick surrender did not come, and by Sunday, British troops were forced to surround as much of the city as possible to prevent Iraqi forces from fleeing or causing further trouble. A daunting standoff, a kind of semi-siege, had begun. Again and again, Iraqi militiamen waved white flags in apparent surrender, then opened fire. Old Iraqi Soviet-made T-55 tanks would lurk just inside the city, then dart out at night to attack. There were reports from British intelligence officers inside the city that Iraqi commanders were forcing their own troops, or civilian irregulars, to fight at gunpoint. Saddam had put his trusted lieutenant Chemical Ali in charge of the city's defense. Allied bombardment had cut the cables running to the city's main water-supply plant, and electricity and water supplies were severely disrupted. Basra's geology made its ground water too saline to drink, and expected delivery of food and relief supplies from the British Royal Fleet Auxiliary Service ship *Sir Galahad* had been held up by continued skirmishing in Um Qasr, twenty-five miles to the south. A severe health and humanitarian crisis was looming. Typhoid, dysentery and other diseases were expected to be a real problem. "A city of that size cannot go without water or electricity for long," said UN Secretary-General Kofi Annan.

All day this Monday, the battle for Basra had raged. Tanks and armored vehicles of the British 7th Armored Brigade—the "Desert

Rats" that had routed Rommel's Afrika Korps in World War II—hovered on the city's outskirts. As billowing black smoke from oil-well fires filled the sky, troops of the Black Watch and the Royal Scots Dragoon Guards came under heavy mortar fire from Iraqi regulars and militiamen as they operated around a bridge over the Shatt al Basra Canal, on the main road leading into town from the west. The Iraqis fired so many rocket-propelled grenades at this spot that the British forces nicknamed the approach "RPG Alley," and troops shuttled back and forth in heavy Challenger 2 tanks and armored vehicles. An earlier plan that weekend for moving into the city proper had been abandoned as too dangerous, and now the British were often unable even to return fire, for fear of hitting residential areas. By day's end, British troops were forced to pull back to avoid a threatened ambush by Republican Guard forces, who were reported to be heading out of town in civilian clothes in an attempt to kill or capture British troops. The relentless pounding of the mortar rounds echoed like the boom and aftershock of the blasting bass of a souped-up stereo in a passing car. The shooting had "tightened people's focus and other parts of their anatomy, and blooded us mentally," said Major Lindsay MacDuff.[2]

Still, the British waited, determined to fight the battle their way, avoiding as many civilian casualties as possible. The wait would ultimately stretch for more than two weeks, in a test of some American commanders' patience and at considerable strain on the British troops themselves. The battle drew comparatively little attention in the United States at the time, in part because there were no American reporters embedded with British troops, and only a relative handful of British correspondents. But the British were proud of their tactics and approach, which owed much to their peacekeeping experience in Kosovo and their years of battling guerrilla war in Northern Ireland. While the American forces plowed toward Baghdad, the British were willing to wait, adopting a lower-key strategy of patient probing attacks aimed at isolating Baath Party elements while working cooperatively with others in the civilian population. It was a strategy that they hoped would pay dividends in the postwar period. Then again, British forces had the comparative luxury of waiting, while the Americans set themselves the tougher task of capturing the capital. For the American forces—already stretched thin—it turned out to be a lucky thing the British were on the ground in Basra.

• • •

THERE WERE MORE THAN 25,000 British troops in the Iraq theater. The first of them had begun moving north from Kuwait on the first day of the ground war, along with their American comrades. The British vanguard included 2,000 marines from 3 Commando Brigade, 2,000 paratroopers from the 16th Air Assault Brigade and 6,000 tank troops from the 7th Armored Brigade, moving in 120 tanks and 145 armored vehicles. Together with American marines, British troops advanced on Friday to Um Qasr, where the fighting was sporadic but intense. That same day, hopes rose when it seemed that the commanders of Iraq's 51st Mechanized Infantry Division, one of the regular army's best units, had surrendered at the border town of Safwan. It was the 51st that had helped put down the Shiite revolt in the south at the end of the first Gulf war, and its surrender now would have been a major coup for the coalition. In fact, it turned out that the officers who surrendered were only battalion or brigade commanders, not leaders of the whole division, which was still active.

On Saturday, American marines, backed up by Cobra helicopters, seized the Basra airport after what one marine called "a decent amount of resistance." Plumes of heavy black smoke were snaking over the city from the fires that the Iraqis had set at several oil wells around the town. Hundred of Iraqis surrendered that day, lining up along a roadside to give up their weapons and have their identities checked. But it was soon clear that militiamen and other units loyal to Saddam were still very much in the fight. Specially trained negotiators, including Iraqi exiles, from MI6, the British intelligence service, were in radio communication with Basra's defenders, attempting to persuade them to surrender. By Saturday night, British commanders pronounced that they had effectively taken control of the city by lightly encircling it, but their optimism proved premature. The great fear was that some Iraqi forces had simply thrown away their uniforms and melted back into the populace, as the Americans were finding in Nasiriya and elsewhere. That night, the British took machine-gun fire from two Iraqi positions at a military complex near a canal on the city's western edge, and replied with cannon fire. British forces moved in to try to secure the barracks, and the Iraqis fired back—in room-to-room fighting for more than two hours. The retreating Iraqis had planted plastic explosives around the pilings of the bridge over the canal, but failed to detonate them. Captured Iraqi troops told British commanders they had tried to surrender on Friday but were instead rounded up by their commanders, sent back to their barracks and forced at gunpoint to return to the front line.

By Sunday, explosions echoed throughout the city, and civilians streamed out across the western bridge in loaded trucks and battered cars. The Arab television news channel Al Jazeera was already broadcasting horrific images of what it described as civilian casualties from the British shelling, including pictures of a child with the back of his head apparently blown off. In the suburb of Zubayr, fifteen miles west of the city, British forces found a huge cache of weapons at a heliport, including Russian-made missiles and giant antishipping mines, stored in dozens of bunkers. Some of the boxes were date-marked 2002, a sign that they had been stockpiled in anticipation of just such an invasion. In a bitter twist, other boxes, full of rocket-propelled grenades, bore the name of Wallop Industries Ltd., a British arms manufacturer based in Hampshire. Continued Iraqi fire made it impossible for British forces to move any farther than the western areas outside the city proper.

Even as the main body of troops remained stuck outside the city, British intelligence officers were providing information about leadership targets loyal to Saddam. In the wee hours of Tuesday morning, March 25, British forces staged a surgical raid in Zubayr. Soldiers of Company D of the Black Watch, in a Warrior armored personnel carrier, smashed through a three-meter-high perimeter wall of a two-story building that housed the local Baath Party headquarters. "Everything was going in, grenades, Warriors laying down 30-millimeter fire, anti-tank weapons, everything," said Lance Corporal Colin Edwards.[3] But it was far from clear what was really happening inside the city. As Tuesday wore on, there were tantalizing, fragmentary reports that a local uprising of Iraqis against the regime might be under way. But other reports told of Iraqi soldiers shelling crowds with mortars and using machine guns to cut down protesters. "We are not getting much information out of there, and we have not had much joy in getting our message in there," one senior British military official complained. "We have got to be extremely responsible in the way we do this."[4] As the British tried to advance toward town on Tuesday, men of the Black Watch mistakenly fired on a tank of the Queen's Royal Lancers, killing two of their fellow soldiers and wounding two others.

In the meantime, humanitarian groups were estimating that more than 100,000 children in Basra were facing extreme hardship. The Desert Rats were carrying 5,000 emergency ration packs, but could not get into town to hand them out. That Tuesday, there were signs of marked escalation. American F/A-18 Super Hornets dropped bombs on military sites, including a large ammunition dump, and on the Baath Party headquarters. Elements of the Iraqi 51st Mechanized Division were active again, and the British destroyed more than twenty T-55 tanks that had tried to make a breakout.

The plan simply to contain the city was proving inadequate. There was also continued resistance farther south between Basra and the Gulf—in Um Qasr and Safwan, which were supposed to be securely in allied hands. In London, Prime Minister Blair sounded a cautious note. "Basra is surrounded and cannot be used as an Iraqi base," he said. But he warned that pockets of Saddam's most fiercely loyal lieutenants were holding out and "still able to inflict casualties on our troops." Sergeant Dave Smith, an American marine who had fought in Safwan and Um Qasr, summed up the allies' frustration. "It was expected it would last two to eight hours, but it went on for four or five days," he said. "If it takes four or five days to take Um Qasr and Safwan, imagine what it's going to be like to take Baghdad."[5]

BEFORE SUNSET ON WEDNESDAY, MARCH 26, British electronic sensors picked up a frightening development: A convoy of perhaps 120 Iraqi tanks or armored personnel carriers was on the move, heading southeast out of town on the main road toward the Iranian border. What was their objective? Were they escaping the city? Or headed to strike the British troops who had secured the Fao Peninsula, fifty miles to the southeast? Was it a retreat or a daring counterattack? "We have no idea why this column has come out at the moment," said Major Mick Green of 40 Commando. "Their intentions or motives are totally unclear but they have adopted an offensive posture and do not want to surrender, so we have attacked them."[6] British Harrier and Tornado GR4 jets and American A-10 Warthog tank busters pounded the Iraqi column, which by 9 o'clock that night had scattered into the open countryside. It turned out that the sensors had wildly exaggerated the number of Iraqi vehicles, but at least three were destroyed. The earlier reports of an uprising inside Basra were turning out to be exaggerated, too. Now came word that the violence may have been sparked because Chemical Ali had killed a tribal leader, a Shiite Muslim, on the grounds that he was not doing enough to prevent desertions, and his followers had lashed back.

By Thursday, March 27, British troops were able to deliver boxes of water, milk, juice and baby food to desperate residents in the suburb of Mushirij, six miles west of Basra. "The biggest problem we are having is getting it out of their minds that the Baath Party is returning," said Major Duncan McSporran of the First Fusiliers Zulu Company. "I've got an enormous amount of sympathy for them—they've lived under a reign of terror for thirty years. They don't know who to trust."[7]

That same day, Iraqi tanks again tried to break out toward the southeast of the city, toward the Fao Peninsula. But the Iraqi column of fourteen T-55s was no match for an equal number of British Challengers. The British tanks each had guns that could fire eight armor-piercing depleted-uranium rounds in under a minute, from a range of up to two miles. The shells whizzed out at a mile per second, in what was billed as perhaps the biggest British tank battle since the end of World War II. The battle was over in no time. All fourteen Iraqi tanks were destroyed, along with their three-man crews.

By now, Iraqi families inside the city were desperate, and began flooding out of town through the British checkpoint on the western side. "It's been *pow, pow, pow* all the time," said one resident, named Maklim Muhammad, as he crossed the bridge leading out of the city. "I can't stand it. I'm nervous and I'm thirsty."[8] Over the weekend of March 29–30, residents clutching overstuffed bags and whatever possessions they could carry streamed out of town. "Civilians are afraid to leave their houses because police wearing civilian clothes form patrols with fedayeen," said Nathim Jaber, an oil industry worker. He said Iraqi officials had been attempting to bribe people with $10,000 promissory notes—IOUs that were no doubt worthless the moment they were written. "They find people, give them a weapon and force them to fight," he said.

After more than a week of allied bombardment and steady skirmishing, Saddam's loyalists were still in control of the city center. The British began making their deepest incursions of the campaign, establishing forward observation posts and sending back intelligence. On Saturday, during a raid into central Basra, eleven tanks from the Scots Dragoon Guards destroyed a twenty-five-foot cast-iron statue of Saddam and knocked out a radio tower. Some commanders were ready to do more. Major McSporran of the First Fusiliers summed up the sentiment: "We've got to go in."[9]

BEFORE DAWN THAT SUNDAY, MARCH 30, British commanders decided to try something new. After days of targeted strikes and sporadic engagements, the Royal Marines launched the single largest British operation of the campaign, the largest all-out British ground assault since the Falkland Islands war in 1982. The goal: to take control of a large Basra suburb, Abu al-Kacib, home to 30,000 people, on the southeast side of town. With a bit of whimsy, the action was code-named Operation James—as in Bond. It began at 3 A.M., and three rifle companies, each with more than 120 men, moved forward on foot at dawn. They fought their way across a wide front under heavy fire from as many as 3,000 Iraqi soldiers. Their goal was to trap the Iraqi forces against the Shatt al Arab waterway. Sniper and machine-gun fire raked down on the marines, and within an hour, two senior Iraqi officers were taken prisoner, four T-55 tanks were destroyed and at least one Iraqi bunker was blown up. At least seventy Iraqis were killed and 300 taken prisoner, with just a single British soldier killed. Later in the day, the Iraqis staged a counterattack, when three patrol vessels attacked a Royal Marine landing craft on the Basra canal, setting it afire with a rocket-propelled grenade, killing one marine and injuring three.

"The planning assumption had always been that the advancing coalition forces would simply sweep past Basra and it would implode by itself," said Brigadier Jim Dutton, the commander of 3 Commando

Brigade. "It became apparent to me that we could do more than that—get the message across that we can go in there and get rid of the regime."[10] On Monday, March 31, British forces destroyed another twenty-five Iraqi tanks and left 200 dead and wounded in massive air and artillery attacks on the north and west sides of the city. There was a week of fighting in Basra still to come. But the raid on Abu al-Kacib had begun to turn the tide.

Chapter 12

SECURING THE NORTH

In northern Iraq
Wednesday, March 26, 2003

The fleet of giant C-17 transports plowed through the night skies over Kurdish-controlled territory. Inside each plane, nearly 100 paratroopers in desert camouflage waited, loaded with weapons and equipment. One by one, the planes dropped low and the jumpmasters called out: "Go! Go! Go!" A thousand men from the 173rd Airborne Brigade parachuted out near Harir Airfield, about 220 miles north of Baghdad, at last opening the allies' long-promised northern front. The brigade's commander, Colonel William Mayville, had told the paratroopers before their takeoff from Aviano, Italy, "Americans are asking you to make the world a better place by jumping into the unknown for the benefit of others. Our cause is just and victory is certain."[1]

The 173rd had earned its nickname, "Sky Soldiers," from the Nationalist Chinese paratroopers with whom it trained in the 1960s, and it had been the Army's first ground combat unit to serve in Vietnam, in 1965. Under Tommy Franks's original war plan, the 173rd was to have supplemented the main thrust of the northern advance, the state-of-the-art armor of the Fourth Infantry Division rolling in from Turkey. But with the Turks' refusal to grant the United States the use of its bases, the 173rd was standing in for the entire advance, while the troops of the Fourth Infantry remained stateside and their equipment was still making its way to Kuwait—weeks away from being able to join the fight.

A real northern front would take weeks to mount, and so this jump was not simply a military operation but also a publicity stunt, a psychological operation to unnerve the Iraqis with its suddenness and speed. Harir was what parachutists call a "cold zone"—friendly territory—and had been securely in friendly hands since 1991. The Iraqi forces' front lines were perhaps fifty miles to the south, and the American troops

153

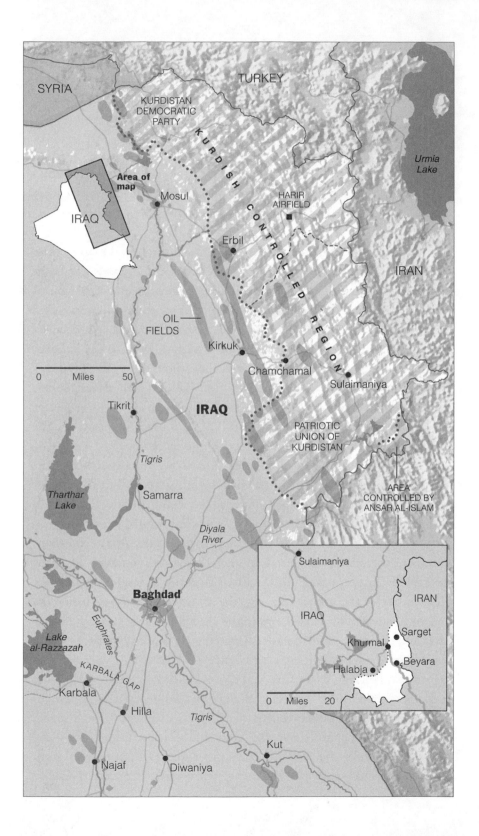

faced no hostile fire as they parachuted in. Special Operations forces had already been operating in northern Iraq, and planes operating with the 173rd had already landed at Harir Airfield; with time, the troops of the 173rd could easily have arrived without jumping. Instead, by sending the paratroopers plunging down into this broad valley lined with snow-capped mountains, Tommy Franks and his generals were making the statement that they could come and go as they pleased in Iraq. This was the largest American parachute drop since the invasion of Panama in 1989, and one of the largest since World War II.

Working with the ragtag but gritty Kurdish forces known as pesh merga, or "those who face death," the Sky Soldiers had several objectives. One was to discourage any interference by the roughly 40,000 Turkish troops massed just across Iraq's northern border. Once the war had begun, Turkey finally relented and granted the United States overflight rights, sparing allied planes a more diplomatically provocative route over Israel and Jordan, but the Turks were still causing headaches in the north. Turkey was threatening to invade Iraq if Kurdish forces moved to take Iraqi territory or solidified their control of the semi-autonomous zone that had grown up in the north since the 1991 war. The 173rd's second objective was to counter threats of terrorism from Ansar al-Islam, a Muslim extremist group with suspected ties to Al Qaeda, which had been attempting ambushes, bombings and political assassinations in an attempt to destabilize the region. And the third objective for the American forces was to freeze in place perhaps 90,000 Iraqi troops positioned along the border of the Kurdish-controlled region, and keep them from moving south to join the defense of Baghdad. The Iraqis, including a Republican Guard division near Mosul, had already been weakened by American air strikes. Northern Iraq's big prize was Kirkuk, the oil-rich city that had long been the subject of interethnic feuding. "Kirkuk is key," said Major Mike Hastings of the 173rd. "The Iraqis want it. The Kurds want it, the Turks want it and various other ethnic groups also want it. What this drop means is that we can secure it until we are relieved by other forces."[2]

When the 173rd landed, the prospects of any such relief seemed remote. The American forces in central and southern Iraq were pinned down by the unexpected resistance in places like Nasiriya. Forward elements of the Marines were pushing up the east side of the Euphrates toward the towns of Diwaniya and Kut, while troops from the Third Infantry had surrounded the city of Najaf and were seeing unexpected action there.

And for two days, American troops all over Iraq had been stopped in their tracks by one of warfare's oldest and least predictable enemies: the weather. On Monday, March 24, cold, dry air sweeping south from northern Europe had collided with warm, moist air over the Mediterranean to produce punishing sandstorms that barreled into Iraq, trapped by the funnel-shaped lines of mountain ranges in Turkey, to the north, and in Iran, to the east. For more than forty-eight hours, much of the country was enveloped in blinding swirls of whirling, blowing grit that grounded helicopters, jammed weapons, stopped tanks and forced troops to use their handheld GPS devices just to find their way around makeshift encampments. The 101st Airborne was stuck at its gunship base in central Iraq. On Tuesday, only the sand was flying, and it was breaking speed limits of fifty miles an hour and more. At one point, when the winds let up for an hour or so, it was possible to see about twenty-five yards into the distance. In early evening, when it suddenly rained, what fell was not water but mud, the suspended sand particles pulled into wet globules. The temperature hovered just below 100 degrees, saunalike for the troops in protective chemical suits, body armor, boots and helmets. If sand were measured like humidity, it would have been 100 percent. "The wrath of Allah," Lieutenant Colonel Steven E. Landis of the Third Infantry wryly called it.

In Washington, the air was thick with another kind of storm: recriminations about the course of the war. The ambush in Nasiriya, the British standoff in Basra, the long supply lines and now the blinding sand had prompted a wave of doubts and second-guessing about the war plan from anonymous generals in the Pentagon—and from the ranks of generals-turned-television-commentators who were busy analyzing the war for the networks and cable channels. There were not enough American boots on the ground, the warnings went, and not enough heavy armor; Rumsfeld had put American men and women at risk in his determination to "transform" the armed forces. From his office at the Pentagon, Rumsfeld brushed off the criticism. Even Secretary of State Powell, the advocate of overwhelming force in the last Gulf war, dismissed the doubts as "the usual chatter," adding, "Every general who ever worked for me is now on some network commenting on the daily battle. And frankly, battles come and wars come and they have ups and downs."

All the same, the back talk—and the combat situation on the ground that fueled it—was putting political pressure on the White House. On Wednesday, March 26, President Bush flew to MacDill Air Force Base in Florida, the headquarters of the U.S. Central Command, to deliver a message of American resolve. On the flight down, the White House press secretary, Ari Fleischer, told reporters aboard Air Force One that the president would declare that the military campaign was "ahead of schedule," based on "progress that is being made on the military battlefield, the advance toward Baghdad and the success we are having in engaging enemy units." Hours later, when Bush delivered his speech to an audience of friends and family members of troops serving in the Gulf, he dropped that reference. Instead the president said, "The path we are taking is not easy, and it may be long. Yet we know our destination. We will stay on the path, mile by mile, all the way to Baghdad, and all the way to victory."

FOR MOST OF THE 1990S, the Kurds of northern Iraq had existed not only in a state of standoff with Saddam's regime but in wary cooperation or outright civil conflict among themselves. Constituting roughly 20 percent of Iraq's population, the Kurds had been at odds with Baghdad for most of the twentieth century. A mountain people whose origins have been lost in myth and uncertainty, they lacked a homeland or even a single language to call their own, instead speaking several dialects of an Indo-European language related to Persian. Despite periods of relative autonomy, including the decade after the first Gulf war, the Kurds had never been able to resolve their own internal and tribal rivalries enough to manage real self-rule, instead bemoaning their fate as "a thousand sighs, a thousand tears, a thousand revolts, a thousand hopes."[3] The two main political factions were the Patriotic Union of Kurdistan, led by Jalal Talabani, and the Kurdistan Democratic Party, led by Massoud Barzani. In the mid-1990s, Talabani had been backed by Iran in what amounted to a civil war with

Barzani's faction, which was eventually backed by Saddam. Each faction ultimately made overtures to Saddam that had allowed the Kurds to maintain a tenuous control of the territory in the north of Iraq, which they called Iraqi Kurdistan. Their hegemony was backed up by American and British enforcement of the northern no-fly zone. But rule was divided: In essence, each Kurdish faction operated a relatively autonomous, parallel, rival government—able to barely exist beyond the reach of Saddam's regime but without any real unity.

The Kurds viewed the prospect of a second Persian Gulf war with decidedly mixed feelings. If Saddam were to be removed, and Washington remained committed to preserving the territorial integrity of Iraq, the Kurds worried about being reshuffled into a new Iraqi government in which they would be a minority, and losing what they saw as the gains of the 1990s. At the same time, if Saddam felt cornered by an American advance, the Kurds feared that they would once again be the first victims of a chemical or biological attack as had happened at Halabja during the Iran-Iraq war. And they knew all too well their own limitations as a fighting force, one unlikely to be called on by the Americans. The Kurdish military was made up of men like twenty-one-year-old Borhan Chato, a would-be guerrilla still trying to adjust to life as a conventional soldier. One day in December 2002, he had occupied the last Kurdish position on the front lines separating Saddam's Iraq from Kurdish territory. He was supposed to have been with five other soldiers, but they had all gone home for lunch. He had a rifle and five rusting magazines holding 150 cartridges, with no helmet, first-aid kit or radio. His mission, should he become suspicious of Iraqi movements, was to telephone his headquarters, a thirty-minute drive away. He was not much of a sentry.

Chato was fairly representative of the pesh merga ranks. "If America attacks Iraq, they will not need our help, because we are not so strong," said Hamid Afandi, minister of the pesh merga for the Kurdistan Democratic Party, which controlled the western part of the Kurdish zone.

As if the Kurds' own internal feuds were not enough, they also had to contend with the fighters of the militant group Ansar al-Islam, whose roughly 650 fighters had taken control of a tiny corner of Kurdish territory near the Iranian border and imposed a harsh,

Taliban-style rule on the 8,000 residents there. According to Kurdish accounts, which were mostly unverifiable, Ansar banned music, alcohol, television and dancing; defectors from the group reported that men had to assemble in mosques for prayer five times each day and that shops could not display products with labels bearing images of women. American officials believed that Ansar had directly collaborated with Al Qaeda, a claim supported by Al Qaeda documents found in Afghanistan by *The New York Times*. In his presentation at the United Nations in February, Secretary Powell had described an Ansar camp near Sarget as a poisons and explosives factory supported by both Baghdad and Al Qaeda, and he offered its existence as a reason to consider using force against Saddam if he failed to disarm. Kurdish officials claimed that the camp was used to experiment with toxins on animals, but Ansar fighters who escorted Western journalists through the rickety compound after Powell's speech dismissed the American claims, showing off crude buildings with no plumbing. As the threat of an American invasion loomed in late February and early March, Ansar fighters reportedly assassinated several Kurdish officials and took others hostage.

Now, with war under way, it was this unsettled reality that faced the American Special Operations soldiers and the newly arrived paratroopers of the 173rd Airborne Brigade. On March 20, the first day of the war, Kurdish forces near Chamchamal, a city facing the Iraqi front lines, mostly just milled about, with only three fighters to be found. Up and down a thirty-five-mile stretch of the front line outside the Iraqi-controlled city of Mosul, Kurdish men asked where the American forces were. They felt vulnerable to an Iraqi attack and wanted American troops deployed in significant numbers to deter chaos. "If there were American soldiers here, people will feel peace and feel secure," said Mazin Hamad, the mayor of the village of Bardarash. "We have a very, very small number of pesh merga."

By the next day, American bombardment of Iraqi targets south of the Kurdish front began. Ansar al-Islam positions near the Iranian border were hit as well. On Saturday, March 22, in apparent retaliation for a strike by American cruise missiles against Ansar, at least three Kurds and an Australian television cameraman were killed when a car filled with explosives detonated at a Kurdish military checkpoint outside Khurmal, a checkpoint crowded with civilians who were flee-ing the area. On Monday, March 24, two days before the 173rd's jump, American forces announced that they had established a military command in the north to "provide a stabilizing influence," in the words of the newly named commander, Major General Henry P. Osman of the Marines.

With Turkey threatening to send its own armed forces into the north to deliver aid, stabilize the region and prevent refugees from flooding across its border, as they had in 1991, the American command was a largely symbolic holding action against that possibility. The American message appeared to be having some effect. By Thursday, March 27, the first crack in Saddam's once-formidable northern defense line appeared: the Iraqi soldiers manning a checkpoint on the main highway into Kirkuk suddenly abandoned it. That opened the road into Kirkuk, and Kurdish civilians and fighters streamed toward the city. But though the Iraqis were gone, there were not enough American forces to assure control. No one knew what might happen next.

THAT SAME THURSDAY, AT A makeshift camp outside Najaf, two top American field commanders held a sober conference. General Wallace, the V Corps commander who controlled all Army units in the theater, had come to meet with General Petraeus, the commander of the 101st Airborne. The generals were troubled. The ambush attack on the Apache helicopters earlier in the week had shaken them badly. "We're dealing with a country in which everybody has a weapon, and when they fire them all into the air at the same time, it's tough," Wallace said. Almost as troubling were Iraqi hits on two of the Third Infantry's Abrams tanks. It was the first time an Abrams had ever been lost in combat.[4]

Was the Iraqi military turning out to have a better capacity than the Americans thought? Speaking to reporters, Wallace said that in the fighting that week in Najaf, Iraqis in pickup trucks with nothing more than light arms had taken on the best American tanks, behavior that he termed "bizarre."

"Technical vehicles with .50-caliber weapons—any kind of weapon—leading the charge," Wallace said, incredulous. "They were charging tanks and Bradleys!" He added: "I'm appalled by the inhumanity of the Saddamists—Baath Party militia or officials—have shown . . . giving out weapons and forcing people to fight and threatening their families. It's very disturbing to understand that someone could be that brutal. It's also very disturbing that the people have put up with this for twenty-five years. I think the people are numb."

Wallace said something else that somber day, something that angered some of his superiors and created a media firestorm in Washington. "The enemy we're fighting is a bit different than the one we war-gamed against, because of these paramilitary forces," the general said. "We knew they were here, but we did not know how they would fight."

Already that Thursday morning, official Washington had had a rude shock delivered to its doorsteps, in the form of a front-page headline in *The Washington Post* that declared, "War Could Last Months, Officers Say." Quoting anonymous senior military officials, the story went on to warn that the war would "require considerably more combat power than is now on hand" in Iraq and Kuwait. Food, water and supplies were said to be running low in frontline units, with resupply efforts delayed by the terrible sandstorm and the fog of war.[5] The doomsayers struck a nerve with President Bush, who met that day at Camp David with Prime Minister Blair for the first time since the war began. When a reporter asked Bush how long the war might take, the president responded bluntly, "However long it takes to win." Pressed whether that could mean months, the president grew testier: "However long it takes to achieve our objective. And that's important for you to know, the American people to know, our allies to know and the Iraqi people to know." Pressed yet again, Bush said, "This isn't a matter of timetable; it's a matter of victory. And the Iraqi people have got to know that, see?"

Now Wallace's candid words about the military's having been taken somewhat by surprise by the extent of the Iraqi guerrilla tactics unleashed a new whirlwind of doubts and finger-pointing around the world. "They thought they would be greeted as liberators and that the regime would collapse like a house of cards," declared President Jacques Chirac of France. "But they underestimated Iraqi patriotism. They would have been better off listening to us." Former senator Gary

Hart of Colorado said that the setbacks vindicated his warning in 2001 that, in envisioning a war with Iraq, the administration had to be prepared for "several tens of thousands of American casualties and hundreds of thousands of civilian casualties in downtown Baghdad."[6]

But at the Pentagon—where senior officials were in fact privately braced for thousands of American casualties and for a conflict of as long as four months—the war looked very good indeed. The tip of the Third Infantry was just fifty miles from Baghdad, despite the storms and delays. The southern oil fields were secure, with minimal losses. More than 1,000 Special Operations forces had moved into the western Iraqi desert from Jordan to deter Iraq's capacity to launch missiles that could imperil Israel or allied troops. The port of Um Qasr was finally secure and almost ready to open, and Basra was surrounded. Finally—and perhaps most crucially—despite the sandstorms, American bombers and missiles had continued to pound away at Baghdad and at the defenses of the Medina Division of the Republican Guard. Though these results were not yet fully clear, General Franks and his commanders suspected that they would be gratifying. To a far larger degree than the public or most politicians in Washington could imagine at the time, "air power was able to continue with the battle plan while the ground force stopped for needed rest and re-supply," said retired General Ronald R. Fogleman, a former Air Force chief of staff.[7] "It may seem to people that it's a lot longer than just under a week," Tony Blair said at Camp David. "But actually, it's just under a week. And in just under a week, there is a massive amount that already has been achieved."

Outside Najaf, Colonel William F. Grimsley, commander of the Third Infantry's 1st Brigade, felt much the same way. "You're only bogged down when you've lost the ability to do things on your own initiative," he said. "We ain't there yet."

AT 5 A.M. ON FRIDAY, March 28, roughly 10,000 pesh merga assembled in a remote mountain valley near Beyara, under the guidance of Task Force Viking, a unit of 100 American Special Operations troops. Their mission was to capture a series of villages from Ansar al-Islam, and they advanced in six simultaneous thrusts. All manner of American firepower was brought to bear. Backed up by intensive bombardment from mortars, artillery, B-52 bombers and attack jets, the American and Kurdish forces swiftly produced a mismatch. Commanders judged that as many as fifty Ansar militants were killed, and a swath of border territory was restored to Kurdish control. As the Ansar forces moved back, trying to consolidate their position on a mountain near the Iranian border, a pilotless drone observed them and beamed live video back to the frontline command post, allowing the Americans to order more precise attacks.

Long before the afternoon shadows lengthened, the Ansar fighters' position was untenable. Columns of Kurds and American pursued them, and one by one the villages fell: Sarget, Glup, Zardahar. Two Kurdish fighters died in a land-mine explosion, and at least twenty others were wounded, but the Americans escaped casualties. Among the items captured in Beyara was a memorandum, taped to the wall of an Ansar barracks, which described a religious justification for the attacks of September 11, in Koranic script. "Allah promises in the Koran to destroy the places of those who do not believe in Islam," one passage read. Before sunset, the weary Kurdish fighters had smiles on their faces as they set up checkpoints on the hills, and the Americans slipped back into their sport utility vehicles and sped away. Resistance had been lighter than expected. It had been a good day.

The next day, Saturday, the fighting continued in intensive pockets in the mountains, but American commanders said that the battle against Ansar was all but over. Kurds said that more than 250 Ansar fighters in all had died, and another 150 had surrendered to Iranian authorities at the border. Pockets of resistance could still be heard returning fire, but Kurdish commanders said the outcome seemed certain. "They will be finished because there is no choice," said General Mustafa Said Qadir, commander of military forces in the eastern Kurdish zone. "There is just death."

But the swift American and Kurdish victory over Ansar did not immediately translate into comparable gains against the regular Iraqi forces. Fearful of antagonizing either the Turks or the Americans, the Kurdish forces decided not to mount an advance on Kirkuk. "We don't want to have any problems with our American friends," said Jalal Talabani of the Patriotic Union of Kurdistan. "We don't want to have any quarrels with our Turkish brothers." Even as Kurdish forces held positions perhaps ten miles outside Kirkuk, they showed restraint, and except for occasional Iraqi artillery shelling—random and not especially accurate—the situation was calm. By the following Wednesday, April 2, Iraqi forces had pulled back several miles from their positions around Mosul, mirroring their withdrawal from Kirkuk the week before. Kurdish forces and American Special Operations soldiers were now within twenty-five miles of the city, Iraq's third largest. By this point, another 1,000 paratroopers were on the ground in the north, but even an American force of 2,000 was too small to secure and police Mosul and Kirkuk and their strategic oil fields, so the troops waited.

The next day, forty swaggering Kurdish fighters and four American Special Operations soldiers set out to seize control of territory abandoned by the retreating Iraqis outside Khazir, but found themselves instead engaged in fierce fighting. Iraqi mortar fire pinned down two Americans, and American warplanes responded with air strikes. Without American air power, the Special Ops troops knew, they were relatively powerless. If they had any doubts about this, they could ask their colleagues fighting near Mosul, where 380 Special Operations troops and several thousand Kurds were facing up to 80,000 Iraqi troops. One well-timed Iraqi artillery shell landed only 500 yards to the south of some Special Operations soldiers. If the Iraqi gunner adjusted his shot just slightly, the next round would land on top of the Americans. "All right," a commander said, "let's get these vehicles off the ridge." After the American trucks moved below the ridgeline, the next Iraqi shell fell even closer. "They've got this ridge zeroed in," a Special Operations solider said. Within seconds, the Americans climbed into their vehicles and retreated. The reason was simple: With American planes ten minutes away, the Americans on the ground were all but helpless. They could hold off the Iraqis with machine guns and antitank missiles, but without air power, their position would eventually be overrun. Whenever American planes were not overhead, the Iraqis sensed this vulnerability. They would fire off artillery shells, then move their guns to disguise the source of the incoming. "These guys are tough," a Special Operations soldier said as night fell. "We give them a beating and they keep coming back."

Chapter 13

SAVING PRIVATE LYNCH

Nasiriya, Iraq
Wednesday, March 26, 2003

After days of rough fighting, the marines of Task Force Tarawa had proclaimed Nasiriya secured. Critical American supply convoys were now moving through "Ambush Alley" and over the two bridges north toward Baghdad. The stretch of road across the Euphrates and the Saddam Hussein Canal was still a turkey shoot, and the convoys of armored vehicles took no chances. Every soldier not holding a steering wheel held a rifle or a sidearm, and drivers barreled through at more than sixty miles per hour. After being fired on more than once by guerrillas, a marine guarding the road was so wary that he simply opened fire when one jitney bus came barreling toward him and refused to stop. He killed everyone inside, but when the bodies were searched, no weapons were found.[1]

On this Wednesday alone, a contingent of about 120 marines trying to make it to the first bridge had come under fire from assault weapons and rocket-propelled grenades; about fifteen of their Humvees and seven-ton trucks were destroyed and more than sixty marines were wounded. "Nasiriya was supposed to be a six-hour fight," said Gunnery Sergeant Tracy Hale. "It's already been five days. Five days of non-stop, twenty-four-hour fighting."[2] The fighting was sometimes block-to-block, against a mix of fedayeen paramilitaries and regular soldiers—often in civilian clothes. Always, there was the battle against what one American doctor called "industrial strength flies." Brigadier General John Kelly, assistant commander of the First Marine Division, distilled the challenge from the Iraqis: "There is an organized pattern of resistance. They are sent out to do this with the express purpose of slowing us down." Still, convoys could cross and the marines had a tenuous control.

Then at sunset, just south of town, 1,000 Iraqi soldiers staged what turned out to be the largest, most organized attack yet on the American positions in Nasiriya. Marine units had been blocking roads that could be used by the Iraqi fighters, but they had not closed off a railroad line. "That's how they're coming in," said Lieutenant Josh Cusworth, an intelligence officer, as he looked up from his map in a cramped command tent. "That railroad. We're not monitoring it whatsoever. We don't think they're using it. That's how they're getting in." The Americans took machine-gun fire, and American artillery opened fire in return. For hours into the night, the fighting wore on. Two American infantry units fought so close together at one point— with the enemy in between—that there was fear that friendly artillery fire had struck the marines. At another point, American batteries feared they might be overrun. A communications officer entered the tent of Colonel Glenn Starnes, the artillery commander who had been helping to lead the fight in Nasiriya since Sunday morning, and pulled several small electronic boxes from a safe. They held the codes for the cryptographic system that was used to keep radio transmissions secret, and if the command were overrun, they would have to be destroyed. The officer left a book of matches and an empty ammunition box for burning code documents, if it came to that. "On your command, sir," he told Colonel Starnes, who nodded. But then just as quickly as the fighting began, it seemed to ebb. More than thirty Americans were injured, but none were killed. Iraqi casualties were unknown, as usual.

By dawn, wreckage from the battle lined the road: two burned-out American Humvees and several shelled Iraqi tanks, their top hatches thrown open. The marines began taking new defensive measures, digging in physically and psychologically. But Colonel Starnes nixed a plan to pull back to a safer spot farther south. "I don't want to appear to be running from the battle," he said.

Lieutenant Mark Empey summed up the mood: "It's going to get worse. Everybody thinks so. They know we're here now."

FARTHER NORTH, BEYOND THE BATTLE in Nasiriya, the brutal sandstorm continued to engulf American forces. Forward Marine elements kept up their two-pronged march along the east side of the Euphrates, with one column bypassing Diwaniya and the other heading toward

Kut. The 101st Airborne's troop-carrying Chinook and Blackhawk helicopters remained grounded, which meant that the Screaming Eagles could not advance from their forward operating base south of Najaf. One of the three major frontline American units was thus effectively out of commission.

In Najaf itself, the Third Infantry Division was facing ferocious fighting from Iraqi forces and paramilitary irregulars—resistance that the division commander, Major General Buford Blount III, called the Army's toughest test so far. Over the past three days, the division's 7th Cavalry Regiment had led the American attack and killed as many as 700 Iraqis, without American casualties. But the sandstorms had allowed Iraqi fighters to advance undetected within a hundred meters of the 7th Cavalry's tanks, in what amounted to ambushes. In twenty-four hours of tough fighting that began Tuesday, the cavalry had managed to seize and hold a bridge across the Euphrates—to keep Iraqi forces from descending on Najaf from the north—and by this Wednesday, other units of the Third Infantry had taken two other bridges; Najaf was essentially encircled. In the south, the British were facing continued tough fighting around Basra, while in Baghdad, two large explosions detonated in a working-class district, killing seventeen civilians, wounding forty-five and setting off a scramble by Iraqi officials to blame the United States for indiscriminate bombing. American commanders could not rule out an errant bomb or missile, but said the explosions might also have been caused by a faulty Iraqi missile or antiaircraft fire falling back to earth.

As they struggled to secure Nasiriya, the marines kept hearing tantalizing rumors. Earlier in the week, they had raided a military hospital on the outskirts of town, where they took 170 Iraqis captive, found 200 weapons, loads of ammunition and 3,000 chemical protective suits and a tank. The head doctor told the marines that the hospital had treated two wounded American soldiers, but that gunmen had taken them away. So began a detective story that would consume the Americans for days. Who were the wounded, and where were they now? Could they be some of the missing soldiers from the 507th Maintenance Company, so brutally ambushed the previous Sunday?

In fact, they were: Private First Class Jessica Lynch and her friend, Private First Class Lori Piestewa. Within three hours of their capture, they had been taken to the Iraqi military hospital near Nasiriya. Both were unconscious, suffering serious shock and trauma, and Piestewa was bleeding from the eyes, with bruises all over her face. At 10 A.M., shortly after arriving at the hospital, Piestewa died. Lynch was still alive, but she had multiple fractures and a minor head wound. Adnan Mushafafawi, a brigadier in the Iraqi medical corps and director of the hospital, led a team of Iraqi doctors who worked on her. The doctors gave her blood and intravenous fluids; they took X rays, partly set her fractures and applied splints. If they had left her untreated, they thought, she too would have died. Lynch briefly regained consciousness but appeared very scared. Dr. Mushafafawi suggested that he might set her broken leg better, but she said "she didn't want us to do anything more," he would later recall. "She was very scared. We reassured her that she would be safe now." Three hours later, an ambulance transferred her to Nasiriya's main hospital, Saddam Hussein General, across town.[3]

Lynch's ordeal was just beginning. Saddam General was open but stretched to the limit. Only a dozen doctors from a staff of sixty were coming to work, and electricity was spotty.[4] The doctors and nurses who were there were amazed to see a blond, blue-eyed, female American soldier in their midst. She was unconscious again, and the first two doctors to examine her both thought she would die. Since they knew nothing of the ambush, or the terrible car crash that had smashed her legs and arms, the doctors could not be sure of the cause of Lynch's injuries. They thought she might have had a gunshot wound. They knew she had pulmonary edema, and they gave her two units of blood and operated on her broken legs. Hours later, she woke up to find a twenty-four-year-old Iraqi doctor, Harith al-Houssona, watching over her.

"Hello, what's your name?" the young resident physician asked her in English.

"Please don't hurt me," Lynch replied. She seemed terribly afraid, and psychologically fragile. Dr. Houssona assured Lynch that he was her doctor and would keep her safe. Another doctor, Anmar Uday, also twenty-four, asked her what she wanted. Orange juice, she said—

and she wanted to get back to her unit. "She was also very truthful," Dr. Uday later recalled. "I asked her if she liked the Iraqi people, but she said, no, she hated them."

But gradually, as she got stronger, Lynch formed a bond with the young doctors, who spoke a bit of English and seemed entranced with their exotic patient, who was only five years younger than they were. The hospital staff was mostly Shiite, and hated Saddam's regime. They assumed the Americans would win the war, and that it would be in their interest to take good care of an American prisoner. And, of course, they were doctors, sworn to do their best to heal. Over the next few days, Lynch cried a lot, but she also laughed. She told Dr. Houssona that her injuries would help her lose weight. She spoke of her family and friends in West Virginia, and of her boyfriend, Ruben, a fellow soldier, and of her love for something called Tex-Mex food. Dr. Houssona told her he felt like her brother; she said he seemed more like a mother to her. The staff kept her alone in a single room, and the nurses would sing to her at night, and rub talc on her shoulders. She was in pain, and ate only sporadically, asking for juice and crackers, and insisting that packages of food be opened in front of her.[5]

Abdul Hadi was the ambulance driver who had brought her in. He was a bear of a man, with seventeen children by five wives, which astonished Lynch. He would go periodically to the market to buy her orange juice or other small items. She told Hadi not to take risks because his children needed him. But each time he went to the market, he told everyone in earshot that he was shopping for a young American prisoner. Gossip began to spread and soon Lynch's presence at the hospital was the worst-kept secret in town.

ALL WEEK, THERE WAS TENSION between the hospital's medical staff and the Iraqi military officials who were using the hospital as an operating base. On the night of Thursday, March 27, a crisis arose. An Iraqi lieutenant colonel ordered Private Lynch to be taken away by ambulance at 3 A.M. the next morning, supposedly to the maternity and child hospital in town. But the medical staff was suspicious, and the ambulance drivers refused to follow the order. Then the lieutenant colonel told another officer and an ambulance driver named Sabah Khazal to take Lynch in an ambulance, shoot her and burn the ambulance. They drove away from the hospital, but Khazal told the military officer not to shoot her, and the officer agreed, peeled off his uniform and deserted the Iraqi army on the spot. Khazal thought of trying to deliver Lynch to an American military checkpoint, but there were firefights on the streets so he turned around and took her back to the hospital instead.

By this point, the Iraqi military was collapsing in Nasiriya in the face of the American military pounding, and Lynch's doctors talked about trying to get her into American hands. They broached the notion with her, but she did not want to be moved. On Monday, March 31, nine days after Lynch's capture, the Americans launched an AC-130 gunship attack on an Iraqi security complex in Nasiriya, and more than 2,000 additional marines from the 24th Marine Expeditionary Unit were sent into town to crack the remaining Iraqi resistance. That same morning, the last Iraqi military officers had fled the hospital, and Lynch's doctors told her that they would take her to the Americans the next day.

In the meantime, American military and intelligence agents kept hearing rumblings about a prisoner in Nasiriya. One tipster was a thirty-two-year-old Iraqi lawyer named Mohammed Odeh Rehaief. He told American officials he had seen Lynch in the hospital on Thursday, when he went to visit his wife.[6] But hospital officials would later dispute this account, saying Rehaief's wife did not work there and speculating that he had simply heard the rumors from the marketplace. In any case, Rehaief walked across town until he found some marines, and he told them about Private Lynch. They sent him back to the hospital several times to sketch a map of the site. The tip was solid, and American commanders decided to try to bring off the first successful rescue of an American prisoner from behind enemy lines since World War II. On the afternoon of Tuesday, April 1, Franks briefed his field commanders on the mission by videoconference, emphasizing the tight security. In Washington, Secretary Rumsfeld called President Bush to tell him not to get his hopes up, but they might have a chance of pulling this off.

Conditions in Nasiriya had been so violent and chaotic that the

Americans could not be sure what they would find at Saddam Hussein General Hospital. There had been intelligence reports that Chemical Ali had visited the hospital, and footage from unmanned Predator drones that had been flying overhead suggested that the Iraqi military had been using the grounds as some kind of command-and-control facility. So American commanders assigned the rescue mission to Task Force 20, a covert Special Operations unit that worked on the war's highest priorities, like the hunt for chemical and biological weapons, and the search for Baath Party leaders. The commandos were loaded for bear, and the brass was concerned enough about trouble that they ordered a contingent of marines to make a diversionary feint elsewhere in Nasiriya, including a barrage aimed at Baath Party headquarters.[7]

After midnight, blacked-out Blackhawk helicopters protected by low-flying AC-130 gunships dipped toward the hospital grounds. Marines on the ground fanned out to make an exterior perimeter while Army Rangers made a second defensive line just outside the hospital walls, taking light fire from nearby buildings.[8] Suddenly Dr. Houssona and his colleagues heard a huge explosion, and the American commandos burst into the hospital, charging from room to room with shouts of "Go! Go! Go!" They stopped and handcuffed everyone they found with plastic ties. Following the map their tipster had sketched out, the Americans found their quarry. "Jessica Lynch!" one of the commandos cried out, as she peeked from under her sheets. "We're United States soldiers and we're here to protect you and take you home." As the soldier approached the bed, and took off his helmet, Lynch replied, "I'm an American soldier, too."

For the American commanders—and the politicians back in Washington—it was by far the best news of a bad week. Special Operations troops had videotaped most of the rescue operation, beaming back live pictures in eerie green night vision to commanders at Franks's headquarters. Soon enough, thanks to the media-savvy operatives at CENTCOM, reporters in Qatar were rousted from their beds and the whole world would see those pictures, along with color images of Lynch's young, frightened-looking face peering above an American flag tucked over the stretcher on which commandos carried her out of the hospital. The rescue was front-page news in every major newspaper, and the cover story of magazines, with one variation or another of the quintessential headline: "Saving Private Lynch." Lynch herself was still in fragile condition, apparently unable to remember her ordeal, as she was whisked off first to an American military hospital in Germany and then to Walter Reed Army Medical Center in Washington. Her family in West Virginia was flooded with flowers and cards and book and movie offers.

But the rescue news was not all good. When Specialist Shoshana Johnson's family first heard the media rumors that a female POW had been rescued, their hearts leapt. As far as they knew, Johnson was the only woman known to have been captured. Lynch and Lori Piestewa were just listed as missing. When they realized their mistake, "it was heartbreaking," Johnson's sister Nikki said.[9] Nor was there any word about the other four known prisoners from the 507th, or about David Williams and Ronald Young, the downed Apache pilots whose pictures had also been aired on Iraqi television. And for some American families there would soon be much worse news: During Lynch's rescue, commandos had been led to eleven American bodies, two in a hospital morgue and nine in a freshly dug grave.

THE NASIRIYA CAMPAIGN WOULD STAND as the bloodiest of the war for the Americans. By the time the city was securely in American hands, more than thirty soldiers and marines had been killed there, and more than sixty injured. The battle was far bloodier for the Iraqis, though a reliable tally of Iraqi dead and wounded may never be known. At the peak, Saddam Hussein General Hospital was receiving 200 casualties a day. Like other distant place names from Anzio to Mogadishu that were unknown to most Americans before they became metaphors for a certain kind of bloody combat, Nasiriya was now more than just a geographical location; it was a symbol. It was the place where Tommy Franks's battle plan, with its swift advance and long supply lines, briefly came to seem too dangerous to sustain. The Sunday morning ambush and the subsequent days of fighting rang alarm bells from the frontline troops to some quarters of the Pentagon.

But in the end, Nasiriya was also among the places that proved the war plan's workability. The Americans' advance was slowed there, but it was not stopped. Even as marines stayed for days to help secure the city, they kept traffic moving north across the bridges toward Baghdad and maintained a measure of control. By the time Private Lynch was rescued, there had been no substantial fighting in Nasiriya for a couple of days. Some neighborhoods were not yet cleared of what Donald Rumsfeld liked to call "dead-enders," but resistance was fading. Iraqi civilians were helping the Marines locate dangerous remaining irregulars. Troop and supply convoys needed at the front were now pouring across the bridges. "We can pretty much use the bridges—the bridge over the Euphrates and the bridge over the Saddam Canal—and the road in between, at will," said Lieutenant Colonel John O'Rourke, a regimental executive officer. There would be tough fighting still to come, but the road ahead was clear and so was the next goal: the "Red Zone," the ring of Iraqi defenses outside Baghdad itself.

Chapter 14

THROUGH THE KARBALA GAP

Near Najaf, Iraq
Thursday, March 27, 2003

At last, the sandstorms had ended and the Third Infantry Division should have been on the move again. Instead, it was fighting to protect its rear. Since leaving Kuwait, the vanguard of the U.S. Army's forces had stayed steadily on the west side of the Euphrates River, roughly parallel to the path the Marines had taken on the east. Now, to get to Baghdad, the Third Infantry would have to cross the Euphrates in force. The chosen spot: north and east of the city of Karbala, less than fifty miles south of the capital. It was at Karbala that the open desert narrowed into a slender plain between the Euphrates on the east and Lake al-Razzazah on the west. It would be the American forces' gateway to Baghdad, and everyone assumed it would be deadly. Commanders expected to encounter the vaunted Republican Guard. They were prepared to endure the pounding of rockets and artillery. If Saddam intended to use chemical or biological weapons, he would surely do so here, where he could trap the invaders in a relatively enclosed space. Captain Joseph A. Simmons, the assistant intelligence officer of the Third Infantry's 1st Brigade, had participated in seven simulated attacks on Karbala—war games conducted on computers and tabletops, first in Germany and then in Kuwait. Every time, he had lost. "I died here, like, seven times," he said.

Before the advancing Americans could even get to Karbala, though, they had to get past Najaf, a city of 500,000 that was a holy site for the Shiites. The vanguard of the 1st Brigade had crossed the escarpment north of the city on Sunday, March 23, but the bulk of the Third Infantry had been stuck there ever since, first by the sandstorm and then by the intense and unexpected fighting. Najaf itself was not a strategically important objective, and the Army had no intention of occupying it. In fact, the Americans badly wanted to avoid inflicting any damage on the city, which was the burial place of Ali, the son-in-law of the prophet Mohammed and the founder of the Shiite branch of Islam. But Najaf sat squarely overlooking the key supply routes leading north to the Karbala Gap, and Iraqi forces had chosen to make a stand here, suggesting that Saddam's government still had some control over its army. Their resistance was proving pronounced enough that the Third Infantry's commander, General Blount, knew he would have to surround the city and cut it off to protect his rear columns and the long supply lines still snaking up from the south.

Lieutenant Colonel Rick Schwartz, the commander of Task Force 1-64 Armor of the division's 2nd Brigade, had led his troops in two days of brutal fighting around Najaf, beginning under the orange sky of the sandstorm, and he had seen it all: Iraqi fighters using women as human shields, firing from mosques, using buses and minivans for cover. "That was a piss," he would say later. This battle was nothing like the ones Schwartz had experienced as a tank company commander in the Gulf war twelve years earlier. Then, in his words, he had fought against "an undisciplined and poorly trained enemy who didn't have the will to fight," and "those that chose to fight did so and died at 2,000 meters." Now, it was "close quarters fighting against an enemy that has nothing to live for."[1]

The battle for the city had begun in earnest late Monday, when the 1st Brigade sent an armored scout company across a bridge north of the city, near the village of Kifl, to cut the main roads into Najaf from the north and thus prevent the Iraqis from sending reinforcements from Baghdad. The mission seemed simple enough, but after three American vehicles passed, the Iraqis detonated explosives, trying to blow up the bridge. It only buckled, but the vehicles were temporarily cut off from the rest of the American forces, and Iraqi fighters came rushing forward to engage in a firefight. The fighting flared for four days, all through Tuesday and Wednesday into Thursday. It was the fiercest battle so far for the Third Infantry, and commanders estimated that 1,000 Iraqi fighters were killed. One American, a tank loader, died in a skirmish on Monday. Early Wednesday morning, the Iraqi commander inside Najaf telephoned his superiors in Baghdad to say he was surrounded, but as many as 1,000 fighters, many of them believed to be militia, remained active inside the city. That day, the Third Infantry's artillery, backed by American air strikes, repeatedly fired on Iraqi troops, destroying more than two dozen Iraqi vehicles, and killing scores. Corporal Benjamin R. Richardson, among the engineers who had arrived to repair the damaged bridge, saw two Iraqi civilian vehicles with armed men inside drive straight toward the Americans. An American tank simply flattened one of the cars, while a Bradley armored vehicle raked the other with fire. Corporal Richardson saw a medic shoot an armed Iraqi fighter, then bandage him and put him in the back of an armored vehicle. "That was my first combat experience," he said, "and I didn't like it very much."

In Kifl, the concussive force of the American tanks' rounds had sucked everything off the sidewalks and into the middle of the village's dusty main road. Blasts shattered the plate glass window of a small barbershop, and outside it sat a sedan with its paint burned off and two charred skeletons inside, one piece in the trail of dead that littered the town. One tank captain who gave his name only as Cobra Six summed up the scene: "A little piece of hell."

Meantime, miles to the east, the Marines were also meeting unexpected resistance—and disturbing evidence that Iraqi troops were being forced to fight by their commanders on pain of death. Near the city of Diwaniya, 100 miles south of Baghdad, an Iraqi shot in a firefight with American troops was discovered to have a small-caliber bullet wound in the back of his head. Fighting had raged all day there on Wednesday, and another wounded Iraqi in an American field hospital said simply, "The officers threatened to shoot us unless we fought. They took out their guns and pointed them and told us to fight." Even so, the Iraqi arsenal was hardly up to the task of seriously slowing the advancing American forces. In one overrun Iraqi trench, there were only a few hand grenades, some rocket launchers and three dozen magazines for Kalashnikov rifles. Of the Iraqi prisoners who huddled together amid the filthy mattresses and moldy blankets, only a few wore uniforms. Most had only tattered clothing and beat-up shoes. Still, as the Americans drove north, the Iraqi ambushes seemed more frequent, the soldiers more desperate. At night, the perimeter of the Americans' camps echoed with the sound of mortar fire and the yips of wild dogs. "The closer we get to Baghdad, the crazier it gets," said Sergeant Robert Gardner, an American marine.

But once again, the bigger picture looked all right. "The enemy adjusted," said Major General William Webster, the deputy commander of the allied ground command back in Kuwait. "The conditions changed. And we are staying on the balls of our feet."

ON THIS THURSDAY, MARCH 27, the feet of the Third Infantry were planted firmly around Najaf. The village of Kifl was virtually a shadow town, a burned-out shell of itself. American forces controlled the two-lane bridge across the Euphrates, and the main road running through town, but they had no desire to venture into the smaller side streets, where the enemy still lurked. "It sort of depends on how you define enemy," said Captain Darren A. Rapaport, commander of Company C of the 2nd Battalion, 69th Armored, sitting on his tank, his turret scanning the village. "He could be right around the corner. He could be up the street. He could be a few kilometers down the road." Lieutenant Colonel Jeffrey Randall Sanderson of Waynesville, North Carolina, the battalion's commander, summed up the mood: "Son of a bitch is still shooting at us," he said. "I'm not going to clear the village. I'm not going to put American soldiers in there. I'll be here a month and a half."

In the street, an American armored Humvee with loudspeakers blasted out a warning, urging civilians to stay inside and soldiers to surrender, declaring: "Your cause is lost." But the Iraqis did not give in. "He's broadcasting, 'Surrender, surrender, surrender,' and they ain't surrendering," Colonel Sanderson said. "I don't know why not. If they want to fight it out, we'll fight it out."

The standoff allowed uncomfortable time for reflection on the fighting just passed. Sergeant Mark N. Redmond of the 1st Brigade, for one, could not shake his memory of the fighting. He had joined the Army three years earlier, after doing odd jobs around his hometown outside Gainesville, Florida. The recruiter had suggested that he become a forward observer, calling in artillery and air strikes, close enough to the front to see it but not in the thick of it. The thick of it, though, was where he and his fellow soldiers had found themselves as they crossed the bridge at Kifl Monday night. Redmond was in his Humvee on the bridge when the Iraqis detonated their explosives underneath it, and had felt a sudden, wrenching fear. The irregular Iraqi fighters came rushing forward the moment Troop C crossed the river, and Redmond shouted *"Qiff,"* Arabic for halt. But the Iraqis did not halt. They kept coming, as if bent on suicide. Redmond fired, using every weapon on his Humvee, including a .50-caliber machine gun, an M-4 rifle and a grenade launcher; everything except the shoulder-fired antitank missile. But now, on Friday, he was troubled. "Look at me today," he said. "When I go home, people will want to treat me like a hero, but I'm not. I'm a Christian man. If I have to kill the other guy, I will, but it doesn't make me a hero. . . . I mean, I have a wife and kids to go back home to. I don't want them to think I'm a killer." He did not want to dwell on the details.

That same Friday, forty miles to the east, some marines outside Diwaniya had fewer qualms. "We had a great day," said Sergeant Eric Schrumpf, a twenty-eight-year-old sharpshooter. "We killed a lot of people." He and a fellow marksman, twenty-year-old Corporal Mikael McIntosh, sat on a sand berm, swapping combat stories. Both marines were frustrated at the Iraqi tactic of using women and children as shields. They thought it was cowardly, but agreed it had been effective. Both talked about not shooting at soldiers for fear of hitting innocent civilians. "If the risks outweigh the losses, then you don't take the shot," Corporal McIntosh said. But sometimes the choice was not so clear. Sergeant Schrumpf told of an Iraqi soldier standing among two or three civilians. The sergeant and other men in his unit opened fire. One of the women standing near the Iraqi soldier went down. "I'm sorry," Schrumpf said. "But the chick was in the way."

THAT FRIDAY MORNING, U.S. AIR Force jets bombed an oil depot south of Karbala. The remnants of a huge plume of black smoke began drifting in a gentle wind toward the desert camp of the Third Infantry's 1st Brigade outside Najaf. Sensors on a specially outfitted armored vehicle registered traces of a nerve agent, and the camp's warning horn blared out, accompanied by instructions telling the soldiers to put on the gas masks, hoods, rubber gloves and protective boots that were always at hand. Suddenly, one soldier, unrecognizable inside his bulky gear, shouted out in relief: "There's a bird flying around us!" What kind of bird? "A living one," the soldier said. It had been a false alarm.

If the Third Infantry was unwilling just yet to enter Najaf, it was determined to keep tight control over the roads leading into the city, so the Americans had established checkpoints on the approaches to the city to prevent Iraqi fighters from reinforcing the militia inside. Just before noon on Saturday, March 29, an American checkpoint on the north side of town was not quite bustling, but busy. A minivan full of passengers had just been turned around and was waiting on the shoulder while troops debated whether to send them back north. A man in a white pickup had also been stopped, but he refused to leave and was sitting in the median, claiming his leg was injured. A man on a bicycle was pedaling by. Then a taxi approached. The driver stopped at the roadblock and waved for help, indicating his car had broken down. Four American soldiers approached, and ordered him out of the car, so they could search it. When the driver followed the troops' orders to open the trunk, the car exploded with a huge white blast, killing all of the Americans and the driver.

It was the first successful suicide bombing of the war, and it seemed an ominous new portent. The force of the blast pressed a crater in the asphalt highway, and the taxi landed fifteen feet down the road. Within minutes, three other taxis tried to bolt through another Army checkpoint on the road into Najaf, but were destroyed by American Bradleys. Colonel Grimsley, the 1st Brigade commander, said that those taxis did not appear to be packed with explosives, but he speculated that they might have been part of a coordinated attack on the American defenses. "It certainly happened near simultaneously," he said. Indeed, no sooner had the first taxi exploded that the Iraqi vice president, Taha Yassin Ramadan, appeared in Baghdad to declare that such attacks would become "routine military policy," and the Iraqi government awarded two posthumous medals to the bomber, an Iraqi military noncommissioned officer named Ali Jaafar Nuamani.[2] In an hour-long speech of defiance and threat, Ramadan warned: "I say to the United States administration, that it will turn the whole world into people who are willing to die for their nations. The aggressors think that their B-52s carry bombs of such weight that they are capable of killing an unlimited number of people. Should we wait until Arabs are capable of making bombs to counter that? No, all they can do is turn themselves into human bombs."

The Americans swiftly denounced the new tactic as beyond the pale. "To me, this is not an act of war," said Captain Andrew J. Valles, the 1st Brigade's civil and military affairs officer. "It is terrorism." The shock was intense, and understandable. Up until now, the entire Third Infantry Division, more than 15,000 strong, had lost only two soldiers, one killed by a reconnaissance sniper and the other when his Bradley plunged into a ditch. Valles expressed frustration not only at the Iraqi tactics, but at the stalled American advance. "This is what happens when we just sit here," he said.

The Pentagon just as swiftly announced that it would tighten security at all roadblocks and checkpoints. At the checkpoint where the Americans died, a new sign went up in Arabic: ROADBLOCK AHEAD. LEAVE THE AREA OR WE WILL FIRE. A route that had been open to anyone who did not seem to pose a threat was now closed to everyone. Up to this point, American troops had tried to protect themselves with minimum measures and had resisted cutting off civilian traffic, in an effort to let "the local people get on with their lives," in the words of Colonel Grimsley. Now that would change. Lieutenant Colonel Scott E. Rutter, commander of the 2nd Battalion, Seventh Infantry, whose men had died, bluntly summed up the new rules for Iraqi drivers. "Five seconds," he said. "They have five seconds to turn around and get out of here. If they're there in five seconds, they're dead."

ONE BIG THING WOULD NOT change for the Americans that Saturday, March 29: President Bush's determination to stick to General Franks's plan and keep pressing toward Baghdad. The days of sandstorms, the stiff resistance in Nasiriya and elsewhere in the south, the failed Apache mission and concerns about rear-area security and the stretched supply lines—all this had led at least some commanders, in the field and at the Pentagon, to wonder whether the best strategy might be to pause and wait a bit before moving on the Iraqi capital. Already, events had forced Franks to put off the final dash toward Baghdad, which had been scheduled for this weekend. Some Army officers in particular were urging a further postponement, believing it would be best to rest the troops, consolidate positions and wait for the Fourth Infantry Division's heavy tanks and high-tech equipment, which were completing their sea journey from the Mediterranean to the Gulf and would be ready to come rolling up from Kuwait within a couple of weeks.

It was a big choice: wait for reinforcements or press on, keeping the advantage and the element of surprise. Now, on this Saturday morning, Bush and his war council met at Camp David, with Franks participating by secure videoconference. The news of the suicide bombing lent a new urgency to the discussions. In the meeting, Bush listened. He was "not an impatient person," one senior administration official recalled. "He was prepared to let things unfold."[3] At stake was not only the press to Baghdad, but Donald Rumsfeld's larger campaign of military transformation, his effort to prove that wars could be fought with lighter, more flexible forces. Some administration officials felt so good about the state of the campaign that they had questioned whether there was even a need for the weekend meeting. In contrast to the early stages of the fighting in Afghanistan in the fall of 2001, when some at the Pentagon feared that some in the White House or State Department might be "going wobbly," there was broad consensus that Franks's plan was working, and had enough built-in flexibility to keep working.

In the end, Bush backed the plan to press on toward Baghdad as fast as possible. The president, having set his course, was seldom one to doubt it. Colin Powell, who dined alone with Bush that week, would later remember that the president was never lacking in confidence, never rattled, and that he never lost confidence in his commanders. The president would pepper officials with questions, but mostly to make sure they were confident of their plans. If they were, he left them alone. One senior White House aide would recall a National Security Council meeting around this time when Bush was asked when American forces would engage Republican Guard troops on the ground. The president had replied, "I don't know. Tommy hasn't told me yet." "Not, 'We haven't decided,' " the aide said, "but 'Tommy hasn't told me yet.' " That was significant, the aide thought, as a sign of Bush's trust.

That weekend of the Camp David meeting, Franks got news that stiffened his resolve to move forward. The bomb-damage assessments began coming in from the relentless air campaign against the Medina Division of the Republican Guard and other targets south of Baghdad, which had gone on despite the sandstorm. The news was astoundingly good. The Americans had hoped the Medina Division's capacity might be degraded by 50 percent. Instead it was down to less than 25 percent of its fighting force, and its support divisions were all but destroyed. The Iraqi forces had simply been no match for the massive, if largely invisible, American air power that had steadily done its lethal work all week. "They didn't just destroy them a little bit," said General Abizaid, Franks's deputy. "They were obliterated in a way that's fairly significant in military terms."[4]

ON THE SAME DAY THAT the suicide bomber attacked the checkpoint north of Najaf, help arrived for the Third Infantry. The sandstorm having abated, troops of the 101st Airborne Division had moved up to help secure Najaf, thus freeing the forward units of the Third Infantry to continue their press north. With the 101st available to tighten the cordon around Najaf, the Third Infantry would begin its first probing attacks toward Karbala, testing the defenses on the last bottleneck on the road to Baghdad. The plain between the Euphrates and Lake al-Razzazah was less than twenty-five miles across, and the Americans would have to slip through it before their final approach to the Iraqi capital. They did not want trouble behind them.

So on Sunday, March 30, American tanks, artillery and planes began barraging Najaf. The battle began at 10 A.M., when tank fire blew a hole in the abandoned Agricultural Research Institute on the southern edge of town, and the 101st spent most of the day clearing surrounding buildings of the Iraqi fighters holding out there. Para-militaries lobbed back mortar fire. The Americans did their best to avoid civilian and religious targets, but there were reports that a large cemetery near Ali's tomb was being used as an assembly site for Iraqi forces, and maps showed an amusement park and a school near the local Baath Party headquarters.[5] "We went into this hoping to keep collateral damage and civilian casualties to a minimum," explained General Blount, the Third Infantry's commander. "They've not let us do that."

That same Sunday, on the approaches to Baghdad, American planes bombed the Medina, Baghdad and Hammurabi Divisions of the Republican Guard more than 500 times. And to the east, the Marines were in furious battle with Iraqi forces, finally pushing them back from around Diwaniya north toward Baghdad. The next day, the American bombardment of Najaf escalated, but again, the effort was complicated by the delicacy of the city's holy places. American air strikes were hitting targets a scant half mile from Ali's tomb, and Special Operations teams inside the city were reporting that fedayeen militiamen were converting the tomb itself into a stronghold.

All that Monday, fighting stretched eighty miles across a diagonal east-west line from Karbala, where the Third Infantry was pressing, to Kut, where the Marines had stopped. The main column of the Marines had begun moving from Diwaniya, bypassing the city itself, heading north toward Hilla, a town between Najaf and Karbala. After five days of standoff, electricity filled the air as the Marines moved within seventy miles of Baghdad. "We're in bad-guy country," Colonel John Pomfret said. "I like it." Some fifteen or twenty miles to the northwest, the leading edge of the Third Infantry was even closer to Baghdad, just fifty miles south in the town of Hindiya, population 80,000, firing at dawn from tanks and Bradleys as they crossed the Euphrates and met stiff Iraqi resistance. In Baghdad, Saddam's presidential compound was again under remorseless air attack from American planes.

That same day, at a checkpoint in Najaf on Highway 9, near where the four American soldiers had been blown up on Saturday, an unidentified four-wheel-drive vehicle came barreling toward American troops. The suicide bombing had left everyone on edge, and every car was treated as a potential threat. Captain Ronny Johnson was agitated. From his position at the nearby intersection, he radioed to Bradley vehicles up ahead to fire a warning shot. But the vehicle kept coming, and the Americans fired no shots. Finally, Captain Johnson yelled, "Stop him!"

When it was over, ten of the fifteen Iraqis packed inside the vehicle were dead, including five children. Captain Johnson roared at the platoon leader, "You just fucking killed a family because you didn't fire a warning shot soon enough."[6] No one meant it to happen. The Americans had taken great care to avoid inflicting civilian casualties when they could, though it may never be possible to know how many

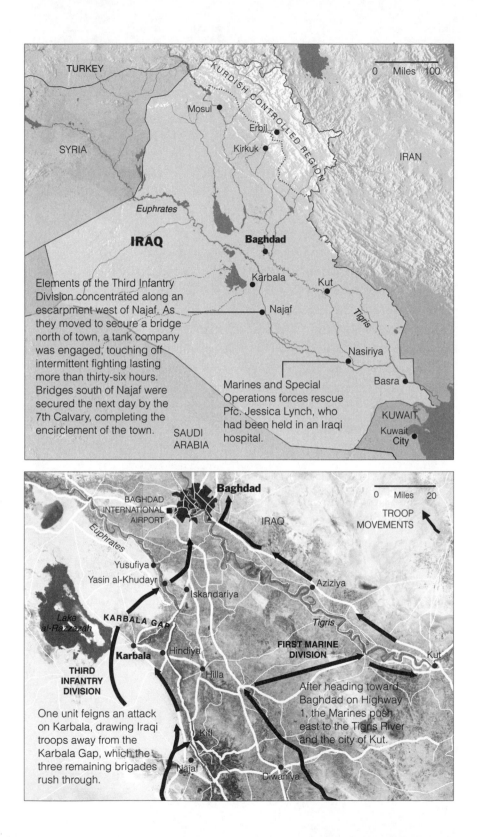

TURKEY

KURDISH CONTROLLED REGION

Mosul

Erbil

Kirkuk

SYRIA

IRAN

Euphrates

IRAQ

Baghdad

Karbala

Kut

Najaf

Tigris

Elements of the Third Infantry
Division concentrated along an
escarpment west of Najaf. As
they moved to secure a bridge
north of town, a tank company
was engaged, touching off
intermittent fighting lasting
more than thirty-six hours.
Bridges south of Najaf were
secured the next day by the
7th Calvary, completing the
encirclement of the town.

Nasiriya

Basra

SAUDI
ARABIA

Marines and Special
Operations forces rescue
Pfc. Jessica Lynch, who
had been held in an Iraqi
hospital.

KUWAIT

Kuwait
City

0   Miles   100

---

0   Miles   20

Baghdad

BAGHDAD
INTERNATIONAL
AIRPORT

IRAQ

TROOP
MOVEMENTS

Euphrates

Yusufiya

Yasin al-Khudayr

Iskandariya

Aziziya

*Lake
al-Razzazah*

KARBALA GAP

Tigris

Karbala

Hindiya

**FIRST MARINE
DIVISION**

Kut

**THIRD
INFANTRY
DIVISION**

Hilla

One unit feigns an attack
on Karbala, drawing Iraqi
troops away from the
Karbala Gap, which the
three remaining brigades
rush through.

Kifl

Najaf

Diwaniya

After heading toward
Baghdad on Highway
1, the Marines push
east to the Tigris River
and the city of Kut.

Iraqis died because they were in the wrong place at the wrong time. This was a tragic—perhaps inevitable—bookend to the suicide bombing. In a word, it was war.

In Najaf, the American firepower was proving overwhelming. The days of air strikes and periodic raids had had their effect. On Tuesday, April 1, American planes dropped 2,000-pound bombs on three buildings believed to be strongholds of Iraqi resistance, and later, seven Abrams tanks backed up by Apache attack helicopters crashed into town in a show of force. Before the day was out, the Americans had seized the southern edge of the city, and curious citizens milled about as soldiers of the 101st Airborne drove through the narrow streets. That afternoon, the 101st's commander, General Petraeus, drove in an armed convoy into town and pronounced Najaf "very much contained."[7] Twenty-four hours later, more troops from the 101st marched back in. The American visitors asked one Iraqi man what the arriving troops would bring to Najaf, now that the Baath Party had been toppled. What would come next? "Democracy," the man said, his voice rising with each word. "Whiskey. And sexy!"

THE AMERICAN NOOSE WAS TIGHTENING on Baghdad. On Tuesday, April 1, the same day the 101st entered Najaf, a regiment of American marines moved up to the southern edge of Kut, which guarded the southeastern approach to Baghdad, while other regiments that had seemed to be heading north circled back and hit the Iraqi rear. The Americans were getting ever closer to the biggest prize, the capital itself. On Wednesday, American intelligence intercepted an ominous transmission from Baghdad to a senior Iraqi commander believed to have control over chemical weapons. It consisted of just one word: "Blood." Was it an order to launch a gas attack against American forces? Commanders thought it might be.[8]

To get to Baghdad, the Americans would have to "shoot the gap" at Karbala, and Franks and his ground commanders had a plan. Early that Wednesday, the Third Infantry moved north, feinting a head-on attack against the Medina Division outside Karbala. At the other end of the American front lines, in Kut, the First Marine Expeditionary Force moved directly on the Baghdad Mechanized Division of the

Republican Guard. With the Iraqis thus occupied, the bulk of the Third Infantry rolled swiftly through the Karbala Gap, racing full steam ahead to cross the twisting Euphrates and move thousands of American troops and tanks through the gap and toward Baghdad. The Third Infantry faced virtually no resistance from a Republican Guard force that had all but crumbled in disorganization. The Iraqis were simply overwhelmed, and the Americans had just a single casualty on their race through the sandy plain.

Ten hours later, at a sharp bend in the Euphrates at the town of Yasin al-Khudayr, the Americans reached their next big objective: a bridgehead code-named "Peach," the last geographic obstacle on the road to Baghdad, which was now just twenty miles away to the north.

But in contrast to the smooth roll through the Karbala Gap, this was a fight, and a fierce one. Beginning in early afternoon, American artillery fired on concentrations of Iraqi forces dug in on the far bank of the river, backed up by American A-10 attack jets, which dropped 500-pound bombs on Iraqi vehicles defending the double-span bridge.

"Six lanes to Baghdad!" shouted Lieutenant Colonel Thomas P. Smith, commander of the 1st Brigade's 11th Engineer Battalion. "We'll be home soon." But his exuberance was short-lived, as Iraqi artillery rounds began landing with a shuddering crack on the river-bank. Worse, the bridge had been rigged with explosives, and now Iraqi soldiers detonated the charges packed inside the bridge's southern span, shearing its steel girders and making it impassable. As Apache gunships flew overhead and American Bradleys sprayed the opposite bank with covering fire, Lieutenant Colonel Ernest "Rock" Marcone, commander of the 1st Brigade's Task Force 3-69 Armor, ordered the first contested river assault by American infantrymen in years. While smoke generators created a covering haze, American soldiers and engineers crossed the Euphrates in rubber boats, attacking a squad of Iraqis under the bridge's pilings. "For about forty-five minutes, we had every kind of contact imaginable happening at once," Marcone said, "and that bridge could have gone either way." Finally, the Americans cut the detonation wires just as the Iraqis were preparing to blow the northern span.[9] A column of American tanks and armored vehicles began slowly lurching over the bridge.

"We'll have to do with three lanes," Colonel Smith said.

Chapter 15

THUNDER RUN

Baghdad
Thursday, April 3, 2003

It was dark and strangely quiet on the grounds of Saddam Hussein International Airport, on the western edge of Baghdad, ten miles from downtown. In fact, the whole city itself was dark for the first time since the war began, its electricity at last interrupted by a mysterious blackout.[1] The only light was the intermittent white flash of American bombs and red Iraqi antiaircraft fire in the distance. But under the cover of the late-night darkness, something profound had changed: American Special Operations troops were busy attacking key leadership targets on the outskirts of the city, and the 1st Brigade of the Third Infantry now controlled the military section of the airport's western side—a taxi ride from the heart of town. An invading foreign army was at the gates of Baghdad for the first time since the British occupied Iraq in 1941.

The first tanks of the Third Infantry had arrived at the airport, codenamed "Objective Lions," at 7:30 P.M., punching through the outer wall of the sprawling compound. They had expected resistance, but faced only light opposition at dusk, and then virtually no resistance at all. Where were the city's defenders, the vaunted layers of Republican Guard troops? "This is weird," said Colonel Grimsley, the 1st Brigade commander. "It's like spooky weird." Captain Michael J. MacKinnon, a staff officer with the brigade's tactical command post, said simply, "I'm flabbergasted." Before the American troops arrived, four 2,000-pound bombs had been dropped on the headquarters of the Special Republican Guard on the airport's east side. Still, the silence was baffling, and unsettling. "They're there," Sergeant Major Gary J. Coker, an engineer, said as he stared out into the blackness. "They're out there right now." As if in response, six Iraqi antiaircraft rockets soared across the sky, exploding harmlessly beyond the American troops.

All along, the Americans had assumed that Saddam's regime would try to make a last stand in Baghdad, and the Iraqis had more or less advertised their intention to do so. The American objective was to encircle the capital to prevent retreating Iraqi forces from melting back into Baghdad's streets and alleys, where block-to-block fighting would be tough. The Americans were closing on Baghdad like a giant pincers, with the Third Infantry curving up from Karbala, in the southwest, and the Marines marching up from Kut, in the southeast. The Marines were headed toward the Tigris River, which flowed through the heart of Baghdad, on a line running roughly from southeast to northwest, with most of Saddam's presidential compounds on the western side. On the northern side of the city, American Special Operations troops were throwing up roadblocks to prevent Iraqi fighters from fleeing north to Tikrit, Saddam's hometown and the seat of his most intense supporters. American commanders already knew that Iraqi forces had been considerably weakened by two weeks of fighting, and by the relentless American air campaign. Intelligence estimates said that more than 1,000 of Iraq's 2,500 tanks had been destroyed, and on the advances up from Karbala and Kut it was clear that many Iraqi soldiers had deserted or abandoned their equipment. Hastily shed uniforms were also found discarded by the sides of the roads. But no one could be sure what the future would hold, and American commanders were rushing to get at least some of the late-arriving troops of the Fourth Infantry up from Kuwait and into position for the final assault on Baghdad.

Swift as it was, the Army's final advance toward Baghdad had hardly resembled a victory march. After intense fighting overnight on Tuesday by the 1st Brigade at the bridgehead over the Euphrates at Yasin al-Khudayr, the Iraqis attacked the bridge again late Wednesday night and into this Thursday morning, firing on the American tanks. The 1st Brigade's lead battalion, the 3-69th Armored, killed the Iraqi commander and perhaps 500 Iraqi troops. The Americans held the bridge, paving the way for the 2nd Brigade to race on to its attack position on the southern outskirts of Baghdad at the intersection of Highways 10 and 8, a key southern approach into town. This position was designated "Objective Saints," after the New Orleans football team, just as the airport drew its designation from Detroit's team name. As the 2nd Brigade moved toward Baghdad, it encountered resistance from several thousand Iraqi troops, members of the Republican Guard's Medina and Hammurabi Divisions, and at least one Abrams tank was destroyed by an Iraqi rocket-propelled grenade. The tank's crew escaped, but two other Americans were killed and four were wounded when rocket-propelled grenades struck their Humvees.

The land between the Euphrates and Baghdad was a patchwork of lush fields and palm groves, interlaced by levees, canals and berms, and the burned-out shells of Iraqi military vehicles littered the roadway as the American forces moved forward. Along the road into one village, Yusufiya, Iraqi civilians mingled on the roadside, some of them waving and cheering, brandishing leaflets that American planes had been dropping by the millions. But most Iraqis glared, whether in awe or anger, at the advancing Americans. Lieutenant Colonel James E. Lackey, the 1st Brigade artillery commander, had an explanation: "I expect some of them were wearing uniforms a couple of days ago," he said.

The Third Infantry's commander, General Blount, was beginning to feel that the Iraqis' resolve was softening and wanted to press ahead. In his forward command post, Blount's boss, the V Corps commander, General Wallace, worried about once more exposing American forces to a possible counterattack, without full reconnaissance or solid intelligence about what lay ahead, at the airport or in Baghdad beyond. But Wallace gave Blount permission to proceed, and the 1st Brigade, having fought two battles since Tuesday with barely three hours' rest, headed for the airport.[2]

EVEN AS THE ARMY ADVANCED from the southwest, the Marines were moving up along the Tigris from Kut, in the southeast. At one point, the advance was so swift—forty miles per hour—that the amphibious troop carriers shredded the outer skins of their treads. But the mood changed quickly when the Marines ran into a large force of determined Iraqi troops guarding the approach to Aziziya, about forty-five miles south of Baghdad. The Iraqis were elements of the Al Nida Republican Guard, and the fighting lasted much of the day, with temperatures inside the marines' vehicles rising above 100 degrees. In the end, the Americans won the day after calling in air strikes from B-52s, Super Cobra helicopter gunships and carrier-based F/A-18 fighter-bombers. By the time the Marines passed through the city in the late afternoon, Iraqi guns had fallen silent and the Iraqi forces were retreating north toward Baghdad. But on Highway 6 heading south out of the capital, Iraqi civilians were streaming out in whatever conveyances they could find. One man drove himself and his family in a motorcycle and sidecar, another in a 1954 Dodge pickup truck. A third man, standing in the bed of another pickup as it whizzed down the road, shouted what appeared to be the only words of English he knew: "George Bush!" Another man, named Alawih Hussein, told the marines: "You have saved us, you have saved us from him," and his wife was even more effusive, panting and weeping, "I love you. I love you." By nightfall, the lead elements of the First Marine Division were within twenty-five miles of Baghdad.

For the retreating Iraqis, there was little respite. "I wouldn't want to be in their shoes right now," said Major Matt Feringa, in charge of coordinating air support for the First Marines. "They are being bombed all the time. If they move, we'll go after them. If they just stay there, we'll find them." As the remnants of the Medina Division and other Republican Guard units fled northward by whatever routes they could find, they could not escape the Americans' reach. Overhead and unseen, unmanned American drones followed the Iraqis from the sky, relaying images in real time to coordinators in the V Corps forward tactical headquarters tent. There, in the darkness of this Thursday night, the operations chief relayed the targeting information to the air commanders, and soon, precision-guided bombs would be on their way to the targets. Commanders could watch the resulting video images in real time, and sometimes a cheer went up in the tent at a successful strike. But the deputy operations chief, Lieutenant Colonel Rob Baker, was under no illusions about what was on the video screens. "It's a helluva thing," he said, "watching people die."[3]

BY FRIDAY MORNING, APRIL 4, 75 percent of Saddam International was in American hands, and had been informally renamed Baghdad International. The Americans had taken the elaborate VIP terminal, and most of the Iraqi forces had been dispersed and were fighting in small groups. But there had been some vicious firefights, and the sun rose with quaking blasts of Air Force bombs dropping less than a mile away, as pockets of Iraqi resistance offered bursts of rifle fire and periodic mortar blasts. More than 300 Iraqis had been killed, and the sounds of shooting still echoed from the control tower. At one point, three Soviet-era T-72 tanks approached from the center of Baghdad, but these were destroyed, two of them by American soldiers launching shoulder-fired antitank missiles called Javelins. Air strikes destroyed another dozen armored vehicles northwest of the airport. The Americans were clearly in charge, and the Iraqis were on the run. "We think they woke up this morning and, like General Custer, said, 'Where the hell did all the Indians come from?' " said Colonel Grimsley.

The troops were running on sheer adrenaline, determined to finish a job that many had already been working at for months. Elements of the Third Infantry had come to Kuwait more than a year before, earlier than almost any other unit in the fight, and at the V Corps forward tactical headquarters, officers joked about the division commander's determination. "If General Blount and the Third ID aren't reined in at the airport, we're afraid he'll turn his tanks toward downtown Baghdad and keep going," said Colonel Stephen Hicks, the operations officer for the tactical headquarters.[4]

American intelligence was recording intercepts of Iraqi commanders ordering the remnants of the Republican Guard to fall back into the city for a final defense of Saddam's regime. But very few replies were heard from the field. As the American forces rolled up from the southwest, they captured whole Iraqi brigades, their guns facing due south, as if the Iraqi commanders were shocked that they had been outflanked. At the airport, the Americans began clearing the runways to prepare for arriving airlifts of needed supplies. The Iraqis had piled heaps of sand and gravel in the center of the landing zones to prevent planes from touching down, and the U.S. Air Force had done an even more lethal job with its bombs, which left craters fifteen feet deep along both main runways. Soldiers tried to find what shade and shelter they could in the airport's giant maintenance hangars, but even here, so close to Baghdad, conditions were arduous, with scorching heat and no running water. GIs searched the airport for duty-free booty, like cigarettes made with "Vergina Tobacco" and innumerable souvenir portraits of Saddam Hussein.

Above all, the Americans wondered, what had become of the Republican Guard? American tanks had rolled virtually unopposed along both the Tigris and the Euphrates, killing hundreds of Iraqis who fired small arms at the passing columns. American commanders believed that two of the six Republican Guard units—the Baghdad and Medina Divisions—had been virtually destroyed by the American bombing. About 2,500 Iraqi troops, assumed to be remnants of the Baghdad Division, had surrendered to the Marines on the road up from Aziziya, and other Republican Guard elements surrendered at Kut. But it also seemed clear that some of the Republican Guard troops simply disappeared or deserted, and never put up a fight. The Americans could hardly believe it.

In Washington, top Bush administration officials were squabbling semipublicly about just how soon an interim Iraqi government could be installed. The Pentagon favored a quick approach that would rely heavily on returning exiles, some of whom it had supported. But the State Department and the CIA had grave doubts about the effectiveness and reliability of some of the exile leaders, and they opposed that idea. President Bush himself thought it was unfair that exiles who had sat out Saddam's tyranny should have an advantage in postwar politics. Now Condoleezza Rice was sent out for a public briefing aimed at settling the internal administration feuds. Making it clear that she was speaking for the president, Rice insisted that the administration would pursue a balanced, deliberate approach involving exiles as well as soon-to-be liberated Iraqis.

The conditions on the ground in Iraq made it clearer than ever that the day of liberation from Saddam was coming, and that questions about the postwar political order would soon have to be answered. On the outskirts of Basra, the British were in intensified fighting with militia elements, while in northern Iraq, Kurdish forces with American assistance took the town of Khazar, near Mosul. Outside Nasiriya, Tallil Air Base had opened as an important refueling stop for American aircraft. American commanders said the route north from Baghdad to Tikrit had effectively been closed by a combination of Special Operations raids and air strikes. On the eastern side of Baghdad, a column of marines was moving to seal off the city from that direction. The encirclement of Saddam's capital was nearly complete.

There was also some bad news: at the Haditha Dam, 120 miles northwest of Bahdad, a suicide bomber killed three Special Operations troops. The dam had been captured to prevent Iraqi forces from blowing it up and releasing waters that would have flooded the Euphrates and disrupted the American advance. A car with two women in it approached the American checkpoint, and one woman, who was pregnant, stepped out and began screaming in apparent fear. When the Americans approached, the car exploded. Soon Al Jazeera was airing videotaped statements from the two women, one of whom vowed to "be a suicide bomber who will defend Iraq."

But the day's biggest mystery was the twelve-minute videotape that Iraqi television began airing over and over again that Friday evening. In it, a paunchy, mustachioed man with a loping gait and a Tikriti accent was shown walking, relaxed and cheerful, on the streets of Baghdad, stopping to exchange greetings with ordinary Iraqis. Two bulky men in sports shirts, armed with Kalashnikovs, accompanied him. At one point, a small, curly-haired boy of two or so was thrust into the man's arms, and like any politician in a crowd, the man held the child up, beaming. Was the man Saddam? The television announcer said so, and while it was all but unheard of for the president to walk among the public with such a light security escort, many Iraqis who saw the tape thought it was Saddam himself. On the tape, black smoke filled an overcast sky that looked like that day's Baghdad; the tape showed the president's car driving past streets of shuttered shops that had been open before the war began, and at least one section appeared to show the man near an auction house in the wealthy Mansour district—almost halfway to the airport from the ruins of the main presidential palace.

For better or worse, it was the clearest sign yet that Saddam might well have survived the war's first-night strike intended to kill him. Hours before the tape of the walkabout began playing, Iraqi state television had broadcast other images of a man it said was Saddam, this time with a new speech, from what appeared to be the same low-ceilinged bunker from which he had last been seen on March 24. This time, he urged Iraqis to fight for Baghdad. "Strike them with the power of faith wherever they approach you, and resist them, O courageous citizens of Baghdad," the man said. "With the grace of God, you will be the victors, and they will be the vanquished. Our martyrs will go to paradise, and their dead will go to hell."

Even as Saddam spoke, the Iraqi information minister, Muhammad Said al-Sahhaf, described the American advances on Baghdad as nothing more than part of the Iraqi plan to lure the invading troops toward the capital for a catastrophic defeat. The airport, he said, would be "the Americans' graveyard now."

At the airport, some soldiers of the Third Infantry could not shake a sinking feeling. "Why do I not feel any closer to home?" asked Master Sergeant Russell B. Carpenter, who was handling liaison between Air Force and Army units with the 1st Brigade. They had come so far, endured so much, survived so much, and they had achieved the objective—seizing the airport—that had been assigned to them when they crossed the border from Kuwait two weeks earlier. But would they prevail? And what would come next? Lieutenant Colonel Steven E. Landis, the executive officer of the 1st Brigade, distilled the mood. "This," he said, looking around, "was the end of our plan."

But now the American commanders had a new plan. And the Third Infantry had yet another big job ahead.

GENERAL FRANKS LIKED TO SAY that "speed kills." Already, on the 350-mile advance from Kuwait, speed—and the surprise that came with it—had killed Iraqi forces, and sapped Iraqi strength. Now, with American troops on the outskirts of Baghdad, commanders knew they would have to "make a transition," as one of them put it. Instead of maneuvering in the open desert, where forces could see 3,000 to 5,000 yards in front of them, troops would now be moving in urban areas where visibility might be limited to 300 or 500 feet. Tanks, so useful in open country, could get trapped in tight corners. Formations would have to be smaller, and less spread out. The American forces now arrayed around Baghdad were strong, but hardly overwhelming. The bulk of the Third Infantry, and elements of the 101st Airborne, was at the airport, while less than a division of marines was on the southern outskirts of the city. In all, American commanders had about twenty thousand troops at their disposal—to take a city of nearly five million people. In Nasiriya, Najaf and elsewhere, ground commanders had seen all too clearly the potential hazards when their forces were stretched thin. Yes, they would have air power to back them up, not only more precision strikes on targets in Baghdad, but now twenty-four-hour-a-day American air patrols over the capital to offer close-air support as well. Yet there was no sign that the Iraqis would be willing to give up if the American forces simply tried to outwait them. The suicide bombings had already shown the range of tactics at the Iraqis' disposal, and now the regime was threatening more such unconventional attacks.

So Tommy Franks once again felt a need for speed. The idea was a "reconnaissance in force," a venerable military tactic intended not so much to take on an enemy directly as to smoke out his defenses and his will to fight. If you could shake him up a bit, so much the better. The ill-fated Allied landing at Dieppe, in France, in August 1942 was a reconnaissance in force intended to explore the techniques that would be needed to break through Hitler's Atlantic defenses. There were heavy Allied losses, but the operation amounted to an early dress rehearsal of the D-day landings in Normandy nearly two years later. Now Franks and his commanders had a similar notion: to send an armored column probing into Baghdad. "To do a raid like that unhinges the other guy, but you also find out what he's got," said General Peter Pace, the vice chairman of the Joint Chiefs of Staff. On Saturday, April 5, at dawn, troops from the 2nd Brigade would go crashing into Baghdad to see what they could see.

LIEUTENANT COLONEL RICK SCHWARTZ—HOLDING his position south of Baghdad at Objective Saints that Friday night—was tired. He and his men had traveled overnight Wednesday from Karbala on an unimproved road in pitch-black darkness. Speeding past lost or abandoned vehicles from the 1st Brigade, they had lost two fuel-tanker trucks but raced on to the outskirts of Baghdad anyway. Now the 2nd Brigade commander, Colonel David Perkins, summoned Schwartz to the tactical operations center, his forward command post. As Schwartz entered, the command post was quiet, which was rare. "Something big is up," he thought to himself. Colonel Perkins drew Schwartz over to a map, with the brigade staff looking over their shoulders, and told him that he wanted Task Force 1-64 to attack into the city the next morning, "to show that we mean business."

It was a surreal feeling: Schwartz's Desert Rogues would be the first American troops in Baghdad. His first instinct was to ask Perkins, "Are you kidding?" The colonel wasn't. Quickly, Schwartz screwed his head back on and began putting together a plan. "Truthfully, I was scared shitless," he would remember. "But I knew we could do it." Schwartz took a deep breath and went back to his own head-quarters. This was the moment the Desert Rogues had trained for, and Schwartz addressed his company commanders. He knew he had to sound convincing, to inspire his men to do something they nor-mally wouldn't do. He told them his initial plan and gave them a minute to digest it. He spent a lot of time looking into their eyes. He wanted "to make sure they knew we could do this."[5]

When Schwartz's troops heard the word, they, too, thought it was a joke. When Captain Jason Conroy told his lieutenants the plan, they all dropped their briefing books in surprise.[6] But hours later, at dawn, the Desert Rogues were driving straight up Highway 8, headed to town, 761 men in Abrams tanks and Bradleys. Their goal, Schwartz said, was to keep moving, and keep fighting. At first, as the tanks passed through industrial neighborhoods, the streets were virtually empty. The few Iraqis the soldiers saw were obviously surprised. Some waved. But soon enough, irregular fighters began hitting the Amer-icans with everything they had. The Iraqis were firing with small arms and shoulder-fired rockets, seemingly from everywhere. The Americans engaged hesitantly, careful to avoid civilian targets, but it quickly became clear that the Iraqis were determined to ram them. Enemy fighters ran out into the streets to throw grenades and sachel charges at the passing column. Schwartz's tank was hit by two rocket-propelled grenades. It rocked back and forth but kept rolling. With their Bradleys' 25-millimeter guns, the Americans blasted Iraqi posi-tions and bunkers with high-explosive rounds. At least three civilian cars tried to crash into the northbound American columns, while doz-ens of others sped south on their way out of town. One Iraqi man in a white headband with explosives strapped to his chest was shot dead in his car, hit by perhaps five hundred American rounds. "That car was cheese," said Sergeant Carlos Hernandez.[7]

Bodies were littered all over the roadways; American commanders

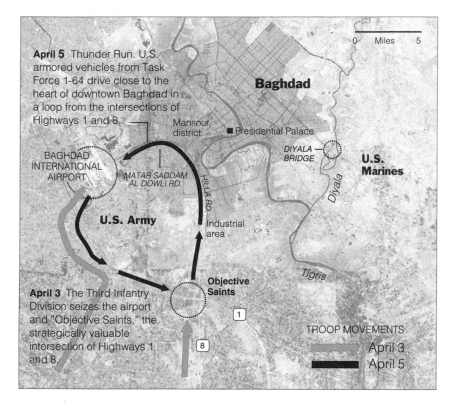

April 5 Thunder Run. U.S. armored vehicles from Task Force 1-64 drive close to the heart of downtown Baghdad in a loop from the intersections of Highways 1 and 8.

Baghdad

Mansour district

■ Presidential Palace

DIYALA — BRIDGE

U.S. Marines

BAGHDAD INTERNATIONAL AIRPORT

MATAR SADDAM AL DOWLI RD.

Hilla Rd.

Diyala

U.S. Army

Industrial area

Objective Saints

1

April 3 The Third Infantry Division seizes the airport and "Objective Saints," the strategically valuable intersection of Highways 1 and 8.

8

Tigris

TROOP MOVEMENTS

April 3

April 5

0   Miles   5

would later estimate that 1,000 to 3,000 Iraqis were killed. Colonel Perkins thought that as many as 100 Iraqi vehicles were destroyed and a number of antiaircraft batteries gutted. Every American vehicle was hit by Iraqi fire. Halfway through the fight, American A-10 Warthog attack planes, the thrumming, thudding craft known as tank-busters, swooped in to take out the Iraqi batteries. Many Iraqi tanks and troop carriers were simply abandoned. One American tank commander, sitting in his open hatch, was killed when a grenade or mortar exploded in his face; at least six other Americans were injured. One Abrams tank took a rocket-propelled grenade to the rear access panel near its engine. "We got flames on the inside of the tank!" a crew member called out on his radio. "Request permission to leave it!" The tank had to be abandoned, its crew piling into another tank under heavy small-arms fire from the Iraqis. But that was the only time the Americans stopped in three hours of blistering death and destruction.

The Thunder Run ended only when the American column swung

around to the west and headed along the Matar Saddam al Dowli Road to the airport, where the rest of the Third Infantry was waiting. The surprise raid had effectively rewritten a tenet of Army doctrine on urban combat, which held that battles in cities should be fought only by dismounted light infantry, not big armored vehicles. Now, one colonel thought, "I wouldn't want to go into an urban area without heavy armor."[8] Lieutenant Shane Williams, standing next to a tank with the words CREEPING DEATH painted on its cannon, said simply, "It was a very good hunting day."[9]

For one day, it was enough. "We're not ready to go in and occupy the city," said the Third Infantry's gratified commander, General Blount. "We don't want to occupy it." The daylight raid had done its work. Though the Iraqi opposition was sometimes intense, it was also scattered and disorganized, not coordinated. And to the residents of Baghdad who saw the rolling American columns, the message was clear and unmistakable: The Americans were not afraid to enter the capital and would do so at a time of their choosing.

Toppling Saddam and taking Baghdad would still be "a real challenge," Rick Schwartz thought, but "we'll do this again and again until he's completely isolated."[10] Even Schwartz could not know just how soon that would be.

Chapter 16

THE FALL OF BAGHDAD

Baghdad
Sunday, April 6, 2003

After two weeks of relentless attacks from the sky, new sounds filled the air in Baghdad. The earth-shattering thud of bombs and missiles had given way to the more distant rumble of artillery and rockets, the staccato of machine-gun fire and the scream of American jets flying low-level close-air support for the troops on the ground. The Iraqi information minister, who on Saturday was contending, ludicrously, that the Americans had been routed at the airport, was now claiming that the Republican Guard was "tightening the noose around the U.S. enemy." Once again, precisely the opposite was true. The Third Infantry had consolidated its hold over the renamed international airport, and its 1st Brigade had moved north to seize Highway 1, a major route out of the city that linked Baghdad with Mosul. American commanders reported that more than a hundred Iraqi fighters—remnants of the Hammurabi and Adnan Divisions of the Republican Guard—had been killed, and twenty-three enemy tanks and more than ninety armored troop carriers, artillery pieces, antiaircraft batteries and trucks had been destroyed in the clash over Highway 1.

While the U.S. Army was attacking from the north and west, the Marines were busy in the east. The 1,500 troops of the 3rd Battalion, Fourth Marines, were struggling to cross a 150-yard bridge over the Diyala River, a small tributary that flowed into the Euphrates on the eastern outskirts of Baghdad. Once across it, the Marines would be just nine miles from the heart of town. But now there was sharp fighting, under dark plumes of smoke from exploding American mortar rounds that made Sunday noontime seem like twilight. Iraqi forces on the north side of the bridge kept firing rocket-propelled grenades, and the Americans just kept moving their tanks and firing back. "We're killing them like it's going out of style," said Lieutenant Colonel Bryan McCoy, the battalion's commander. "They keep reinforcing, these Republican Guards, and we're killing them as they show up. We're running out of ammo."[1] One of the bridge's main pylons had been badly damaged, and the Marines would have to lay pontoons to cross the river in their heavy armored amtracks. So McCoy and his men dug in on the southern side of the bridge, to plan an assault for Monday morning.

American forces had now blocked virtually all major routes in and out of the capital. "We have isolated the city from the Tigris in the north to the Tigris in the south," said Lieutenant Colonel Peter C. Bayer, the Third Infantry's operations officer. Lieutenant Jay G. McGee, a division intelligence analyst, said that the Republican Guard appeared to have more or less collapsed. No one seemed to be in control of Iraqi defenses. "Right now, you're looking at a paper army," he said. Colonel Grimsley, the 1st Brigade commander, said, "It just must be on autopilot. No one is in charge. The inmates are running the asylum." Still, there were pockets of fierce opposition. Third Infantry troops moved into an area of military barracks on the north side of the airport without resistance, but the American forces were still within reach of Iraqi artillery batteries closer to town. Commanders said the enemy guns were scattered in residential neighborhoods, and they did not fire back for fear of causing heavy civilian casualties. Saddam himself—or a double— again appeared on television in his field marshal's uniform, presiding at a meeting of senior officials. This time, he read a statement offering a reward of 15 million Iraqi dinars—roughly $5,000—to any Iraqi who destroyed an allied tank, armored personnel carrier or artillery gun, and he directed any Iraqi fighter losing touch with his unit in battle to "join a unit of the same kind that he is able to join." If that was an exhortation against desertions, it was not working.

All over Iraq, the fighting was going well for the Americans this Sunday. In Karbala, the 101st Airborne won a lopsided battle against irregular forces that had been fighting for two days. One American soldier was killed and half a dozen others wounded, but commanders estimated that 400 Iraqi fighters had died. In Basra, the British seemed close to gaining full control, after a day of intense fighting in which tank battalions and Royal Marines shot their way into the center of the city, surrounded the already-destroyed Baath Party headquarters and stayed unchallenged. But in the north, allied fighters suffered a terrible accident when an American Special Operations fighter traveling with a convoy of Kurdish leaders mistakenly called down an air strike on the column—instead of the intended target, an Iraqi tank nearby. The blast killed eighteen people and wounded forty-five, including three Kurdish military commanders.

Even with fighting still going on, the Americans were beginning to turn their attention to Iraq's political future. With American help, Ahmed Chalabi, the leader of the exiled Iraqi National Congress, who had long been supported by the Pentagon, slipped into Nasiriya with a group of fellow exiles that the Americans said could help form the nucleus of a new Iraqi army. It was a controversial move. Chalabi and his forces had been flown into Nasiriya on American aircraft. Officials at the State Department, the CIA and the National Security Council— all of whom were skeptical about Chalabi's potential as a postwar leader—were taken aback. Chalabi had left Iraq in 1958 and had lived in London for many years, trying to rally the Iraqi exile cause. Paul Wolfowitz and Donald Rumsfeld liked him, but many other officials in Washington saw him as a self-promoter and operator, and they saw this sudden airlift as an attempt by Chalabi's patrons in the Pentagon to help stack the deck in his favor. But Dick Cheney had concurred in the decision to send Chalabi in, and so it was done.[2]

In Washington, Wolfowitz made the rounds of the Sunday talk shows and said it would probably take more than six months to set up a new Iraqi government, once allied forces had full control of the country. "Six months is what happened in northern Iraq," he said, referring to the aftermath of the 1991 war and the time it took for the Kurds to take control of their territory. "This is a more complicated situation. It will probably take longer than that."

Already there was controversy brewing over the postwar administration of Iraq. The Bush administration, having fought the war, intended to organize the peace. But in Britain, Tony Blair was pressing for a greater role for the United Nations. France, Germany and other Western European nations that had opposed the war were girding for another round of diplomatic squabbles. The Bush administration was willing to have the United Nations play a part in providing food, medicine and emergency aid to postwar Iraq, but it was deter-

mined to reserve for itself the principal role in political and govern-
mental administration. UN Secretary-General Kofi Annan and others
were warning that UN involvement in establishing postwar order
would be essential to establish the legitimacy of any new Iraqi government. All sides agreed, however, that the paramount goal was to
assure that Iraqis ultimately controlled their own country's destiny.

LATE THAT SUNDAY, AMERICAN COMMANDERS sketched a plan for
another Thunder Run into Baghdad. Once again, the 2nd Brigade of
the Third Infantry got the job. Rick Schwartz and his Task Force
1-64 would be joined this time by another battalion of like size and
would thrust all the way into the sprawling government complex on
the west bank of the Tigris, which housed Saddam's Republican Palace, the military parade ground and Baath Party headquarters—the
inner sanctum of the regime's power. Once again, the Americans
would test the Iraqi defenses, and draw out enemy fire. But now the
goal was not just one quick pass through town. This time, the Americans wanted to stay the night, and the brigade commander, Colonel
Perkins, decided that if they could, they would.

Before dawn on Monday, an American column rolled once more up
Highway 8, heading straight into town along the route Schwartz had
followed on Saturday. The two tank battalions were in the front, racing
ahead, curving off to the right and passing under the giant arch of
crossed sabers Saddam had built to commemorate his war with Iran.
Behind them were other Third Infantry units whose job was just as
important: to take and hold three key cloverleafs at which Highway 8's
curving north-south path linked up with major east-west roadways
across town. That move would secure the road so American trucks could
resupply the tanks in the center of town, and these troops, in their Bradley fighting vehicles and armored Humvees, would be the sole line of
defense between the brigade's forward elements and whatever threats
might surround them in Baghdad. It was a deadly serious mission, but
the names that the Americans gave the three cloverleafs struck a note of
manic absurdity: Moe, Larry and Curly, the Three Stooges.

In the hatch of his armored Humvee, manning its .50-caliber
machine gun, Private First Class Cody Ruiz of the 2nd Brigade's 3rd

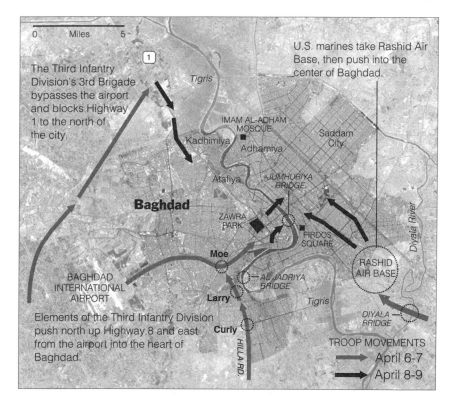

The Third Infantry Division's 3rd Brigade bypasses the airport and blocks Highway 1 to the north of the city.

U.S. marines take Rashid Air Base, then push into the center of Baghdad.

Elements of the Third Infantry Division push north up Highway 8 and east from the airport into the heart of Baghdad.

TROOP MOVEMENTS
April 6-7
April 8-9

Battalion had a question for his staff sergeant, Jason Giles. Days ago, the men had been ordered to remove all rings, lest their hands get pinched and injured in guns or machinery, but now Private Ruiz was on his way to secure the intersections and he was worried. "Sergeant, no kidding," he said. "If I get hit today, will you put my wedding ring back on my finger?" Without missing a beat, Sergeant Giles answered, "Yes, I will."[3] The 3rd Battalion's commander, Lieutenant Colonel Stephen Twitty, called out a warning to his troops on the radio: "They know we're coming."

So they did. The two tank battalions at the front of the line took fire from Iraqi mortars, rocket-propelled grenades and small arms, but soon they were in the midst of the presidential compound. Colonel Schwartz's Task Force 1-64 controlled Zawra Park, including Saddam's parade grounds and the Tomb of the Unknown Soldier, near the Baghdad Zoo, while the 4th Battalion's Task Force 4-64 moved to attack the presidential palaces before linking back up with

Schwartz's men to make a defensive cordon.[4] The troops walked the palace grounds, surveying the gaudy, ornate riches of Saddam's regime. They sensed the end was near. One of the tanks fired on an equestrian statue of Saddam. "It was a tremendous show of force," Schwartz said.[5]

But on Highway 8, the fighting at interchanges Moe, Larry and Curly was intense, and it dragged on for hours, sometimes in a swirling dust storm. From trenches and hastily dug bunkers, from surrounding buildings and speeding civilian cars, Iraqi irregulars attacked again and again. Some of the Americans recognized the pattern of Iraqi fighting. The enemy was trying to cut the Americans off and trap them downtown. Command Sergeant Major Robert Gallagher had fought as a Special Operations soldier with the 75th Rangers in Somalia in 1993, and he had seen the same pattern of attack in Mogadishu. But here the outcome was decidedly different. At Objective Moe, the northernmost intersection, at the junction of Highway 8 and the Qadisiya Expressway, every American vehicle was hit by at least one rocket-propelled grenade, but only seven Americans were wounded. The Iraqis, in contrast, lost as many as thirty vehicles and 150 to 200 fighters.[6]

A few miles south, at Objective Larry, where a road curved off Highway 8 and led over the Tigris at the Al Jadriya Bridge, seven of seventeen American vehicles were hit, but all kept going and took out at least twenty Iraqi vehicles. Two suicide bombers came racing north up Highway 8: One, a white van, was hit by American machine-gun fire and exploded; the other, a car, came barreling up an off-ramp without seeing a berm that the Americans had built. When it hit the berm, it, too, exploded.[7]

But it was at Objective Curly—the southernmost cloverleaf, where resistance had been expected to be the lightest—that the fighting was most ferocious. Some Americans likened the intensity of Iraqi opposition to the Japanese charges of World War II, and the fight at Curly dragged on for twelve hours or more. The Iraqis charged the American position in taxis, cars, trucks with heavy mounted machine guns, even in motorcycles with rifles tied to the sidecars. American mortarmen fired rounds both north and south to defend their position.[8] Air cover was impossible because of smoky haze and fires from exploding vehicles and oil fires along the Tigris, but with continuing fire pouring in from the Iraqis, commanders called for close American artillery fire from 155-millimeter Paladin self-propelled howitzers in their rear. But one of the rounds fell far short of its target, hitting a stone embankment in the cloverleaf and wounding two Americans, so even the artillery had to be called off.[9]

The troops at Objectives Larry and Moe were critically short of ammunition, and the tanks deeper in the city were running out of vital fuel—partly because of those missing fuel-tanker trucks that Schwartz and his men had lost on the dark, bumpy road from Karbala. The situation was critical, and the supply convoys—by now backed up and blocked by the fighting at Objective Curly—had to get through. Colonel Twitty called for help, and finally Captain Ronny Johnson, the commander of Bravo Company, drove up with another platoon and then some, guns blazing. Johnson reinforced the American forces at the intersection, pushing their perimeter farther out, far enough so that the resupply convoy could begin moving through.[10]

But still, the intersection was not secure. Two American Special Operations pickup trucks, which had been parked under the overpass, took direct hits from the Iraqis and exploded in flames. Scores of Iraqi fighters came barreling into the intersection, and an American ammunition truck, part of the resupply convoy, burst into flames, setting off a chain reaction of powerful explosions and fires that engulfed another ammo truck, a fuel tanker and a Humvee. Captain Steve Hommel, the battalion chaplain, thought to himself: "We just can't get overrun. Surrendering to those guys is just not something we can do."[11] Finally, Lieutenant Colonel Scott Rutter arrived with more troops, traveling a long, roundabout route from his position near the airport. He assumed control at Curly, while Captain Johnson escorted the remaining resupply trucks on to Objectives Larry and Moe, and finally to the tank battalions at the presidential compound.

"There are no American infidels in Baghdad," Information Minister al-Sahhaf insisted. Just blocks away, Rick Schwartz was being interviewed live on Fox television, and he volunteered to come right over and introduce al-Sahhaf to 700 of his closest friends.

Many of the captured Iraqi fighters turned out to be Syrian mercenaries, recruited by Saddam to fight for his regime. American commanders made many of them strip naked, to avoid suicide bomb attempts. The fighting had been grim: 350 to 500 of the enemy fighters were killed. But the Americans had succeeded. A brigade of roughly 5,000 troops had taken and held a position in the heart of a city of five million. Gone was the determination to wage a patient, probing campaign against Saddam's expected defenses. The days of Thunder Runs were over. The full-court press was on. "That was the whole turning point of the war right there," said Major Roger Shuck, operations chief of the 2nd Brigade's 3rd Battalion. "This mission is the one that cut the snake in half."[12]

AT THE DIYALA BRIDGE ON the southeast side of town, the Marines were still struggling in the snake's coils. On their march from Kuwait, they had crossed two of the world's great rivers, the Euphrates and then the Tigris, but now this sixty-meter-wide tributary had stopped a mighty Marine Expeditionary Force cold for the better part of twenty hours. Because the bridge was too badly damaged for heavy armor to cross, the Marines had had to summon engineers to lay pontoons.

Early this Monday morning, the Americans launched another round of heavy artillery barrages to weaken the Iraqi forces holding the northern side of the bridge. In the fight, two marines were killed when an Iraqi shell hit their armored vehicle. Finally, after the Americans had either killed most of the Iraqi fighters or pushed them back into redoubts on the northern side of the river, Colonel McCoy resolved to try a crossing—on foot, in an infantry charge, with troops running and holding their weapons in front of them. "Blue-collar warfare," McCoy called it.

Once across, the Americans found themselves in a neighborhood of low-slung shops and two-story houses, and they were swiftly met with a wave of incoming fire, from small arms and rocket-propelled grenades. Advance units took up sniper positions, while rear units fired mortars and bombs ahead into enemy territory. "Brute force is going to prevail today," McCoy said. His radio crackled, and he listened. "Suicide bombers headed for the bridge?" he said. "We'll drill them." The plan was for the Marine snipers farthest up the road to fire warning shots at approaching vehicles; anyone driving south out of town was considered suspect. The idea was to fire precisely enough to stop a vehicle in its tracks, or send the message that its owner should turn around. But if a car did not stop, the marines just riddled it with bullets until it did. Sometimes the snipers fired. Sometimes, other marines would open fire with their M-16s or machine guns.

Only later would it become clear that the cars were full of civilians, trying to escape the American bombs that were falling behind them, or just getting out of Baghdad altogether. An old man, walking with a cane on the side of the road, was shot and killed. He did not stop—he may have been confused—so he was shot. In all, there were nearly a dozen corpses, all but two of them with no obvious military clothing or weapons. The next morning, survivors lingered by the road. One of them, Sabah Hassan, was digging a grave. He was a chef at the Al Rashid Hotel, the favored stopping point for foreign guests at the height of Saddam's power. He had been fleeing the city when the Americans began firing. "What can I say?" he asked. "I am afraid to say anything. I don't know what comes in the future. Please." He put his shovel back in the ground and kept digging.

A group of marines drifted by. This corner of the war was not a scene of precision bombs or bloodless psychological operations. This was war as it had been for centuries: fierce, bloody, close and confusing. When someone suggested that the civilians should not have been shot, Lance Corporal Santiago Ventura spoke up. He was angry. "How can you tell who's who?" he demanded. "You get a soldier in a car with an AK-47 and civilians in the next car. How can you tell? You can't tell."[13]

ABOUT 2:15 THAT MONDAY AFTERNOON Baghdad time—6:15 A.M. in Washington—American officials once again got a tantalizing tip: that Saddam and his sons Uday and Qusay might be meeting in a house in the Mansour district, an exclusive residential neighborhood on the west side of the Tigris where VIPs from the regime were known to congregate. There was still considerable disagreement and uncertainty about whether the strike on the first night of the war had injured or even killed Saddam. American officials had let it be known that they believed that Qusay, at least, was still alive and leading the country's security forces. Intercepted conversations among top Iraqi military officials included accounts of Qusay giving them orders. The intercepts also revealed that Iraqi generals were feeding their superiors the same mix of fanciful lies and propaganda that Minister al-Sahhaf was feeding the Iraqi public, that American forces had been turned back at the airport. American commanders said that the intercepts suggested that Iraqi commanders were too afraid to give Saddam's leading loyalists accurate information. The decision was made to try a second decapitation strike.

Barely half an hour later, high in the skies over western Iraq, Lieutenant Colonel Fred Swan and Captain Chris Wachter of the Air Force had just finished a midair refueling in their B-1 bomber, nicknamed "Seek and Destroy." Their plane's bays were loaded with two dozen 2,000-pound bombs, and they were preparing to head off to another target. Then their radio brought the word: They were to change course and head for a "priority leadership target" in central Baghdad. "Stand by for coordinates," the radio said.[14] Colonel Swan, the plane's senior weapons officer, had been flying for twenty years, fifteen of them in the B-1. Now all his training—and the adrenaline rush—kicked in. His plane had already dropped 2,100 bombs in this war, but targets like this did not come along often. "Let's get the job done," he thought. There was not a lot of time for reflection; they entered the coordinates. In twelve minutes, the plane would be over its target. Just two minutes before they reached it, the crew got another message, from the top American commander of the air war: "Don't miss."

A total of just forty-five minutes had elapsed since the first intelligence report came in. Baghdad was covered with clouds. The B-1 crew could hardly see anything from nearly 30,000 feet in the air. They dropped four bombs, two that pierced the building's roof, and two more with 25-millisecond fuse delays, which allowed them to penetrate deep into the target before exploding. Colonel Swan thought, "Well, you know, this could be the big one. Let's make sure we get it right."

The bombs landed where they were supposed to, but in the aftermath, no one could be sure whether the Americans had gotten it right or not. The windows of the Al Saah, one of the few Baghdad restaurants that had still been open, were blown out, like those in all the buildings around it. Clumps of heaved-up earth and glass and debris were scattered over blocks, and there was only a giant pit where neighbors said four houses had once been. Residents wept and tried to console one another. There were no immediate signs of Saddam or his sons.[15]

Saddam Hussein is a topic of conversation as George W. Bush consults with his senior advisers at Camp David on September 15, 2001. *Left to right:* Attorney General John Ashcroft, Vice President Dick Cheney, President Bush, Secretary of State Colin Powell, Secretary of Defense Donald Rumsfeld, Deputy Secretary of Defense Paul Wolfowitz.
(J. Scott Applewhite/Associated Press)

Saddam Hussein and his sons, Uday (*left*) and Qusay (Iraqi News Agency)

TOP: The British foreign secretary, Jack Straw (*left*), was Colin Powell's most consistent ally as the Bush administration sought a United Nations resolution on Iraq. (Librado Romero/*The New York Times*)

ABOVE, LEFT: The French foreign minister, Dominque de Villepin, opposed military action in Iraq. (Vincent LaForet/*The New York Times*)

ABOVE, RIGHT: Hans Blix (*left*), the chief UN weapons inspector, and Mohammad ElBaradei, the head of the International Atomic Energy Agency, listen during Powell's presentation at the Security Council on February 7, 2003. (Elise Amendola/ Associated Press)

In December 2002, A UN weapons inspector looks through metal tanks at a pesticide factory near Falluja, Iraq, which were believed to have been used in Iraq's chemical weapons program in the 1980s. (Tyler Hicks/ *The New York Times*)

Antiwar protesters (*left*) fill the streets of London on February 15, 2003, demonstrating against the policies of Prime Minister Tony Blair (*above*). (Left: Peter Macdiarmid/Reuters; above: Associated Press Television News)

BELOW: President Bush meets with top aides after authorizing military action in Iraq on March 19, 2003. Left to right: Stephen J. Hadley, deputy national security adviser; Karen Hughes, adviser; General Richard B. Myers, chairman of the joint chiefs of staff; Dan Bartlett, communications director; Vice President Cheney, President Bush; Secretary Rumsfeld; Condoleezza Rice, national security adviser; Secretary Powell. (The White House)

Commander Bill Dooris flies over Kuwait on his way to Iraq from the USS *Abraham Lincoln* in an F/A-18 Hornet carrying bombs and Sidewinder missiles. (Cmdr. Bill Dooris and Vincent LaForet/ *The New York Times*)

Severe sandstorms slowed a convoy of armored vehicles from the headquarters battalion of the First Marine Division, which took twenty-seven hours to make a twelve-hour trip to its destination north of the Euphrates River. (Ozier Muhammad/*The New York Times*)

Pinned down during a gun battle in Nasiriya on March 23, 2003, marines from Task Force Tarawa duck as an American Cobra helicopter fires a missile that destroys a building behind them. (Joe Raedle/Getty Images)

Rumsfeld and Wolfowitz (*above, foreground*) confer in a secure room at the Pentagon moments before a videoconference with General Tommy R. Franks, seen at left at his wartime headquarters in Doha, Qatar, along with several of his top commanders. (Above: Stephen Crowley/ *The New York Times*; left: Tim Aubry/Reuters)

Lieutenant Colonel Eric C. Schwartz, the commander of Task Force 1-64, an armored battalion within the Third Infantry Division's 2nd Brigade, sits inside his Abrams tank. Schwartz led Task Force 1-64 on the Thunder Run incursion into Baghdad on April 5, 2003, the U.S. Army's first "reconnaissance in force" into the Iraqi capital. (Courtesy of Lt. Col. Eric C. Schwartz)

ABOVE: Murad Mohamad, a Kurdish pesh merga fighter, keeps an eye on Ansar al-Islam fighters whose trench is just over a kilometer away, near the Iranian border in northern Iraq. (Chang W. Lee/*The New York Times*)

RIGHT: Iraqis loot goods from a warehouse after the fall of Baghdad. (Tyler Hicks/ *The New York Times*)

BELOW: Corporal Edward Chin of the 1st Tank Batallion, First Marines, drapes an American flag over the face of a statue of Saddam Hussein in Firdos Square on April 9, 2003, just before the statue is pulled down in front of a cheering crowd. (Ramzi Haidar/AFP-Getty Images)

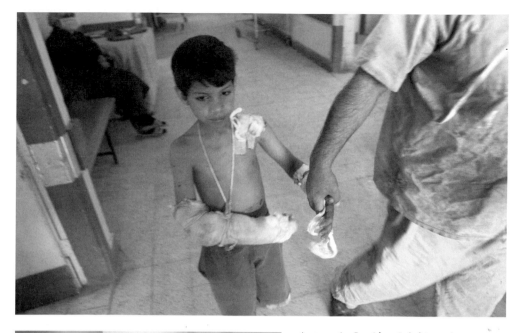

ABOVE: An Iraqi boy is led into the operating room to have his arm amputated at a hospital in Hilla, Iraq, the apparent victim of cluster munitions. (Tyler Hicks/*The New York Times*)

LEFT: Hundreds of bundles of human remains, most of them Iraqis executed by Saddam's regime after the 1991 Shiite uprising, await examination in Musayib, Iraq, in late May 2003. (Ruth Fremson/*The New York Times*)

BELOW: A Shiite man cries over the remains of a relative found at a mass grave in Mahawil, about sixty miles south of Baghdad, where 3,000 bodies were uncovered. (Tyler Hicks/*The New York Times*)

President Bush arrives on the USS *Abraham Lincoln* off San Diego on May 1, 2003, to announce the end of major combat operations in Iraq. (Vincent LaForet/*The New York Times*)

An American holds off an angry Shiite man who got too close to a line of marines and military police at a military post in Najaf during a demonstration in July 2003 protesting the American occupation. (Tyler Hicks/ *The New York Times*)

Shiite pilgrims march in a ritual of self-mutilation in a processional in Karbala, commemorating the death of the Shiite martyr Hussein, 1,400 years ago. Such ceremonies had been banned under Saddam Hussein. (Ozier Muhammad/ *The New York Times*)

• • •

ALL AROUND THE COUNTRY, IRAQI control was collapsing. In Hilla, the 101st Airborne encountered resistance and tough skirmishing with fedayeen fighters. General Petraeus called the Sunni town "a black hole." But American forces had stabilized Najaf and Karbala, while in Basra, the British at last pronounced themselves in control. "The Baathist regime is finished in Basra," said the British theater commander, Air Marshal Brian Burridge, and residents cheered a 300-man British patrol that walked without incident through the markets of the Old City, though it could not stop widespread looting. "The relationship between Basra and Baghdad is very intimate, in that we characterize Basra as the outskirts of Baghdad," Burridge said.

Tommy Franks himself made his first tour into Iraq, flying into Najaf, the southern town of Numaniya and the outskirts of Basra, before heading back to his base in Qatar. Aboard his plane on the return flight, the general showed off two aerial photographs of Baghdad, both depicting long lines of blue rectangles representing American troops. In one, the rectangles ringed the city; in the other, a miles-long line representing the Third Infantry stretched into the heart of the capital like a spear.

"Baghdad," Franks said, "is completely isolated by U.S. combat units."

IN THE WEE HOURS OF Tuesday morning, April 8, fighting erupted on the grounds of the Republican Palace, despite the 2nd Brigade's presence there. By dawn, massive gunfire echoed in the presidential compound near the planning ministry. Rick Schwartz and his men had expected such skirmishing; by now it was routine business.[16] Bombs and rockets rained down on more government buildings in the center city, setting the planning ministry ablaze. On the southeast side of town, marines now poured across the Diyala River, destroying several Iraqi T-55 tanks and capturing Rashid Air Base, to use as their operations center the same way the Third Infantry was already using the international airport on the west side of town. At a military prison in the Rashid base, marines found discarded American uniforms that

they believed might belong to some of the other prisoners who had
been captured with Jessica Lynch in Nasiriya, and who remained unaccounted for.

In the north, American Special Forces and Kurdish pesh merga
fighters gathered around Mosul and Kirkuk in anticipation of an
assault, and American transport planes airlifted more tanks into the
north to help in the expected fight against perhaps 100,000 remaining
Iraqi soldiers there. Special Operations troops also began moving to
block principal crossing points into Syria, to prevent senior members
of the Iraqi regime from escaping across the border.

Whatever Saddam's fate or whereabouts, until the minute American troops arrived in Baghdad, agents of the regime were working as
usual. Even as marines moved into the southeast part of the city, in the
Shiite neighborhood of Amin a group of Iraqis were being tortured by
police, who beat them, gouged them with wires and burned them with
cigarettes inside a local jail. By the time the marines arrived,
the jailers had fled and the captives, some still shackled and blindfolded,
were set free. Hamid Neama, a laborer, said he had been picked up that
morning in front of his brother-in-law's house, blindfolded, driven ten
minutes away, accused of having connections to the Americans—and
had then been beaten all over his hands and body. "The Americans saved
me," he said, holding out his hands. They were swollen like overripe
fruit.

ON WEDNESDAY MORNING, APRIL 9, something remarkable happened: Information Minister al-Sahhaf did not show up for work. No
one knew where he was. It hardly mattered. At midmorning, one of
the minister's minions, a burly, thirty-nine-year-old Iraqi named Qifa,
paused to grip the hand of an American reporter to whom he had
been assigned as a minder. He watched the flaming inferno that had
been the headquarters of Iraq's National Olympic Committee, the
domain of Uday Hussein. "Touch me, touch me," Qifa said. "Tell me
that this is real. Tell me that the nightmare is really over." Tears
streamed down his cheeks.

Suddenly, all over Baghdad, everything had changed. Marines on
the southeast side of the city awoke ready to attack, block by block

if necessary. "Our goal is to kill as many of the bad guys as possible," said Lieutenant Ty Moore. Before dawn, they pushed into urban neighborhoods where they expected house-to-house fighting. But there was nothing, and by noon, they had rolled through all the territory they had planned to cover in an entire day. But Corporal Bryon Adcox was skeptical. "A few hours ago, they were shooting at us," he said. "Now they are having a party. Are they truly happy we are here?"

Clearly, not everyone was. In the Atafiya district, five miles north of the presidential compound on the west side of the Tigris—a neighborhood that American troops had not yet penetrated—journalists who wandered into crowds were confronted by angry residents who shouted a scathing insult in Arab culture: "Bush down shoes!"—meaning that the president was only good for being walked on.

And yet a kind of euphoric chaos descended on the city. Several of Uday Hussein's racehorses—chestnut, gray and white—broke free from the crowds that had stolen them from the Olympic Committee headquarters and raced down the highway to an uncertain fate in a hungry country. At the infamous Directorate of General Security, the secret police headquarters, no one showed up for work, though crowds did show up to loot everything from new police cars to foam-rubber mattresses—even a plastic Santa Claus. Saddam City, the vast Shiite slum on the east side of town, essentially fell without the Americans ever having to fire a shot. By lunchtime, more than a thousand people had gathered around the cool courtyard of the Al Mohsen mosque, which had been closed four years earlier after Republican Guard units opened fire on Shiites protesting the killing of a Shiite cleric. The mosque's imam, Sheik Amer al-Minshidawi, ascended a raised wooden throne to declare, "We must teach the world that Islam is a religion of peace and tolerance and love."

At 11:30 Wednesday morning, Generals Wallace, McKiernan and Conway convened a videoconference to plot the final assault on Baghdad. The Army would come from the west and the Marines from the east, and they would meet in the middle in four days. By 6:30 P.M., the generals met again, but their plan had been overtaken by events.[17] In Firdos Square, on the east side of the Tigris, a crowd had surrounded a towering statue of Saddam. The people were trying to pull it down. Suddenly Corporal Edward Chin, a twenty-three-year-old marine from the Dyker Heights section of Brooklyn—a member of Bravo Company of the 1st Tank Battalion out of Twentynine Palms, California—clambered up the arm of a giant tank-recovery vehicle. Corporal Chin's parents had left Burma just before he was born, and he was deeply proud of the country that had welcomed his immigrant family. Now he draped an American flag upside down over the statue's head. The picture was beamed around the world. Precisely 138 years to the day after Robert E. Lee surrendered to Ulysses S. Grant at Appomattox, the Yankees had won again.

Cooler heads realized that this spontaneous gesture of symbolism was wrong: This was a liberation, not an occupation, as the Bush administration had always been careful to say. So an old Iraqi flag was found instead. Then the marines tied chain and a thick rope around the statue and used the massive M88—a wrecker for tanks—to pull it down. The statue bent, then buckled. "All the way down!" said a blacksmith named Muhammad Abbas, who watched with his two young children. Then the statue broke at the knees, tumbling over to reveal its hollow insides and the pipelike column that had held it up. "Very good!" Abbas said. "A good day." Crowds dragged the broken head through the streets, slapping it with their shoes. Saddam down shoes.

In the White House, President Bush watched the statue's fall on television. "They got it down!" he told his aides. At the Pentagon, Secretary Rumsfeld declared, "Saddam Hussein is now taking his rightful place alongside Hitler, Stalin, Lenin, Ceausescu in the pantheon of failed, brutal dictators, and the Iraqi people are well on their way to freedom."

But the crowd in Firdos Square was not quite as big as it looked on television, and the moment in Iraq was not quite so euphoric. One Iraqi man who had survived the American assault on Hilla said simply, "We hate Saddam but we hate the war." Of the Americans, he said two things: "We want them to finish Saddam Hussein" and "We want them to leave." Across the street from the ministry of telecommunications, Ibrahim Hussein, a sixty-one-year-old taxi driver, sat in a stacking chair amid the ruins in front of his home. He surveyed the abandoned street, strewn with glass and metal from bombs and looting. "These people will need someone tough," Hussein said. "A soft man will not be able to govern. He will need a stick."

Chapter 17

THE AFTERMATH

Baghdad
Thursday, April 10, 2003

For twenty-four years, Saddam Hussein had ruled Iraq with iron discipline, imposing an order enforced with the constant threat of death. Twenty-four hours after his regime's sudden collapse, all semblance of order had evaporated from the capital. Bands of looters ran free through broad areas on both sides of the Tigris in the heart of Baghdad. Looters broke into at least six government ministries and set several afire. Crowds ransacked the mansions of Uday and Qusay Hussein, and those of other members of the ruling elite, making off with liquor, guns, appliances, rugs, videotapes and paintings of half-naked women. The sprawling Al Kindi Hospital, overflowing with Iraqi civilians suffering from blast and shrapnel wounds—and its morgue filled with uncounted dead—lost beds, electrical fittings and all manner of other equipment.

The looters stripped the German embassy and the French cultural center—special symbols to some Iraqis of Western equivocation about Saddam's evils—of furniture, curtains, decorations and anything else that could be carried away. "Security in the city is very bad, and people are not daring to go to the hospitals," said Nada Doumani, an official of the International Committee of the Red Cross. "Small hospitals have closed their doors, and big hospitals are inaccessible." American marines were tightening their hold on the eastern sections of the city, and the Third Infantry troops that had swung into Baghdad on Monday were even more dug in around the government complexes on the west bank of the Tigris. But in northern riverside areas like Atafiya and Kadhimiya, and to the west in Al Mansur, pockets of paramilitary fighters still loyal to Saddam and the Baath Party lurked down the side streets, in building entrances and bunkers. Veronique Taveau, a United Nations official, summed up the situation: "There is absolutely no security on the street." One Marine officer standing on a tank at a checkpoint in eastern Baghdad said that the locals had repeatedly asked him why his unit had done nothing to stop the rampant looting; he had explained that he had no orders to do so. "I tell them the truth," the officer said, "that we just don't have enough troops."

The troops that were in the city were busy. If the Fourth Infantry had managed to move down into Iraq from Turkey as originally planned, things might have been different now. As it was, something less than the full force of two American divisions—the Third Infantry in the west and the Marines in the east—was holding down a city of five million people, with other American forces scattered southward. A suicide bomb attack at an American checkpoint on the east bank of the Tigris, about a mile from Firdos Square, where Saddam's statue had been toppled only hours earlier, left four marines severely injured. In northwest Baghdad, another marine was killed and more than twenty injured in a firefight outside the Imam al-Adham mosque in the Adhamiya neighborhood. The Americans had surrounded the mosque and an adjoining house early on Thursday morning after reports that Saddam might have taken refuge inside. An American jet later dropped a bomb that destroyed the mosque's main dome, but there was no sign of Saddam.

Overall, about one-third of Iraqi territory was still outside American and British control. The British were in command in Basra, but there, too, looting and revenge killings had broken out. The local police force and government in the city of more than a million people had been destroyed, and British soldiers were doing the best they could to maintain order. But some residents were looking to settle old scores, chasing down Baath Party members in retaliation for years of torture and repression. "One by one, we will kill them," vowed a twenty-four-year-old man who gave his name only as Khalid. "We will catch them by our hand and we will kill them by our mouth—not by a bullet, but by our tooth."

In western Iraq, near the town of Qaim, on the Syrian border, 200 miles west of Baghdad, American Special Operations troops and British commandos were fighting soldiers from the Special Republican Guard and the Special Security Services. In the 1980s, the town had been home to a plant used for uranium processing, and American officials now feared that the fighters might be trying to shield weapons programs or fleeing Iraqi leaders from scrutiny. Iraqi forces were still in charge in Tikrit, Saddam's hometown north of Baghdad, and American commanders were braced for a potentially dangerous fight there with the regime's die-hard supporters. In Najaf, the holy Shiite city that the 101st Airborne had worked so hard to pacify, a prominent newly returned Islamic cleric, Sheik Abdel Majid al-Khoei, was killed on Thursday by members of a rival Shiite group outside a mosque. To some Iraqis, Khoei seemed guilty of a double crime: He was cooperating with the invading Americans, and he had tried to establish his authority by reconciling with the caretaker of Ali's tomb—a man widely condemned by Najaf's Shiites as a collaborationist with Saddam's regime. The murder was an ominous sign that Iraqis who had suffered under Saddam might not be quick to accept the ministrations of outsiders, Iraqi or otherwise.

Even the good news tended to be tinged with complications. In northern Iraq, there was hardly a bigger prize than the oil-rich city of Kirkuk. After three weeks of American bombardment and harassing fire from Special Operations troops and Kurdish fighters, the Americans had planned to take the city ridge by ridge if necessary. Instead, the city's Iraqi defenders simply collapsed and fled in the hours after midnight on Thursday, just as local residents were beginning to hunt for them. The collapse was so fast and so total that a raucous army of Kurdish fighters rolled into the city in pickup trucks, abandoning their original plan of keeping the city under siege. With so few Kurdish and American forces in place, civil authority immediately collapsed. Homes, businesses and government offices were looted, and by nightfall the Kurdish cities of Erbil and Sulaimaniya were crowded with hundreds, perhaps thousands, of cars and trucks crammed with stolen goods.

The Kurdish presence in Kirkuk set off fresh political tensions with Turkey, which had feared just such scenes. Turkey remained adamantly opposed to Kurdish domination of the region, fearing it could be the first step in pressing for a Kurdish state that would encompass Turkey's own Kurdish population. The Americans had pledged that they, rather than the Kurds, would take control of Kirkuk, and the Turkish foreign minister, Abdullah Gul, noted, "We have reminded them of their guarantee." By Friday, the city of Mosul had fallen to Kurdish fighters after the surrender of the last elements of Iraq's V Corps, and American paratroopers took over control of the occupation in Kirkuk. But in both places looting continued. Even in the chaos, however, there were also scenes of jubilation. In Kirkuk, Ali Azad, a Kurdish man who appeared to be about seventy, hugged all the foreigners he could find. He said he had hated Saddam, but now was rid of him. "I was born today!" he shouted. "Today is the first free day of my life."

IN BAGHDAD ON FRIDAY, THE mood remained mixed. Some fedayeen fighters stayed on the prowl, but angry civilians chased them off. Ordinary residents of Baghdad were still reaching out to the arriving Americans. "These people couldn't be more friendly," said Lieutenant John R. Colombero, a marine on patrol downtown. Asked for evidence, he brandished a freshly plucked wildflower that had been stuck into the front of his bulletproof Kevlar vest by some effusive local. "See that?"

But the American presence was powerless to stop a fresh wave of looting. Three more government agencies were set afire by mobs—the Information Ministry, the Ministry of Planning and the Higher Education Ministry. At the Ani Mosque, the imam, Hamid Adel Mustaf, complained, "We have no security here. Listen to the gunfire outside. We cannot even pray in our mosque without hearing the gunfire in the street." Some of the most frenzied looting took place at the Sajida Palace, the one named for Saddam's wife, a structure that was especially grand and gaudy even by Saddam's standards. There, huge crowds carried out nearly every piece of furniture or adornment that could be lifted or ripped from the walls: gilded eighteenth-century-style chairs, wall friezes, beds, tableware. By no means were the looters limited to the lower classes. "I don't feel any guilt at all," said a pharmacist who came with her husband, an obstetrician, and their two children, to help themselves to brocaded sofas and stacks of Wedgwood china. "We paid for these things a hundred times over. Not a hundred times. A thousand times."

On Sadeh Street, near the Tigris, the opulence was almost too much to describe, and it drew repeated visits from some looters. Both of Saddam's sons lived on the street, as did the deputy prime minister, Tariq Aziz, and Saddam's private secretary, Abid Hamid Mahmoud, who had helped Qusay make the huge withdrawal from the Central Bank before the war began. Haidar Arubay said he went to Mahmoud's house five times over three days, just to gawk. "I can't help myself," he said. "I keep coming back. For so long, I've been looking at this place from the outside that my eyes can't get enough." The only thing he admitted taking was a first edition of Saddam's biography. "I wanted," he said, "to read about his miserable life."

In Washington, Secretary Rumsfeld sounded a note of both defensiveness and defiance. "You cannot do everything instantaneously," he said. "It's untidy. And freedom's untidy. And free people are free to make mistakes and commit crimes and do bad things. They're also free to live their lives and do wonderful things."

No one may ever know whether a more robust American military presence might have prevented the worst of the looting and violence. Soldiers are trained for war, not peace, and the plain truth is that in the days after the regime's fall, combat conditions persisted in much of Baghdad and the rest of the country, which required the troops' undivided attention. Vigilantism has been a fact of postwar life throughout history. But the Americans did manage to secure some government buildings, principally the Iraqi oil ministry. The shortage of troops was the result of Rumsfeld's insistence on a light invasion force and of the Iraqi regime's swifter-than-expected final collapse. The war planners had assumed that it would have taken longer for Baghdad to fall, by which time more American troops would be in place. With more troops on the ground, could they have secured more? Could commanders have deployed their forces more effectively? Those questions will be long debated. This much is clear: The lack of effective security in the early days after the regime's collapse did damage to the invading Americans' image that would endure, and worsen, in the days and weeks to come. At the Ani Mosque, another man, Nabil Abed, said bitterly, "This is what America has brought us—looting and destruction."

No report of looting attracted greater initial attention—or greater international outrage—than that of the plundering of the National

Museum in Baghdad, whose collections chronicled the history of civ-
ilizations in the fertile crescent dating back more than 7,000 years.
Within forty-eight hours of the regime's collapse it was in a shambles.
The initial reports were that 170,000 artifacts had been carried away
by looters, but these numbers turned out to be wildly exaggerated.
Some items had apparently been stolen in inside jobs before Saddam's
government fell. Hundreds of missing artifacts and tens of thousands
of ancient manuscripts would later be found stored in underground
vaults, where they had been stashed for safekeeping in anticipation of
the American attack. In early summer, the ancient treasures of Nim-
rud—gold earrings, necklaces, bowls and flasks dating to about 900
B.C.—would turn up in a secret vault-inside-a-vault, submerged in
sewage water in the bowels of the Central Bank. By July, Colonel
Matthew Bogdanos, a Marine reservist investigating the looting,
would estimate that only about 12,000 items had been stolen—mostly
objects of archaeological significance, like pottery shards and individual beads of lapis lazuli—and that some 3,000 of these had been
recovered. Bogdanos, who in civilian life was an assistant district attorney in Manhattan with a master's degree in classical studies from
Columbia University, said that thirty-two of forty-two "display qual-
ity" items were still missing. In any case, he said, walking through
the battered museum "breaks your heart."

A potentially far more dangerous loss occurred at Iraq's nuclear
facilities. The Tuwaitha Nuclear Research Center, the home of Iraq's
Atomic Energy Agency just south of Baghdad, was inspected more
often than any other site by UN inspectors in the 1990s, and the
International Atomic Energy Agency estimated that it held thousands
of pounds of partially enriched uranium, tons of natural uranium and
smaller amounts of other dangerous radioactive materials. American
marines reached the site on Sunday, April 6, but found it abandoned,
with some of the buildings showing evident signs of looting. In subsequent days, Iraqis cut through barbed-wire fences and made further
intrusions.[1] Most, if not all, of the uranium stored at Tuwaitha was
later accounted for, but other questions remained. In all, American
forces would determine that seven nuclear facilities in Iraq had been
damaged or effectively destroyed by postwar looting, with computers,
files, furniture and equipment carted off, and some containers that

held radioactive materials missing. Many of the facilities held material or scientific information that—in the wrong hands—could aid in the production of a nuclear or radiological bomb. But by midsummer, it remained unclear precisely which materials were missing throughout the country, in part because of jurisdictional disputes between the Americans and the International Atomic Energy Agency over who should conduct detailed site surveys.[2] If the sites contained evidence of Iraq's pursuit of undeclared weapons programs, such evidence might well have gone missing.

ON SUNDAY, APRIL 13, AMERICAN marines moved north toward Tikrit, ready to take on Saddam's ancestral town and the last redoubt of his sympathizers' power. The Americans' orders were clear: Eliminate any remaining vestiges of the regime. A group from the 3rd Light Armored Reconnaissance Battalion approached Samarra, a town about seventy miles north of Baghdad made famous in Somerset Maugham's reworking of an old tale in which a servant flees the specter of death in a Baghdad market and travels north, not knowing that death has "an appointment with him tonight in Samarra." As it turned out, these Americans had a far happier appointment—with life.

As the Marines drew near Samarra, a group of local Iraqis came up to them with word that seven American prisoners of war were being held in the town, and gave directions on where to find them. Look for House 13, the Iraqis said. Creeping through a crowded warren of dwellings, the Americans found a House 11, and a House 12, but no House 13. And as they kept looking, crowds of Iraqis gathered around them. "Something's not right," Lance Corporal Curney Russell told his squad mates. Was it a setup? An ambush? The marines prepared to withdraw. Just then, a man in faded yellow pajamas looked out from a house, trying to attract the Americans' attention. "I'm an American," he said quietly.[3] And so he was. Inside the house, the marines found the five Americans still missing from the Nasiriya ambush—Sergeant James Riley; Specialists Shoshana Johnson, Joseph Hudson, and Edgar Hernandez; Private First Class Patrick Miller—and the two downed Apache pilots, Chief Warrant Officers Ronald Young and David Williams. Johnson had been shot in both feet,

Hernandez had been shot in the right bicep and Hudson had three bullet wounds: two in the ribs, and one in the left buttocks. Now they were safe, and the marines whisked them out of town.

But the prisoners had undergone a frightening odyssey. The members of the 507th, the first to be captured, were swiftly taken together to Baghdad, and isolated in separate cells of a prison with concrete walls. They had no idea what had happened to the other members of their company, and underwent days of interrogation, sometimes blindfolded, sometimes in front of video cameras. They were stripped of all clothing and given unwashed blue or yellow-striped prison pajamas. Their daily diet was water, tea, bowls of rice—sometimes chicken. Sleeping on concrete floors with only blankets, they were not allowed outside. Their guards were menacing at first, but physical abuse subsided and those prisoners with gunshot wounds underwent surgery. "More than once a doctor said that they wanted to take good care of me to show that the Iraqi people had humanity," Johnson recalled.[4] Within a couple of days, Young and Williams arrived.

The members of the 507th did not know who the newcomers were at first, but could tell from the voices in nearby cells that they were Americans. At night, the prisoners heard the pounding of American bombs. The Iraqis had moved an artillery gun inside the prison and into a nearby room, effectively making the compound a target for the American attacks. Williams, as the senior officer present, demanded to be moved to a safer location, but the Iraqis refused. Finally, one night, a powerful explosion about fifty yards away shook the building, and the next morning, after about two weeks of captivity, the Iraqis bound the prisoners and took them to another location—in what would be the first of many moves. For the rest of their confinement, the group was moved nightly, to seven or eight different government buildings or private residences. "We could feel that the whole thing was collapsing," Young recalled. "We were the bastard children of Iraq. Nobody wanted to hold us."[5] As the prisoners kept moving, their treatment got better, and by the time they reached Samarra, their guards were lower-level police officers, who pooled their own money to buy food and medicine. Yet there was constant fear. "I was getting to the point where I believed they would have killed us," Johnson said.[6] Then, suddenly, the American marines were kicking in the door House 13 in Samarra and yelling, "Get down! Get down!" After three anguished weeks, the prisoners— Iraq's last known captives—were safe.

In Alamogordo, New Mexico, Specialist Hudson's mother, Anecita, watching on television, was overjoyed. She had always believed he would survive. "I told myself, 'Hell, no, not my Joseph.'" Now she said, "I'm going to fatten my boy up a bit with some chicken adobo and rice when he gets home."

THAT SAME SUNDAY, A FORCE of several thousand marines attacked Tikrit, backed up by intense bombardment from jets and fire from helicopter gunships. The American forces had moved ninety miles overnight before launching their attack in the afternoon. Commanders thought perhaps 2,500 Iraqi fighters were holed up inside the town, though it was impossible to know for sure. A platoon of fifteen or twenty Iraqi fighters had attempted to attack some of the Marines' 300 light armored vehicles, but without success. As Brigadier General John Kelly explained, "We had to kill them all."

Battles lasted into the night, but then—as almost everywhere else—the fierce resistance disappeared, and the advancing Americans met only empty streets. "There wasn't a lot of resistance," said Major Chris Snyder. "We're not sure where they all went." By Monday, the breeze off the Tigris blew through the empty halls of the grandest of Saddam's palaces. In one room was a tablet of paper, labeled simply, THE PRESIDENT. In a bathroom there were signs of a hurried exit: a cabinet door open, a crumpled towel on the floor, a pair of men's underwear hanging from a rack. Ahmed Farhan, a twenty-two-year-old student, wandered around the grounds. There were two miles of riverfront property, perhaps ninety buildings in all—homes, offices, hotels, servants' quarters. There were lakes, with swans, and rare birds gliding in the breeze. Farhan's eyes were wide and his mouth agape. "All my life I have dreamed of this palace," he said. "We were never allowed to see it." As the day wore on, more and more residents slipped past the Marine guards to loot the palaces. A man named Maaruf Hussein filled his car, a battered taxi, which he loaded down with Persian carpets, lamps and fixtures. "I never had a refrigerator, and today I took one," he said. "I'm going to put cold water in it for my wife. Maybe I will take the day off tomorrow."

IN WASHINGTON THAT MONDAY—TWENTY-SIX days after the war began—the Pentagon declared that major combat operations were over. "The major Iraqi units on the ground cease to show coherence," said Major General Stanley A. McChrystal, vice director of operations for the Joint Chiefs of Staff. "There will be a requirement for combat power for some period of time." But, he added, "Clearly, the requirements for civil affairs, engineer organizations, military police, will be significant."

The situation in Baghdad made that all too plain. By Sunday, looting had seemed to abate a bit, and the street stalls selling eggs, fruits and vegetables were open. There were enough casual motorists and pedestrians to provide the semblance of a normal Sunday. But challenges persisted. One prominent scholar, Wamidh Nadhmi, a professor of political science at Baghdad University, compared the vacuum in Iraqi politics with the period of uncertainty that followed the collapse of Shah Mohammed Reza Pahlavi's rule in Iran in 1979 and preceded the ascendancy of Ayatollah Khomeini. He said that after watching the Americans' failure to curb the looting, many middle-class Iraqis feared "the carelessness shown by the invading power." In his view, things did not bode well for the United States' ability to manage the complicated relations between Iraq's political, ethnic and religious groups. "We would like to see a secular state preserved in Iraq," he said. "We don't think that there is a Khomeini here, because the Shiites are too divided, and we know that a great many Islamists in Iraq accept the idea of democracy and an alternation of competing groups in power through elections." But, he added, "There are others for whom elections are a one-time thing, a way station on the road to the end of democracy. The message we want to get through is that no one represents the word of God—or rather, that it is the people, not the clerics, who represent the word of God."

In the moment between chaos and calm, Iraqi sentiment remained as unsettled as the situation on the streets. Cars plowed through intersections, but the stoplights were not yet working. There were fewer looters, but much less to loot. On Monday morning, about 3,000 former Iraqi policemen gathered at an American outpost to apply for just over 100 jobs. The men, who just weeks earlier had been among Saddam's enforcers, began jumping up and down on a portrait of the deposed leader, calling him "nothing" and "a dog." Chaos ensued, until marines ordered the newly appointed police chief to start over with a list of approved officers. The twist was not lost on the American troops: To restore order, they would have to rely on some of the same forces they had come to overthrow.

"The situation of Iraqis," said Sayid Hashem al-Shamaa, a Shiite leader at the Kadhimiya shrine in Baghdad, "is as if one eye is crying and one eye is laughing."

PART THREE

AMERICA'S CONSEQUENCES

Chapter 18

CATASTROPHIC SUCCESS

Baghdad
Wednesday, April 16, 2003

In the battle-scarred gilt-and-marble splendor of the Abu Ghraib palace on the outskirts of the capital, Tommy Franks convened a meeting of his victorious land, sea and air commanders—the first such gathering since the war began. It was a moment of satisfaction, and Franks smoked a celebratory cigar. "The Republican Guard no longer serves in this country," Franks said. "The Special Republican Guard no longer serves in this country. The regular army in this country no longer functions. In that respect, certainly, the decisive combat portion of the campaign is finished." But Franks knew the situation on the ground was more complicated. After all, he had come to this palace in a heavily armored convoy straight from the airport—and did not go into downtown Baghdad at all—because of ongoing concerns about security. "Every day we see the remnants of what we call Arab fighters, or foreign fighters who have come in from a number of other countries," Franks said. "We see them here in Baghdad. So now we are about the business of rooting them out."

It was Franks's first-ever visit to Baghdad, and only his second trip into a country whose terrain and military capacity he had studied for so long. "I am a lifelong learner," he quipped at one point.[1] Indeed, Franks and his fellow Americans still had a lot to learn about Iraq. A week after the fall of Saddam Hussein's regime, and the triumphant toppling of his statue in Firdos Square, conditions in the country remained profoundly unsettled. The fleet-footed American and British military campaign had overturned a dictatorial regime—seemingly in no time, and with relatively few American casualties—and routed an Iraqi army that had mostly crumbled in the face of the allied advance. But already, winning the peace was proving to be a more complex and challenging task.

"Affairs are natural, things are returning to normal," said a thirty-three-year-old fruit and vegetable vendor named Walid al-Fartousi, selling his wares on a busy market block of Karada Street in the city's center. But al-Fartousi also acknowledged a more ambivalent reality. "Frankly," he said, "the people are beginning to lose their trust in America. Because America promised Iraq to remove the tyrant government, but now things are even worse. Some people are even beginning to wish Saddam had stayed because all the troubles erupted after his departure. Until today, we are sitting in our houses, not safe from killers, looters. American forces stand by and do nothing. There is no security, no order. People do not feel safe."

Besides the fear at the lack of order on the streets, there was also outright Iraqi resentment of the occupying Americans. Even some of those citizens who might have been expected to be most sympathetic were outraged. Amal al-Khedairy, a seventy-year-old, Western-educated Baghdadi who ran a venerable cultural center that had survived Saddam's repression, stood in the ruins of her elegant waterfront home on the day of Franks's visit, and cursed the Americans. She had spent a lifetime appreciating Western culture, teaching French and English literature. She did not speak of whatever compromises or sacrifices had allowed her to maintain a comfortable, even dignified life under Saddam. Now she was unsparing in her rage at the country that had rained bombs on hers. "This is our American liberation!" Khedairy spat, in a voice of full-throated fury as she waded through the half-burned books in her second-floor library. "I never thought you would do it. I went to the American School. I believed in your moral values. And every night you bombed. Every night I ran through the streets, an old woman in my nightgown. Look at my library!"

TOMMY FRANKS AND DONALD RUMSFELD saw as their paramount goal the swift and decisive defeat of Saddam Hussein's military, and they had achieved it, perhaps even more swiftly and decisively than they could have imagined. "Catastrophic success," General Peter Pace, the vice chairman of the Joint Chiefs of Staff, called it. Indeed, the very speed of the American military campaign now contributed to the postwar problems that American troops and officials faced on the ground in Iraq. "We are facing some of the problems brought on by our very success in the war, in particular our ability to use speed to preempt many of the actions that we were afraid Saddam might take," the undersecretary of defense for policy, Douglas Feith, said in a postwar speech. "War, like life in general, always involves tradeoffs. It is not right to assume that any current problems in Iraq can be attributed to poor planning."

But other analysts and critics offered a different view. As the military historian Frederick W. Kagan pointed out in a postwar essay, Rumsfeld's vision of modern warfare focused on destroying an enemy's armed forces and its ability to command and control them—not on the problems of achieving political solutions. "They see the enemy as a target set and believe that when all or most of the targets have been hit, he will inevitably surrender and American goals will be achieved," Kagan wrote. "War is not that simple, however. From the standpoint of establishing a good peace it matters a great deal how, exactly, one defeats the enemy and what the enemy's country looks like at the moment the bullets stop flying. The U.S. has developed and implemented a method of warfare that can produce stunning military victories, but does not necessarily accomplish the political goals for which the war was fought."[2]

In the military campaign, the equivalent of four ground divisions (one British, one U.S. Marine and two U.S. Army units) had conquered a country the size of California, with crucial support from precision-guided bombs and missiles, Special Operations troops and other high-tech tools of war. In purely military terms, the results were impressive indeed, from the Third Infantry's rapid march across the desert to its daring Thunder Runs into Baghdad. The improvised northern front—where paratroopers, Special Operations troops, Kurdish pesh merga fighters and American air power combined to substitute for the originally planned advance of the Fourth Infantry Division—bore sometimes spectacular fruit. On one occasion, the Special Operations commander, Brigadier General Gary L. Harrell, would recall, a dozen Green Berets and a small band of Kurdish fighters took on an entire division of Iraqi troops and kept them from moving to join the fighting in Baghdad and the south. "Twelve guys and some pesh merga took on a division—and moved it," Harrell said, admiringly. Similarly, a single 5,000-strong brigade of the Third Infantry had pierced into Baghdad on Monday, April 7, and taken and held its position on the grounds of the Republican Palace.

In part, the Americans succeeded beyond expectations because the Iraqi forces put up such an erratic, disorganized fight, whipsawed by conflicting orders and strategic miscalculations. As American forces advanced toward one Republican Guard unit outside Baghdad in late March, Saddam's son Qusay issued a new order every morning, directing the unit to reposition its tanks. Each order contradicted the one before it, and every time the tanks were moved from their bunkers, a few more were spotted and destroyed by American air strikes. "These were the orders of an imbecile," an Iraqi commander, Colonel Raaed Faik, recalled. "Qusay was like a teenager playing a video war game."[3]

Even before the war, the CIA, the American military and Iraqi exiles had begun a covert effort inside Iraq to try to forge alliances with commanders and persuade them not to fight, people involved with the effort later said. There were some indications that the Iraqi defense minister, General Sultan Hashem Ahmed al-Tai, might have been willing to cooperate to bring the war to a quick end and help ensure postwar stability. General Hashem's ministry was never bombed by the United States during the war, and the Pentagon's decision to leave Iraqi television on the air permitted him to appear with what some Iraqi exiles have called a veiled signal to troops that they should not fight the invading Americans. General Hashem's fate in the aftermath of the fall of Baghdad was unknown, and the success of the covert American operation cannot be fully judged. Some people involved in the effort, including Iraqis inside the country, said that they had succeeded in persuading hundreds of Iraqi officers to quit the war and send their subordinates home, and some Iraqi military officers confirmed that they had carried out acts of sabotage against Saddam's regime after being contacted by the Americans. In the end, officials in Washington were reluctant to leave any high-ranking officials from Saddam's government in power after the war.

In any event, when the regime fell on April 9, it quickly became apparent that there were simply not enough American boots on the ground to deal with the storm of forces—pent-up relief, revenge, rivalry—that Saddam's defeat had unleashed. The Fourth Infantry eventually arrived, along with other troops. But even so, there was a shortage of military police and civil affairs units. And because of Washington's insistence on fighting the war almost entirely alone, without the backing of the United Nations or most of the international community, other countries were reluctant to send peacekeeping troops, at least not without a new UN mandate. Three months after the fall of the Iraqi regime, roughly 140,000 American troops remained in Iraq, and there was every indication that this level of forces would be needed for a considerable time to come.

PART OF THE PROBLEM WAS unrealistic expectations. The Americans had counted on cheering crowds of Iraqi civilians welcoming them, but these largely did not materialize during the military campaign itself, and certainly not in the aftermath. Instead, the American troops faced dogged resistance from some resentful civilians or Saddam loyalists, both before and long after the fall of Baghdad. In time, Baathist loyalists would actually put bounties on American soldiers' heads and send young Iraqis out to commit what amounted to contract killings of the occupying troops.

The war planners in Washington had not realized quite how battered Iraq's vital infrastructure—power grids, water supply facilities and the like—was after a decade of economic sanctions, nor did they completely anticipate the additional battle damage that had occurred, especially to communications. Though Iraq's power plants should have been able to generate roughly 7,800 megawatts of electricity, even before the war they were producing only about 4,500 megawatts, because of chronic breakdowns, poor maintenance, old equipment and residual damage from the 1991 Gulf war. Power outages were common, and although Baghdad, Tikrit and other cities favored by Saddam received steady power, Shiite areas in the south fared less well. After the fall of Baghdad, deliberate sabotage and looting by opponents of the American occupation led to repeated brownouts, including several in midsummer that left Baghdad sweltering without air conditioning or a reliable water supply, in temperatures approaching 120 degrees. Ordinary Iraqis were hard-pressed to understand why conditions were worse than they had been under Saddam. "They brought thousands of tanks to kill us," complained a shopkeeper named Bessam Mahmoud. "Why can't they bring in generators or people to fix the power plants? If they wanted to they could."[4]

Another problem was planning. The State Department had drawn up detailed plans for postwar Iraq, but the Pentagon, which controlled the effort at President Bush's direction, ignored the State Department's experts and shut them out of key discussions and decisions. Not until late February did all the prospective participants in the postwar administration gather under one roof to go over the state of planning. "The Messiah could not have organized a sufficient relief and reconstruction or humanitarian effort in that short a time," recalled Judith Yaphe, an Iraq expert and former CIA analyst who participated in the effort.[5]

Moreover, as Paul Wolfowitz would later acknowledge, the planners planned for some of the wrong things. They expected a potential humanitarian and refugee crisis and food shortages, which largely failed to materialize. They prepared for environmental damage from oil field fires set by the Iraqis, or dams opened by Saddam to flood the country and block the American advance, but there were minimal oil fires and no broken dams. They also expected that Saddam's removal from power would quickly neutralize the threat posed by Baath Party followers, and that they could swiftly incorporate large numbers of Iraqi police, army units and various civil servants into a postwar civilian administration. After the fall of the Soviet Union, or Nicolae Ceausescu's regime in Romania, the old bureaucrats returned to work under new governments. In Iraq, that, too, largely failed to happen. Demoralized army officers shed their uniforms and deserted, and Iraqi bureaucrats, frightened by the looting and violence on the streets, sat at home.

In hindsight, perhaps the most provocative question is whether Franks's vaunted speed and tactical surprise were really needed to head off what the war planners perceived were Iraq's greatest threats, like Saddam's possible use of chemical or biological weapons. Iraq had not used such weapons because, it seemed certain, it had no ready stocks to deploy. So, in the end, these were not the biggest threats.

The biggest threat—during major combat operations and afterward—was one that the Pentagon largely failed to anticipate: ambushes, suicide attacks and guerrilla resistance from the fedayeen and other irregulars, some of them recruited from Syria or other Arab nations. These were the fighters who attacked American forces as they made their way north through the country from Kuwait to Baghdad in March and April, and who kept attacking for weeks and months after the fall of the regime. Before the war, the CIA had warned that terrorists based in Iraq—possibly including Al Qaeda operatives—were planning attacks on American troops in the event of any invasion, but the alert drew comparatively little notice at the time. If the Bush administration was unwilling to acknowledge explicitly any miscalculations in this regard, it did so implicitly in the summer of 2003, by shelving indefinitely its plans to reduce troop strength in Iraq.

WAR MAY LEAVE NO GREATER scar on the psyche of an invaded nation than the unintentional civilian deaths the battle inflicts. From the outset, American commanders repeatedly emphasized their desire and intention to minimize Iraqi civilian casualties. Indeed, while part of the strategy of the swift land advance was to shock Saddam's regime, another goal in racing past southern Iraqi cities was to minimize gritty close-up fighting that could kill innocent civilians. There is little doubt that the guerrilla tactics of Iraqi irregular and militia fighters greatly complicated the Americans' efforts, and doubtless increased the number of Iraqi civilian casualties—perhaps substantially. So did the Iraqi regime's decision to locate some strategic military or communications targets in or near residential areas, which made civilians more vulnerable to inadvertent bomb damage. A full tally of Iraqi deaths, both military and civilian, may never be known. In the immediate aftermath of major combat operations, the Bush administration made no move to compile one.

There is no reason to doubt the Pentagon's assertions that it sought to avoid civilian casualties whenever possible, consistent with its broader war plan. In Baghdad and elsewhere, there was clear evidence of the precision of American weapons. Bombs plunged deep into government buildings and left nearby houses standing. It is also clear, however, that the effort was not always so clinical or precise. Air war commanders were required to obtain the personal approval of Secretary Rumsfeld if any planned air strike was thought to be likely to result in the deaths of more than thirty civilians. Commanders proposed more than fifty such strikes. Rumsfeld approved them all.

The Pentagon insisted that in civilian areas it scrupulously avoided the use of cluster bombs, which splinter into scores of smaller explosive pieces. In a briefing in late April, General Myers, the chairman of the Joint Chiefs of Staff, said that of about 1,500 such bombs used in the war, only twenty-six were dropped over populated areas (in each case an area where the Iraqis had located military targets), and that there was only one reported death or injury to a noncombatant. But the Pentagon does not keep track of similar explosive devices fired from weapons on the ground, and doctors and international relief workers in postwar Baghdad reported treating hundreds of wounds apparently caused by such explosives. In the weeks after major combat ended, Baghdad residents reported finding dozens of bomblets the size of soda cans, which can explode if picked up.[6] Some incidents remained unexplained. On March 28, a missile landed in a crowded Baghdad market, reportedly killing fifty-eight civilians. Iraqi officials blamed the Americans, but the Pentagon said at the time that it was investigating the matter, suggesting that the missile might have been Iraqi. No definitive explanation came to light in the following months.

On April 8, American forces in central Baghdad fired a single tank round into the Palestine Hotel, killing two European journalists, who had been filming from hotel balconies. American forces said that earlier in the day they had found an Iraqi military radio and had intercepted transmissions indicating that an enemy spotter was calling in the location of advancing American troops. The soldiers saw what they believed to be an enemy observer and sniper on the upper-story balcony of a tall, tan-colored building, and "they also witnessed flashes of light, consistent with enemy fire, coming from the same general location as the building," according to the military's official statement after the incident. Only later did the American troops realize they had been firing at the Palestine Hotel, which was well known as the headquarters for journalists during the war. The U.S. Central Command later concluded that the firing had been a "proportionate and justifiably measured response" to the perceived threat, and fully consistent with the rules of engagement. But the incident sparked sharp objections from journalists' groups and others, who said there was no evidence that hostile fire had been directed from the Palestine Hotel and that the deaths could have been avoided because field commanders in Baghdad were well aware of the hotel's location and its status as a headquarters for journalists.

Before Baghdad fell on April 9, the Iraqi government itself had claimed that more than 1,200 civilians had been killed in the war. A postwar tally by the Associated Press, based on incomplete records from 60 of Iraq's 124 hospitals, estimated that from March 20 to April 20, at least 3,240 civilians died throughout the country, including 1,896 in Baghdad. The AP excluded all counts done by hospitals whose written records did not distinguish between civilian and military dead, which meant that hundreds—and perhaps thousands—of victims in the largest cities and the most intense battles were not reflected in the estimate. The hospital ledgers tracked the wounds and diagnoses of the victims, and also their jobs: carpenter, butcher, student, policeman. Hameed Hussein al-Aaraji, the postwar director of the al-Kindi Hospital in Baghdad, was philosophical about the toll. "Did the Americans bomb civilians?" al-Aaraji asked. "Yes. But one should be realistic. Saddam ran a dirty war. He put weapons inside schools, inside mosques. What could they do?"[7]

COLIN POWELL HAD RELUCTANTLY ACCEDED to the Pentagon's wish to be in charge of postwar planning, because he knew how many of the immediate postwar tasks would involve security. But the military's experience with reconstruction was limited. The man Rumsfeld chose to oversee the occupation was himself a retired lieutenant general, Jay Garner, who had helped safeguard the Kurds of northern Iraq in the aftermath of the 1991 Gulf war. Garner had dispatched a team of experienced officials to Kuwait before the war, to begin planning the postwar administration; by the time the war began, there were close to 200 people involved. Garner had hoped to get quickly to Baghdad after it fell on April 9, but Franks, concerned about security, would not let him go until nearly two weeks later. By the time Garner got to Baghdad, he would recall, seventeen of twenty-one Iraqi ministries had "evaporated" in looting or fire.[8]

When Garner and his team finally did arrive in Iraq, they lacked the most basic necessities to do their jobs effectively. They had satellite phones, which only worked outside and lacked docking stations that would have made them functional indoors. Power and running water were spotty. Clothes had to be sent to Kuwait to be laundered—a five-day round-trip—or wrung out in the courtyards of Saddam's former palaces, which became occupation headquarters. The Army and the Marines were in charge of logistics and security, and some on Garner's team complained bitterly that the military commanders, still busy fending off skirmishers in the streets, were not taking the civilian mission seriously enough.

Timothy Carney, a veteran ambassador, was among the officials sent to help in the effort. His job was to try to get the Ministry of Industry and Minerals up and running again, and he knew enough from past experience in Haiti and the Sudan to take his own supply of baby wipes. But the challenges were almost overwhelming. At one point, in an effort to pump some money into Iraq's paralyzed economy, the American officials worked out a system to provide emergency payments for Iraqi government workers—$20 a head, just under $1 million in all—and Carney delivered the cash in the back of his Suburban. Many senior Baathists had simply stopped going to work, and the Iraqis were impatient with the bureaucratic fine points of getting relief. One day Garner took a walkabout in a Baghdad market, and to the shock of his security team, an Iraqi grabbed his jacket and said, "I believe in God and in you, but you are the one I need now!"[9]

Garner's assignment had always been envisioned as temporary, but things were not working out as planned. Concerns about security were still so high that Iraqis could not easily enter the American headquarters to meet with officials, and many Iraqis remained confused about who was in charge, the military commanders or Garner's team. On April 24, just three days after Garner arrived in Baghdad, Rumsfeld called him to say that President Bush had decided to name L. Paul Bremer, a former State Department counterterrorism official and veteran diplomat, to be the chief American official in Baghdad.[10] Bremer arrived in mid-May and promptly stepped up efforts to restore order. "They recognized that public order had broken down in a far more serious way than they had expected," one official said of Garner's team.

• • •

BY THE FIRST WEEK OF JUNE, Rick Schwartz's Task Force 1-64, and other elements of the Third Infantry's 2nd Brigade, had been sent forty miles west of Baghdad, to Falluja, a town of 200,000 people where resistance to the American occupation remained strong. The same unit that had led the Thunder Runs into Baghdad—and might have hoped to be heading home soon—was now in the thick of things again. They spent their days rumbling through the city in Abrams tanks and Bradley vehicles, trying once again to assert some measure of control through a show of American force. Their mission was to try to root out small teams of enemy fighters who had already killed three American soldiers and wounded more than a dozen before fading back into the city streets—some of which were so narrow that the American soldiers could patrol them only on foot.

The 2nd Brigade had been sent to Falluja after a succession of other American units had failed to bring order. The effort involved far more than just fighting. Rick Schwartz spent one Saturday at the local hospital, trying to turn its director into an ally by discussing plans to restore the facility. He urged the director to spread the word that shooting at American soldiers would simply make it harder to help the town. "I don't believe there is a single organized group," Schwartz said of the guerrillas. "The information that we have is that it may be a collection of folks. It may be Iraqis. It may be Syrians. It may be Palestinians. We believe that Al Qaeda is possibly in there." The 2nd Brigade, he promised, would use its combat engineers to make repairs to damaged buildings, and try to build goodwill. "The strategy is to provide the assets Falluja needs to get back on its feet," he said. "I think providing those assets will change the mind-set. We have also got to get rid of the Baathists, terrorists and street-corner thugs. Unfortunately, they are going to shoot at us, and once they shoot at us, we have got to find them and either detain them or kill them."

FOR SCHWARTZ AND HIS MEN in Falluja, the limits of the light invasion force were readily apparent. At the Pentagon, some commanders confessed to a pair of additional worries. The first was that the military's striking tactical victory in the Iraq campaign would come to be over-shadowed by the politicians' strategic miscalculations—and the result-ing complications in winning the peace. What a shame it would be, they thought, if the troops' brave work in the field could not produce a more lasting victory. The second concern was more subtle. For a quarter century after Vietnam, military commanders like Colin Powell had warned that wars were brutal, bloody, costly exercises, and that to fight and win them, the American public must be prepared for sacrifice—in lives and treasure. But since 1991 the American military had fought three swift and comparatively bloodless wars, for Amer-ican troops at least: the first Persian Gulf war, Afghanistan and Iraq. Would the public—and perhaps civilian Defense Department officials—be tempted to draw the conclusion that all wars were easy, and that exercising America's military might around the world in the future would be uncomplicated? The commanders hoped not.

Secretary of the Army Thomas E. White, a former brigadier gen-eral who had feuded bitterly with Rumsfeld for months over many issues, from weapons programs to the transformation of the military, said that the Pentagon was "unwilling to come to grips" with the scale of the postwar commitment that would be required. "This is not what they were selling" before the war, he declared in June, having resigned abruptly a month earlier. "It's almost a question of people not wanting to 'fess up to the notion that we will be there a long time and they might have to set up a rotation and sustain it for the long term."[11]

For his part, the historian Frederick Kagan invoked Clausewitz's timeless assertion that war and politics were forever intertwined, and warned against any assumption that wars could be fought successfully without due consideration of the human element. "The enemy in war is a group of people," Kagan wrote. "Some of them will have to be killed. Others will have to be captured or driven into hiding. The overwhelming majority, however, have to be persuaded. They must be persuaded not merely of the shocking awfulness of American power, but of the desirability of pursuing the policies the U.S. wishes them to pursue. And they must not be driven away from the pursuit of those policies by the horrors and opportunities presented by a chaotic, lawless vacuum created by our precision weapons."[12]

Chapter 19

SMOOTH LANDING, ROUGH TAKEOFF

Aboard the USS Abraham Lincoln
Thursday, May 1, 2003

The S-3B Viking jet came screaming onto the deck of the giant aircraft carrier at 150 miles per hour, catching the last of four cables that would keep it from taking flight again, or plunging into the Pacific Ocean. Sitting in the copilot's seat was the president of the United States, outfitted in full flight suit, parachute and water survival kit, the interlocking straps and buckles emphasizing his lean frame. "Yes, I flew it," a beaming George W. Bush said after emerging from the plane, holding his flight helmet under his arm like the cockiest pilot in *Top Gun*. The Viking, normally used for refueling, had been designated Navy One for this special mission.

The president was quickly surrounded by cheering crew members of the USS *Abraham Lincoln*, at last returning from nearly ten months at sea. It was an extraordinary moment for Bush, who had learned to fly as a Texas Air National Guard pilot during the Vietnam war, and he basked in the glow of a political photo opportunity that Ronald Reagan himself might have envied.

Hours later, in a golden sunset off the California coast, Bush—now in a business suit—stood in the middle of a vast open space on the carrier's flight deck, with its crew arrayed around him and a giant banner proclaiming "Mission Accomplished" hanging behind him. "In the battle of Iraq, the United States and our allies have prevailed," the president told the sailors and airmen and a live television audience, "and now our coalition is engaged in securing and reconstructing that country." In a twenty-minute speech, Bush spoke not only about the men and women of the armed forces still fighting in Iraq, but also of the victims of the September 11 attacks, and he cast the campaign to oust Saddam Hussein as part of a much broader global battle against terrorism and weapons of mass destruction. "The liberation of Iraq is a crucial advance in the campaign against terror," Bush said. "We've removed an ally of Al Qaeda, and cut off a source of terrorist funding. And this much is certain: No terrorist network will gain weapons of mass destruction from the Iraqi regime because the regime is no more."

Those assertions were dubious, because there had been only the most tenuous evidence connecting Saddam to Al Qaeda, and no weapons of mass destruction had yet been found anywhere in Iraq. For all the brilliance of the American military campaign, the ongoing violence and disorder in much of Iraq made any hint of gloating unseemly. But the president used his speech to restate and amplify the Bush Doctrine, pledging to confront such threats before they reached American shores. "All can know, friend and foe alike," he said, "that our nation has a mission: We will answer threats to our security, and we will defend the peace."

If it was a triumphant moment for Bush, it was also a delicate one. The president took some care not to pronounce the American job in Iraq finished, in part because American forces were still interrogating thousands of Iraqi prisoners of war, and declaring a cessation of hostilities would have required their release under the Geneva Conventions. But the president and his aides were also eager to turn their attention to domestic issues, and Bush's chief political adviser, Karl Rove, had happily anticipated Bush's speech.

Bush was all too aware that his father's stunning victory in the 1991 Persian Gulf war, and the stratospheric approval ratings that followed, had not translated into enough lasting support to reelect him a year later. Now, with the 2004 presidential election just eighteen months away, Bush was determined to refocus his attention on his domestic agenda, including deeper tax cuts, and thereby avoid a similar fate. The president spent the night on the *Lincoln,* but the next day he flew north to California's Silicon Valley for a speech at United Defense Industries, the manufacturer of the Bradley fighting vehicles that had just seen service in Iraq. Hours before Bush spoke, the government announced that the national unemployment rate had risen to 6 percent, and now the president declared, "We need a bold economic recovery package so people can find work."

Bush had barely finished his victory lap before the Democrats accused him of playing politics with the war. The White House had initially said that the president would land on the *Lincoln* by jet because the carrier would be too far out at sea for a helicopter landing. In fact, the ship had already steamed so close to San Diego (and within helicopter range) that it had to be repositioned for the president's speech so that land would not be visible in the background. The president's press secretary, Ari Fleischer, was forced to acknowledge that Bush had simply wanted to experience a carrier landing the way that pilots did. Representative Henry A. Waxman, a California Democrat, demanded a General Accounting Office investigation of how much Bush's trip to the *Lincoln* had cost taxpayers. Senator Robert Byrd, who had been one of the few vocal congressional opponents of the war, now denounced Bush's "flamboyant showmanship." "To me, it is an affront to the Americans killed or injured in Iraq for the president to exploit the trappings of war for the momentary spectacle of a speech," Byrd said.

At the Pentagon, senior officials also were grappling with the politically delicate question of when, and whether, to hold a victory parade for the returning troops. In 1991, after the Persian Gulf war, General Schwarzkopf and his troops rolled through Lower Manhattan in a ticker-tape parade and marched in another celebration in Washington, D.C. But if the battle of Iraq was just one victory in a long campaign against terrorism, was it really an occasion for celebration at all? "What you want to do now is very different than in '91," one senior Pentagon official said.

IN IRAQ, the political fighting was far more complicated. Two weeks earlier, on April 15, the American authorities had helped organize a conference of more than seventy Iraqi notables—exile leaders, tribal sheiks, Kurds and Shiite clerics—in a tent at Tallil Air Base, near Nasiriya, to begin the process of creating a new Iraqi government. But there was squabbling and dissension from the outset. The largest Shiite faction, the Supreme Council for the Islamic Revolution in Iraq, had refused to attend. Even as the group met, thousands of protestors demonstrated in Nasiriya, chanting, "No no Saddam, no no United States." After a daylong session, the group issued a statement outlining thirteen points of agreement toward establishing a "federal system" under leaders chosen by the Iraqi people and not imposed from outside. But there were still broad areas of disagreement, especially over the role of religion. Sunni and Shiite Muslims had competed for power in Iraq for generations, even though secularism had been the official state policy for the past eighty years. "Those who would like to separate religion from the state are simply dreaming," said Hussein Mussawi, a delegate at the meeting.

Saddam Hussein had so repressed Iraq's majority Shiite population that its members now exploded in a mix of joy and defiance. In late April, hundreds of thousands of Shiite pilgrims converged on Karbala to honor their sect's founder, Hussein, the grandson of the prophet Mohammed, wailing and beating and slashing themselves with swords in a celebration long banned by Saddam. For the past two decades, defiant pilgrims had been gunned down on the road to Karbala, but now there was overwhelming emotion in the streets. Even so, nationalist resentment of the American presence seemed to outweigh gratitude for new religious freedoms. "Our celebration will be perfect only when the American occupier is gone and the Iraqi people are able to rule themselves by the principles of Islam," said Sheik Muhammad Thamer, deputy to the Grand Ayatollah Ali al-Sestani, Iraq's most senior Shiite cleric.

It was not clear that Iraq's Shiites would be willing to accept the kind of pluralistic democracy that Washington now envisioned for their country. Many Iraqi Shiites looked to neighboring Iran as a friendly power. A fundamentalist Shiite regime—even one less hostile to the United States than the clerics who ran Iran—would hardly be a desirable outcome to a war fought to advance American interests in the region. Skeptics of American military action in Iraq had long warned of the unpredictability and potential instability of whatever regime would replace Saddam, and now those concerns were being tested. In early April, an Iraqi-born cleric named Kadhem al-Husseini al-Haeri, living in exile in Iran, issued a religious edict, or fatwa, calling on Shiite mullahs in Iraq "to seize the first possible opportunity to fill the power vacuum in the administration of Iraqi cities," as a way of helping to "impose a fait accompli for any coming government." The fatwa warned that "the Great Satan" of America would "try to spread moral decay, incite lust by allowing easy access to stimulating satellite channels and spread debauchery to weaken people's faith." Many Sunni Muslims were just as suspicious of the American occupation. "You are the masters today," said a Sunni cleric in Baghdad named Ahmed al-Kubeisy. "But I warn you against thinking of staying. Get out before we kick you out."

Some Iraqi women, in particular those in Sunni urban areas like Baghdad, worried about their lot in a new Iraq. Iraqi women had enjoyed an unusual degree of liberty compared to their counterparts in other Muslim countries. Women made up a large proportion of Iraq's professional classes, and were free to make basic decisions, like choosing a husband. What would become of those basic rights now? "I want to move freely, live a joyful life out in the open," said Nimo Din'Kha Skander, the owner of Nimo's, a Baghdad beauty salon where Saddam's wife had had her hair done. "I don't want a government of religion." By midsummer, the U.S. Marine Corps, supervising the reconstruction of the city government in Najaf, had to postpone the swearing-in of the city's first-ever female judge after a wave of fatwas from senior Shiite clerics and heated protests from local lawyers, who charged that women were incapable of dispensing justice.

Zalmay Khalilzad, a National Security Council official who was President Bush's official envoy to the meeting at Tallil Air Base, did his best to allay fears that the United States would try to dominate the process of choosing new Iraqi leaders. "We have no intention of ruling Iraq," he said. "We want you to establish your own democratic system based on Iraqi traditions and values." The problem was that Iraqi traditions and values—venerable as they were—had virtually no connection to democracy. Modern Iraq had been created after World War I from three provinces of the defeated Ottoman Empire that had come under British control—Mosul in the north, Baghdad in the center and Basra in the south. The districts were composed, respectively, of Kurds, Sunni Muslims and Shiites, all of whom hated one another—and hated the occupying British colonial power even more. Winston Churchill, who as colonial secretary presided over the creation of Iraq, called the country "an ungrateful volcano."

For their part, the Iraqis had not forgotten that the first British-backed king, Faisal I, had been installed in a rigged plebiscite, and their suspicions of Western powers ran deep. From the beginning,

Faisal was seen as a British puppet, but he had higher aspirations to Arab independence and nationalism. The combination proved impossible. On the one hand, the king was at pains to prove his legitimacy to his new countrymen. On the other, Iraq's majority Shiite population chafed at domination by the Sunni elite that made up the monarch's circle, and feared absorption by the Sunni-dominated pan-Arab world, which viewed the Shiites as heretics. The result was decades of sectarian and ethnic feuding that culminated in the overthrow of the monarchy in 1958, followed by a succession of military and Baath Party coups—all of them brutal—before Saddam Hussein assumed total control in 1979.

Naturally enough, then, many Iraqis now viewed the American occupation, and the attempts to organize a new government, with the greatest wariness. Moreover, the Iraqis had no prism through which to filter their aspirations. Saddam had ruled through fear, intimidation and the exploitation and stoking of tribal and ethnic feuds. Roughly one in twelve Iraqis were members of the Baath Party, more out of fear and necessity than conviction, perhaps, but nonetheless a complicating factor in the creation of any new bureaucracy in a government expected to be democratic. "This is not Afghanistan; this is a country that's functioning," the historian Phebe Marr, author of *The Modern History of Iraq,* said before the war. "They can get the oil up, they can run the irrigation system, they can run the government. But that's very different from a political system. The liberal strand you need—tolerance, compromise—it's just not there."[1]

There were no easy answers in the first weeks after the fall of Baghdad. Some of the country's new self-proclaimed leaders operated at cross-purposes to the American authorities, who wanted to proceed cautiously and deliberately in setting up a new Iraqi government. Muhammad Mohsen Zobeidi, who in April declared himself the mayor of Baghdad and set up committees that he said would run the city under his direction, was arrested by the Americans later that month. Afterward, he issued a statement saying he was not, in fact, mayor and would cooperate with American authorities.

The exile leader Ahmad Chalabi posed a more complicated problem. His airlift by American forces into Nasiriya, while the fighting was still going on, had been controversial because, despite having the support of Paul Wolfowitz and others at the Pentagon, he was viewed with intense suspicion by many Iraqis. In 1992, Chalabi had been convicted in absentia by a Jordanian court of embezzlement and fraud, over the operations of a bank he had founded there. He denied the charges, claiming they were fostered by Saddam's regime, but not everyone believed him. Chalabi had boasted that he had a broad following among Iraqis, but these claims were already proving overstated. In February, he had been smuggled into northern Iraq, where he recruited and began training a small militia, which in turn became the core of the force that he took with him to Nasiriya. Now he and his supporters had set up shop in Baghdad's elite Hunting Club, apparently with the support of his allies within the Bush administration, but he was irritating other American officials with his imperious ways. If he could seize a private building for his headquarters, why shouldn't other groups? If he could have his own militia, why couldn't they? "What we have done is import mafias into Baghdad," one American official said.

On April 28, a gathering in Baghdad of some 300 Iraqis pledged to call a conference for a month later, to select a postwar transitional government—a faster timetable than many at the State Department had initially thought feasible, and one that would prove to be too optimistic. The challenge for the Americans was how to keep the process of transferring power to the Iraqis on track, without seeming to control it. Days later, a forty-two-year-old juice vendor named Abbas Mustafa Hussein seemed to speak for many Iraqis when he said, "I don't want the Americans here forever. But if they left in the next couple of days, there would be even more chaos."

OF ALL THE POLITICAL ISSUES involving Iraq, perhaps none was a greater lightning rod for scrutiny or criticism than oil. Donald Rumsfeld had insisted that the war "has nothing to do with oil, literally nothing to do with oil."[2] Even so, Iraq has the world's second-largest known pool of oil reserves—after Saudi Arabia—and has the potential to become the largest producer if its infrastructure is modernized. Dick Cheney once observed, in warning of Saddam's aspirations, that whoever sits atop the Middle Eastern oil market has a "stranglehold" on the global economy. For much of the past twenty years, Iraq's oil industry—battered first by the Iran-Iraq war, then the Persian Gulf war and the UN economic sanctions that barred oil exports—had been reduced to a shadow of its former self. From 1990 to 1996, Iraq stopped exporting oil entirely. Then the UN Security Council created the "oil-for-food" program, which regulated exports and was supposed to guarantee that the proceeds went to import food and other civilian necessities, and not to foster Saddam's military aspirations or prop up his regime. In fact, Saddam managed to divert proceeds from oil sales to just such illicit uses, pressing the industry to pump as much oil as possible from outmoded and poorly maintained wells. Now postwar looting, some of it apparently the result of deliberate sabotage by regime loyalists, had left the oil industry in the same mess as much of the rest of the country.

The Bush administration was counting on Iraq's oil revenues to finance the reconstruction of the country, and officials from the president on down repeatedly pledged that Iraq's oil belonged to the Iraqi people, and that the revenues from its sale would benefit them. But given the history of America's exploitation of Middle Eastern oil, and the resentments engendered over the decades, skepticism ran deep. "People in the region and beyond have a great suspicion of U.S. intentions, and with the U.S. and the U.K. in control of the second-biggest pot of oil in the Gulf region, those suspicions will be reinforced," said Judith Kipper, a Middle East expert at the Center for Strategic and International Studies in Washington. But because in its conduct of the war the United States acted so quickly to secure oil facilities while allowing other Iraqi institutions to be looted, Kipper added, "The perception that this is about oil is reinforced, and in the Middle East, perception is everything."

In late May, the Bush administration persuaded the UN Security Council to end the economic sanctions that had been in place against Iraq for nearly thirteen years, and to grant the United States and Britain an international mandate to occupy and reconstruct Iraq. The administration saw this as a significant diplomatic victory, since France, Germany and Russia—the main opponents of the war, all of whom had long-standing commercial interests in Iraq—voted to support the measure. But it was also a reflection of their unsentimental acceptance of the hard reality on the ground, and a way for the war's opponents to say to Washington, You asked for it, you got it.

The resolution required that Iraq's oil profits be deposited in a fund to benefit the Iraqi people, to be overseen by the United States and Britain with outside monitors, including the United Nations. But American oil companies remained reluctant to commit money to Iraq because of the ongoing lawlessness and security problems. Lee Raymond, the chairman and chief executive of Exxon Mobil, had predicted in March that "before a lot of money shows up, there's going to have to be a lot of confidence in the economic and political regime. People aren't going to just show up and start throwing money around."[3]

After the fall of Baghdad, that prediction was proving true. The extensive oil field fires that had been feared before the war had not occurred, but the Americans were having trouble stopping postwar sabotage of oil pipelines and refineries, and gasoline shortages were widespread. Oil analysts were now predicting that it would take at least five years, perhaps even twice that long, before Iraq's oil output reached its potential, and that it would cost at least $5 billion to rehabilitate its oil fields and make needed repairs. By late summer, fuel shortages in Basra were severe enough to prompt rioting, and United Nations officials warned that there was a "near certainty" that Iraq would face winter shortages of kerosene, a vital fuel for home heating in northern Iraq, because of the same problems that had led to the gasoline shortages. The black-market price for gasoline in Basra had soared to 60 cents a liter, about fifty times the official price, and the fuel shortages caused power failures at hospitals.

Another source of controversy grew out of complaints at home and abroad that too much of the money that the United States was spending on postwar reconstruction in Iraq was going to companies with business and political ties to the Bush administration. Before the war even began, the Army Corps of Engineers had chosen—without competitive bidding—Kellogg, Brown & Root to extinguish oil well fires and conduct emergency repairs on Iraq's oil fields in the event of hostilities. Kellogg, Brown & Root is a construction subsidiary of Halliburton Company, the Texas-based oil-field services company that Dick Cheney had headed before becoming vice president, and the Iraqi work had been added to an existing contract and justified on the grounds that the company already had the necessary security clearances and expertise. (Kellogg, Brown & Root had helped put out some 300 oil fires in Kuwait after the 1991 war.) But when the contract came to light, many members of Congress, Republicans as well as Democrats, were not happy. Senator Susan Collins, a moderate Republican from Maine, joined Senator Hillary Rodham Clinton of New York in sponsoring a bill that would require federal agencies to publicly explain and justify any closed bidding for reconstruction work in Iraq.

In late June, in part to counter the complaints about lack of openness, the Army Corps of Engineers announced plans to take bids for a new contract to rebuild the oil industry. But in early August, the Bechtel Group, one of the world's largest engineering and construction companies—which had long-standing Republican ties and had itself won an early reconstruction contract for Iraq—dropped out of the running, citing a timetable for the job that effectively favored Halliburton, which was already at work inside the country. That contract also helped to turn around Halliburton's troubled financial performance. The company made a profit of $26 million in the second quarter of 2003, in contrast to a loss of $498 million in the period a year earlier, and it said that revenues of $324 million during this period had come from work in Iraq. Statistics like these caused further erosion of the Bush administration's claims of impartiality in governing and reconstructing the country.

FOR MUCH OF MAY AND June, American officials in occupied Baghdad grappled with how to begin the transfer of political power to Iraqis in the face of the obvious and continuing instability in the country. In mid-May, the new American administrator in Iraq, L. Paul Bremer, announced an indefinite postponement of the earlier plan to form a national assembly and interim government by the end of the month. The United States was supported in this decision by its partners, the British. "It's quite clear that you cannot transfer all powers onto some interim body, because it will not have the strength or resources to carry those responsibilities out," said John Sawers, a British diplomat who had been sent to Baghdad to represent Prime Minister Tony Blair. "There was agreement that we should aim to have a national conference as soon as we reasonably could do so."

In a step intended to fight any resurgence of influence by Saddam's loyalists, Bremer issued an order banning as many as 30,000 top-ranking Baath Party members "from future employment in the public sector." On July 13, three months after the fall of Baghdad and following eight weeks of negotiations with American and British officials, twenty-five prominent Iraqis from a range of political, ethnic and religious backgrounds stepped onto the stage of a convention center in Baghdad and declared themselves the Governing Council, the first interim government of a new Iraq. The council said it would choose a rotating presidency from among its members and as its first act, it banned six national holidays that had been celebrated under Saddam, including the July 14 anniversary of the overthrow of the monarchy in 1958 and the July 17 anniversary of the Baath Party's seizure of power in 1968. The new national day would be April 9, the anniversary of the fall of Baghdad. One of the members, a Shiite cleric named Sayyed Muhammad Bahr al-Uloum, read a one-page statement declaring, "The establishment of this Council is an expression of the national Iraqi will in the wake of the collapse of the former oppressive regime."

The Governing Council would now begin the work of running the government, sending diplomats abroad, establishing a new currency, setting budget policy and drafting a new constitution. It would also move quickly to form a special war-crimes court to try members of the former regime. Within a week, the United States also announced plans to create a new civil defense force of 7,000 Iraqi militiamen trained by the Americans to help put an Iraqi face on the postwar security effort. "We hope that this Council will work for a very short time," said Abdul Aziz al-Hakim, another Shiite cleric who represented the Supreme Council for the Islamic Revolution of Iraq, which had earlier resisted participating in conferences organized by the Americans but now agreed to participate in the new body. "We should have a constitutional government and we should get rid of the occupation."

The council included returning exiles like Ahmad Chalabi, who was the only member to offer public thanks to the Americans and British for toppling Saddam's regime, and veteran Iraqi politicians like Adnan Pachachi, an eighty-year-old former foreign minister and UN ambassador from the pre-Saddam era. It was made up of doctors, lawyers, teachers, engineers, businessmen, a judge and three women. It embraced Shiites, Sunnis, Christians, Kurds and Turkmen. But its very diversity quickly raised questions about whether it could project unified goals and principles in a transitional period of old and new rivalries. In the north, the Kurds wanted to protect the autonomy they had won in the dozen years since the end of the Gulf war; in the center of the country, the Sunnis remained divided by mistrust for the occupation and old loyalties to Saddam; and the Shiites in the south once again feared that their majority status would be submerged by a Sunni elite.

Days later, Bremer said that there was still much work ahead to "undo the enormous economic damage" caused by Saddam's rule. But, he declared, "the timing of how long the coalition stays here is effectively now in the hands of the Iraqi people." In fact, it was not nearly so simple. At least some of the Iraqi people so resented the American presence that they resorted to increasingly violent and daring attacks on American soldiers—attacks that, for the moment, only seemed to guarantee that the Americans would stay longer.

IT BEGAN WITH SABOTAGE AND scattered resistance, the typical, inevitable aftermath of any war. It was looting, and crime, and at first it could be dismissed as such by American military commanders. But as the spring and summer wore on, it was clear that some Iraqis—and others who had come from Syria, Iran, Yemen and elsewhere to join the fray—were waging a dogged and increasingly determined campaign against American troops. The effort may have lacked central direction, but it showed signs of at least local coordination. It did not involve tanks or other heavy armor. Rocket-propelled grenades and small arms were the weapons of choice. But it was brutal, and deliberate, and it was taking a toll. By the Pentagon's account, 138 Americans had died from all causes during the period from the start of the war to May 1, when Bush landed on the deck of the *Abraham Lincoln*. By early September, nearly 150 additional Americans had been killed in the continuing fighting or had died from non-combat causes, and scores of others had been wounded.

Resistance was toughest in the so-called Sunni Triangle, bounded by Baghdad in the east, Ramadi in the west and Tikrit in the north. The organized attacks began to increase in frequency in June. At first, there were on average about a dozen attacks a day, but now that rate had doubled. Commanders even began to worry about keeping their supply lines to Kuwait open. Finally, the Americans felt compelled to begin large-scale operations in response, including one that involved 143 raids across the country and detained almost 700 loyalists of the old regime, together with assorted criminals. Several dozen of the people seized proved to be "high-value targets," former Baath Party officials or other leaders of Saddam's regime.

For American soldiers, the work—and the risks—were grinding. "You call Donald Rumsfeld and tell him our sorry asses are ready to go home," Private First Class Matthew C. O'Dell, an infantryman in the Third Infantry's 1st Brigade, told a reporter in mid-June. But in Washington, President Bush almost seemed to taunt the Iraqi fighters. "There are some who feel like that if they attack us that we may decide to leave prematurely," Bush said in early July. "They don't understand what they're talking about, if that's the case." When a reporter tried to ask him another question, the president said, "Let me finish. There are some who feel like—that the conditions are such that they can attack us there. My answer is, bring 'em on." The next day, an American soldier was killed and at least ten were wounded in two attacks in central Iraq.

Chapter 20

CASUS BELLI

Washington, D.C.
Wednesday, May 28, 2003

I t was an unusual public announcement by the CIA. Two mysterious trailers found in Iraq in April and May, the statement said, were mobile units designed to produce deadly germs, and were "the strongest evidence to date that Iraq was hiding a biological warfare program." For weeks, there had been intense speculation about the purpose and importance of the trailers. Now, the Bush administration seemed to be offering definitive word: The CIA's analysis, done in collaboration with the Defense Intelligence Agency and posted on the CIA Web site, concluded that each trailer could brew enough germs to produce, without further processing, one or two kilograms of dried agent each month. That seemingly small amount—a kilogram is 2.2 pounds—could wreak havoc if released into the wind, or in an urban subway system. By comparison, the anthrax-tainted letters that had killed five Americans and put more than 30,000 citizens on protective antibiotics in the fall of 2001 each contained only about a gram of dried anthrax spores. "If you're looking at kilograms," one intelligence official said, "you're talking about thousands of people."

In an interview with Polish television broadcast two days later, President Bush declared: "We've found the weapons of mass destruction. You know, we found biological laboratories. You remember when Colin Powell stood up in front of the world and he said Iraq has got laboratories, mobile labs to build biological weapons? They're illegal. They're against the United Nations' resolutions and we've so far discovered two. And we'll find more weapons as time goes on. But for those who say we haven't found the banned manufacturing devices or banned weapons, they're wrong. We found them."[1]

If only it were that simple. Even allowing for Bush's presumably unintentional equation of the trailers with actual weapons, within the administration doubts remained about the evidence and its implications. As the intelligence agencies themselves announced their findings, one intelligence official acknowledged that a technical assessment of the equipment alone "would not lead you intuitively and logically to biological warfare." The trailers' hardware presented no direct evidence of having been in contact with pathogens or of having been used to produce weapons. The gear was rusty, perhaps from sitting in the rain. The mobile factories were poorly designed. But the CIA analysts had concluded that the trailers' very inefficiencies were probably conceived with deceit in mind—to bolster a claim, if the trailers were ever discovered, that they had benign uses. The best evidence that the trailers were intended to make weapons was their close resemblance to prewar descriptions, supplied by Iraqi informers, of mobile germ labs constructed by Saddam's scientists.

Within days, the CIA's claims came under stiff international criticism. Other American and British intelligence officials who had direct access to the evidence sharply disputed the CIA's view. These skeptics said that the trailers lacked gear for steam sterilization, normally a prerequisite for any kind of biological production, peaceful or otherwise. Each unit could produce only a relatively small amount of germ-laden liquid, which would have to undergo further processing to make it concentrated for use as a weapon. By late June, word surfaced that the State Department's intelligence arm—which had earlier raised doubts about Iraq's purported attempts to buy uranium in Africa—was disputing the CIA's conclusions about the trailers. And by August, engineering experts from the Defense Intelligence Agency had come to believe that the most likely use for the trailers was to produce hydrogen for weather balloons, which were used in Iraqi artillery practice.

Officials at the CIA and the Defense Department nonetheless stood by their earlier findings. But the continuing debate put President Bush—and his British ally Tony Blair—on the defensive for months. After all, as the president's press secretary, Ari Fleischer, had said the day after Baghdad fell, weapons of mass destruction were "what this war was about." The National Intelligence Estimate in October 2002, representing the government's consensus view at the time, had flatly stated, "Baghdad has chemical and biological weapons." Now the failure to find such weapons—let alone evidence of an active nuclear program—loomed as one of the great mysteries of the aftermath of the campaign to oust Saddam Hussein. There was no doubt that at one time Saddam had possessed and used chemical weapons; the scarred Kurdish residents of Halabja were living proof of that. But where were these weapons now? Had they been destroyed after the 1991 Gulf war, as Iraq had long claimed? Had they been destroyed more recently? Was the American advance so swift that Saddam did not have time to issue orders to deploy chemical and biological weapons? Were they still hidden so effectively that it would take American troops months to find them? Were the "weapons" more accurately a series of seemingly benign industrial or agricultural products that could be assembled into poisons on short notice? In the months after Saddam disappeared, no one could be sure. But it was a question of more than passing interest. It was central to the Bush administration's rationale for the war in Iraq, and had broad implications for judging when—and whether—preemptive action could be justified to keep dangerous groups or nations from obtaining the most deadly weapons.

FOR WEEKS IN APRIL, MAY and June, American troops turned up tantalizing hints and tips about possible weapons: fifty-five-gallon drums of suspicious liquids, caches of powder, gas masks, suspected blister agents, possibly radioactive material, the mobile trailers. In the early days, each discovery was trumpeted as a potential smoking gun. Each in turn turned out to be less than met the eye.

There was a list of nearly a thousand potential sites to search, but the Americans faced daunting problems of execution and coordination. United Nations inspectors had spent the better part of the 1990s looking for weapons in Iraq, but now the Pentagon was determined to keep control of the search in American hands. Some foreign experts, including former UN inspectors, were recruited to join the hunt, but some of them complained that bureaucratic infighting had delayed the effort, and that some military units did not know enough about what they were looking for to conduct thorough searches. Worse, many U.S. search teams lacked Arabic language skills. "They're going to blow it," one would-be inspector said, days after Baghdad fell. "That's the concern of a number of us."

One American military unit, Site Survey Team 3, dug up a playground, raided a distillery and scoured a swimming pool in search of suspected weapons sites. One search of a suspected outpost of Saddam's Special Security Organization led through a series of locked doors and a dank, moldy corridor, only to find a bunch of vacuum cleaners.[2]

In late April, another American military unit in the hunt for unconventional weapons in Iraq, Mobile Exploitation Team Alpha, located a man who said he had been a scientist in Iraq's chemical weapons program for more than a decade, and he made a sensational claim: that Iraq had destroyed chemical weapons and biological warfare equipment only days before the war began. The man also told the Americans that Iraq had secretly sent unconventional weapons and technology to Syria, starting in the mid-1990s, and more recently had cooperated with Al Qaeda. Months later, the man's claims had not been substantiated, and American officials publicly disclosed no more about his identity.

But there were other suggestions that Iraq had continued to pursue illicit weapons. In early June, a former senior Iraqi intelligence officer—a brigadier general—told the *Los Angeles Times* that Saddam's intelligence services had set up a clandestine network of cells and small laboratories in the mid-1990s, with the aim of someday rebuilding the means to manufacture banned chemical and biological weapons. The officer reported that while no banned weapons existed to be discovered, they could have been quickly produced as soon as the UN sanctions against Iraq were lifted.[3]

Similar indications emerged about Saddam's nuclear program—that the scientists who had worked on it before 1991 retained plans and knowledge—though there was no immediate confirmation of an active ongoing effort to build a bomb. In June, the CIA confirmed that an Iraqi scientist, Mahdi Obeidi, who had headed Iraq's uranium enrichment program in the 1980s and early 1990s, had turned over some components of a gas centrifuge, a machine used to enrich uranium for nuclear weapons, as well as blueprints for building and operating such a device. He said that he had been ordered by Saddam Hussein's son Qusay to bury the material in his rose garden in 1991. While the discovery revealed that the Iraqi regime was willing to hide materials that it was supposed to disclose, the components and blue-prints were nonetheless a long way from an actual weapon. They amounted to templates that could be used to build the hundreds or thousands of centrifuges needed to produce bomb-grade uranium. "What's significant," one intelligence official said, "is these documents and components were deliberately hidden at the direction of Iraq's senior leadership with the aim of preserving the regime's capacity to resume construction of a centrifuge that at some point could be used to enrich uranium for a nuclear device." Even so, it seemed clear that Iraq's nuclear program was in deep hibernation. In the period from 1998 to 2002, when UN inspectors had been barred from Iraq, Obeidi was never told to dig up his buried treasures.

That may help explain why Saddam was never willing to satisfy the UN inspectors that he had disposed of his banned weapons, despite the cost of billions of dollars in forsaken oil revenues. By keeping the question open, he may have had three goals in mind: first, to save face and maintain his standing within the Arab world; second, to deter or limit the scope of any military action by the United States; and third, to keep the Iraqi people in a state of fear, the better to control them.

For their part, President Bush and his advisers were simply unwilling to imagine that Saddam had not retained at least some banned weapons. To think otherwise would be to ignore too many years of accumulated evidence—about Saddam and his intentions—and too many unanswered questions, questions that had been raised in part by two separate UN inspection regimes with international support. At the very least, as Colin Powell had suggested, the Iraqi regime's scientists had retained the knowledge needed to produce such weapons. For Bush, trusting Saddam's goodwill was never an option.

IN BRITAIN, TONY BLAIR WAS facing harsh questions about his government's role in gathering and publishing what now looked like suspect intelligence on Saddam Hussein's weapons programs. In late May the British Broadcasting Corporation (BBC) reported that "one of the senior officials in charge of drawing up" the September 2002 government report stating that the Iraqi military could deploy chemical or biological weapons within forty-five minutes now claimed that some in the government had expressed doubts about that information, but that the prime minister's office ordered it to be included anyway, so that the report would be "sexed up." The alleged culprit was Blair's communications adviser, Alastair Campbell, who hotly denied the charge. A huge feud between the Blair government and the BBC followed, along with a parliamentary inquiry.

Blair was under pressure because the decision to go to war had never been popular among the British public. Now that doubts were emerging about the validity of the prewar intelligence estimates and British troops were coming under attack by disgruntled Iraqis in and around Basra (on June 24, six British soldiers were killed after being trapped by an angry mob in the southern Iraqi town of Majar al Kabir), Blair's political opponents were quick to seize the initiative.

In early July, reports began to surface in the British press that David Kelly, an expert in chemical and biological warfare at the British Defence Ministry, had been the source of the BBC's story about the "sexed up" intelligence report. On July 15 and 16, Kelly was summoned to testify before two parliamentary committees, where he underwent harsh questioning about what he knew and to whom he told it. Kelly acknowledged that he had met with the BBC reporter, Andrew Gilligan, to discuss Iraq's weapons programs but said that he did not see how Gilligan "could make the statements he was making from the comments that I made." For one thing, Kelly said, he had not been involved in the final drafting of the September dossier, but had only written a historical section on weapons inspectors and concealment, though he did acknowledge discussing the forty-five-minute claim and Campbell's role in drafting the dossier. Kelly's exchanges with his questioners were tense and sometimes confused. The day after his testimony ended, Kelly did not return from a walk in the woods near his home, and his body was soon found, the left wrist slashed in apparent suicide. Two days later, the BBC asserted that Kelly had indeed been the principal source of its disputed report.

Blair promised a full investigation into the events leading up to Kelly's death, but insisted all the same that his policy on Iraq had been correct. "People need to know that what we did in Iraq was right and justified, and that's a case that we have to not just assert but prove over time."

As THE SUMMER WORE ON, President Bush took to hedging his statements about Iraq's weapons capacity. Barely a week after his assertion that Americans had "found the weapons," the president told troops at Tommy Franks's headquarters in Qatar that the discovery of the trailers showed that Saddam was "capable" of producing biological weapons. Later, Bush took to speaking of his conviction that Iraq had a "weapons program," a formulation that could comfortably cover plans and equipment, without necessarily making a claim about the weapons themselves. By late July, debates over the accuracy of prewar intelligence focused on the sixteen words in Bush's State of the Union address about Iraq's alleged attempts to acquire uranium from Africa, which had been included in the speech despite ample warnings that the evidence backing the claim was suspect. Stephen Hadley, the deputy national security adviser, eventually stepped up to take the blame, but only after a round of finger-pointing between the White House and the CIA. Even so, the president said he was confident that banned weapons would eventually be found in Iraq, and suggested that the effort to find them was motivated more by political reality than moral necessity. "In order to placate the critics and the cynics about intentions of the United States, we need to produce evidence," Bush said. "And I fully understand that. And I'm confident that our search will yield that which I strongly believe: that Saddam had a weapons program."

There were any number of potentially justifiable reasons for going to war in Iraq, including Saddam's brutal and destabilizing effect on his country and the region. The testimony of survivors, the horrific mass graves that American forces helped uncover, the stories of torture, terror and privation after Baghdad fell made that abundantly clear. But President Bush had repeatedly made the case that the United States could not afford to wait to strike Iraq because Saddam possessed horribly destructive weapons and might get more. This was the most urgent rationale for war, and the strongest rebuttal to those critics who argued that Iraq could be contained. In the wake of the September 11 attacks, American policy makers of all political stripes expressed palpable fear that a terrorist armed with even the crudest kind of nuclear device could cause untold havoc. No one could be sure where such material might come from, and many government officials were unsure whether the intelligence agencies had the capacity to find out before it was too late. The CIA and FBI had failed to piece together a potentially telling series of clues leading up to the September 11 attacks. The CIA had also failed to anticipate India's decision to resume nuclear testing in 1998. And many administration officials who had served in the first Bush administration, including Dick Cheney, had never forgotten the CIA's inability to predict the scope of Iraq's nascent nuclear program before the 1991 Gulf war.

Finding reliable intelligence was a perpetual challenge to all governments, but it was of crucial importance to the United States if it sought to justify future applications of the Bush Doctrine. If preemption was justified as the best way to stop terrorists or rogue nations from acquiring devastatingly destructive weapons, everything depended on being able to ascertain, swiftly and correctly, how determined such nations and groups were to get such weapons, and how close they were to having them. The experience in Iraq showed how hard it was to know for certain what the threats might be. And the early months of fruitless searching raised provocative questions, for Bush's supporters and critics alike, about just how high the standard of certainty needed to be before American lives and treasure were committed to a preemptive attack. Perhaps no national security challenge loomed larger in the post–September 11 world, and far from settling the question, the war in Iraq may have created a whole new set of doubts.

THE SECOND MOST URGENT OF the Bush administration's rationales for going to war was its assertion that Saddam's regime was aiding and abetting terrorism, with shadowy links to Al Qaeda, in particular. There were widespread doubts about the veracity of such assertions before the war, and in the period after the fall of Baghdad, considerable new evidence emerged to cast even more pointed doubts on these claims as well. In early June, intelligence officials told *The New York Times* that two of the highest-ranking Al Qaeda leaders in American custody had told the CIA in separate interrogations that their organization had not worked jointly with the Iraqi government. Abu Zubaydah, an Al Qaeda planner and recruiter until his capture in March 2002, had told his questioners that the idea of working with Saddam's regime had been discussed among Al Qaeda leaders but that Osama bin Laden himself had rejected such proposals because he did not want to be beholden to the Iraqi leader. Separately, Khalid Sheikh Mohammed, Al Qaeda's chief of operations until his capture in Pakistan just before the Iraq war began, told interrogators that the group had not worked with Saddam. The Bush administration had never made such statements public, though it had frequently sought to highlight whatever fragmentary intelligence information it could muster that might suggest ties between Baghdad and Al Qaeda.

By late summer, a new and troubling possibility emerged: that whether or not Al Qaeda had been active in Iraq before the war, groups of Muslim extremists with similar motives were almost certainly active there in the aftermath of the war, motivated by outrage at the American occupation and determined to resist it. In early August, a car bomb attack on the Jordanian embassy suggested a possibly ominous new style of terrorist activity in Iraq; American officials said that they were investigating the possibility that elements of the Ansar al-Islam group, which had been routed in northern Iraq during the war, might have fled to Iran but then regrouped inside Iraq, with plans for more large-scale attacks. Ambassador Bremer characterized the group's history in blunt terms: "They do big stuff; they don't do chicken-feed-type stuff." Ansar al-Islam was widely believed to have links to Al Qaeda, and while investigators left open many possibilities, the date of the attack, August 7, had eerie overtones. It was the fifth anniversary of Al Qaeda's 1998 bombing of the American embassies in Kenya and Tanzania and the thirteenth anniversary of the date in 1990 that President Bush's father had dispatched the first American troops to Saudi Arabia, in response to Saddam Hussein's invasion of Kuwait—a deployment repeatedly cited by Osama bin Laden as being at the core of Al Qaeda's grievances against the United States.

The attack on the Jordanian embassy escalated the violence in Baghdad from guerrilla warfare against armed American troops to a more traditional kind of terrorism against a "soft" civilian target. It killed seventeen people and wounded scores more and was the deadliest attack against civilians since the American military took control in Baghdad. The motive was unclear, but Jordan was among the Arab countries friendliest to Washington and had facilitated the American war effort in Iraq. Whatever the reason, American officers were troubled at the prospect that militants from Syria, Saudi Arabia, Yemen and other countries had been crossing into Iraq from Syria. The fear was that young Muslim militants were now being drawn to fight the infidel in Baghdad in much the same way that their fathers and uncles had gone to fight the Soviets in Afghanistan. "Iraq is the nexus where many issues are coming together—Islam versus democracy, the West versus the axis of evil, Arab nationalism versus some different types of political culture," said Barham Saleh, a Kurdish official in northern Iraq. "If the Americans succeed here, this will be a monumental blow to everything the terrorists stand for."

Twelve days later, the threat escalated even more dramatically when an even bigger truck bomb destroyed much of the United Nations headquarters in Baghdad, killing the chief UN envoy to Iraq, Sergio Vieira de Mello, and 22 others and wounding at least 100 people. The suicide attack seemed squarely aimed at destroying any sense of security for the workers charged with reviving Iraq, whoever they worked for and whatever their views on the war. So did the late-August car-bombing of the holiest Shiite shrine, in Najaf, which killed nearly 100 people, including Ayatollah Muhammad Bakar al-Hakim, the most prominent Shiite cleric cooperating with the American reconstruction effort.

THE BUSH ADMINISTRATION HAD FOCUSED on Saddam's potential weapons as a matter of hard-nosed reality and cold-blooded calculation about the risks of leaving the Iraqi regime unchecked. But, in a larger sense, no particular piece of intelligence about the Iraqi threat— whether it involved weapons, terrorism or any other question—was as important in shaping the administration's core policy as the abiding faith of the president and most of his top advisers that Iraq was simply not to be trusted. In an interview with *Vanity Fair* magazine in May,

Paul Wolfowitz seemed to suggest that, in building the case for war, the administration had emphasized the threat of weapons of mass destruction as much for tactical as for strategic reasons. "The truth is that for reasons that have a lot to do with the U.S. government bureaucracy, we settled on the one issue that everyone could agree on, which was weapons of mass destruction as the core reason," he said.[4]

That was true enough, but only part of the explanation. Bureaucracies favor the most dogged advocates, and Wolfowitz, Cheney and Rumsfeld were tireless advocates for taking on Saddam. As veterans of the first Bush administration, the Iraq hawks saw Saddam as unfinished business, and their personal experience convinced them that no one could err by overestimating his malevolence. They were sure that their worst assumptions had to be true.

In 1976, Wolfowitz had been part of a famous CIA working group called "Team B," which questioned the government's official prevailing estimates of the Soviet Union's mind-set and capabilities in its Cold War struggle with the United States. The point of the exercise was to have smart outsiders second-guess the government's conventional wisdom, and one result of Team B's hawkish reports was to cast doubt on the policy of détente, setting the stage for Ronald Reagan's arms buildup in the 1980s, a confrontational strategy that some later credited with helping to bring down the Soviet empire. But with respect to Iraq policy in 2001 and 2002, Wolfowitz and other top Bush administration aides were themselves Team B, pressing the American intelligence community for every shred of potential evidence about Iraq, and viewing Iraqi intentions through the darkest, most skeptical glass. The problem was that there were few advocates of a more conciliatory posture to argue effectively against the hawks, and the policy momentum was clearly in one direction only. Douglas Feith, the undersecretary of defense for policy, who headed the Pentagon's prewar efforts to review Iraq-related intelligence, flatly rejected any suggestion that intelligence analysts had been pressured to tailor their conclusions to fit administration policy. "This suggestion that we said to them, 'This is what we're looking for, go find it,' is precisely the inaccuracy that we're here to rebut. I know of nobody who pressured anybody," he said. But some intelligence analysts did report feeling pressured all the same.

The decision to go to war apparently was not so much dependent on any particular piece of new or old evidence, but rather was the result of a larger global strategy. In testimony before the Senate Armed Services Committee in July 2003, Secretary Rumsfeld said succinctly, "The coalition did not act in Iraq because we had discovered dramatic new evidence of Iraq's pursuit of weapons of mass murder. We acted because we saw the existing evidence in a new light through the prism of our experience on September 11." This rationale was endorsed by large segments of the American public, thanks to the Bush administration's dogged efforts to link the two issues. In the months after the fall of Baghdad, polls showed that a quarter of Americans believed that weapons of mass destruction had in fact been found in Iraq, and that fully half believed that Saddam was personally involved in the 9/11 attacks.

Wolfowitz himself said in the *Vanity Fair* interview that at that first meeting at Camp David after the September 11 attacks, when Iraq came up and the decision was made to focus first on the Taliban, "To the extent it was a debate about tactics and timing, the President clearly came down on the side of Afghanistan first. To the extent it was a debate about strategy and what the larger goal was, it is at least clear with 20/20 hindsight that the President came down on the side of the larger goal."[5]

To some in the administration, it was far from clear just when the president and his advisers passed the point of no return. Richard Haass, who was the State Department's director of policy planning, recalled a discussion with Condoleezza Rice in early July 2002, when he asked her if it really made sense to put Iraq at the center of the foreign policy agenda, at a time when the administration was already engaged in a worldwide campaign against terrorism. "And she said, essentially, that that decision's been made, don't waste your breath," Haass recalled.[6] Evidence like Haass's conversation notwithstanding, Colin Powell arranged to have his first long, private discussion with Bush about Iraq a month later because he was convinced that, whatever Bush's predisposition, no one had yet presented the president with a full range of options. By then, of course, it may have been too late to change the president's course. "Sometimes," one senior official said later, "decisions happen as much as they're made."

Chapter 21

THE PRICE OF GOING IT ALONE

Paris
Tuesday, July 15, 2003

President Jacques Chirac put out the word without being asked, in a meeting with the president of the Czech Republic: France would not send troops to Iraq to help the American-led peacekeeping effort. Chirac's announcement was hardly a surprise, of course. He had been saying the same thing privately in other recent meetings with the leaders of Germany and Russia, and his foreign minister, Dominique de Villepin, had made it clear that France would consider sending troops to Iraq only if they were part of a mission under the authority of the United Nations.

The Americans were determined to maintain control in Iraq. That cost them the support of other nations—rejections that were more troubling than the predictable French response. The day before Chirac spoke, India had refused an American request to send a full army division (17,000 or more soldiers) to Iraq. It, too, insisted on a UN mandate before committing its troops. That was a particular blow because American-Indian relations had recently been flourishing after decades of Cold War tensions, and the Bush administration had hoped an Indian contingent would set a model for participation by developing countries.

By early August, eighteen nations besides the United States had a military presence in Iraq, and the Pentagon had announced that nineteen more had promised to send forces. But there were a total of only about 21,000 non-American troops on the ground in Iraq, 11,000 of them British, compared with about 140,000 Americans. That meant that the other "coalition" partners—nations like Albania, Estonia, Georgia, Latvia, Lithuania, Poland, Slovakia and Spain—had each contributed an average of fewer than 600 troops. The high cost of go-it-aloneism was becoming apparent, and Donald Rumsfeld and other administration officials were facing increasing pressure from Congress to find more partners to share the burden. At a hearing of the Senate Foreign Relations Committee in late July, President Bush's new budget director, Joshua B. Bolten, said it was impossible to predict how many troops would be needed in the coming year, and what they would cost. Senator Joseph Biden, the committee's ranking Democrat, erupted: "Oh, come on now! Does anybody here at the table think we're going to be down below 100,000 forces in the next calendar year? When are you guys starting to be honest with us?"

Money was also becoming an issue. Administration officials expected the cost of reconstruction through the end of 2003 to be about $7 billion, and so far they had managed to finance that from a variety of sources, including Iraqi assets that had been frozen in American banks since the Gulf war, some $900 million found stashed in hiding places in Iraq after the fall of Baghdad, and other money from congressional appropriations. But those funds would run out at year's end, and it was unclear to what extent sales of Iraqi oil would be able to bridge the gap. The administration was hoping to organize an international conference of donors in the fall, to explore additional sources of funding. However, the president of the World Bank, James D. Wolfensohn, suggested during the summer that it would lend money for the reconstruction of Iraq only after the country wrote a constitution and conducted national elections, and restructured or shut down a number of its state-run industries. All that could take well over a year. And in a frank assessment of the task ahead, Ambassador Bremer observed that in the period from 2003 to 2007, the amount of outside money required for reconstructing Iraq would be "staggering."

Paul Wolfowitz, also testifying before the Senate Foreign Relations Committee, said that Washington would welcome a new UN resolution that might attract peacekeepers from countries like India and Pakistan, but only if it did not restrict or dilute the authority of the American administration in Baghdad. "I'd be very enthusiastic about the right kind of resolution," Wolfowitz said, "and very concerned about the wrong kind."

So, having been determined to wage war largely alone, the United States was now being forced to win the peace largely alone, too.

• • •

IN THE AFTERMATH OF THE fall of Saddam Hussein's regime, the watchword in relations between the United States and opponents of the war was "pragmatism," as one American diplomat put it. The two sides still disagreed deeply whether it had been right to go to war, but they would have to deal with the facts on the ground as they now stood and make their respective judgments from that starting point. "We haven't changed our analysis that the war wasn't necessary," one senior French official said in April. "We don't feel guilty. But now is a different time." Despite their unyielding opposition to the war, France, Germany and Russia acceded relatively quickly to the passage of the Security Council resolution on May 22 granting the United States and Britain the authority to administer postwar Iraq. And in August, the Security Council passed a resolution that said the UN "welcomes" the new Iraqi Governing Council, which was seen as a first step toward eventual recognition of it, or its successors, as a new sovereign government. But even that amounted to tepid support for the Americans; the Bush administration had preferred wording that would have said the UN "endorses" the new Iraqi council.

For their part, American officials were warning that dealings with countries like France and Germany on matters from trade to military-to-military cooperation would be complicated, and that there would be "consequences" for opponents of the war, a nonspecific threat that implied retaliation without spelling it out. Some Bush administration officials saw demands by Germany, France and Russia, in particular, for a greater role in postwar Iraq as reflecting a desire on the part of these nations to get more contracts and economic benefits for themselves and their corporations. Of course the Europeans saw the postwar contracts for American companies like Halliburton as reflecting the same sort of self-interest. There was an unmistakable transatlantic chill. President Bush himself said of Jacques Chirac, "I doubt he'll be coming to the ranch any time soon." But Bush also added that he hoped "the past tensions will subside and the French won't be using their position within Europe to create alliances against the United States or Britain or Spain, or any of the new countries that are the new democracies in Europe."[1]

In late July 2003, UN Secretary-General Kofi Annan suggested that the jury was still out on the aftereffects of America's action in Iraq. "Many of us sense that we are living through a crisis of the international system," he said, adding that the UN needed to have a fuller discussion of the issues. He posed the question, if "indeed we are going to make preventive action, or war, part of our response to these new threats, what are the rules?" At one point, Annan said with the barest hint of satisfaction, "I did warn those who were bashing the United Nations that they had to be careful, because they might need the United Nations soon."

During the preceding decade, the United States had always relied on international support for its efforts at nation-building, in Somalia, Haiti, Bosnia, Kosovo and most recently Afghanistan. James Dobbins, who served the Clinton and Bush administrations as special envoy to all these countries, noted that the global context of 2003 was different from that of 1945, when the United States singlehandedly oversaw nation-building in Japan and played the dominant role in Germany at the same time. He pointed out that while the United States produced more than half the world's wealth at the end of World War II—and was thus uniquely qualified to take on the burdens of postwar reconstruction—it now produced less than one-quarter of global wealth, so "burden-sharing is not only more feasible, it's necessary."[2]

IN THE MIDDLE OF THE war, when it seemed that Iran and Syria might be tempted to intercede on Baghdad's behalf, Donald Rumsfeld declared that any "hostile acts" by those countries would prompt severe consequences. When one of President Bush's aides stepped into the Oval Office to warn him that his blunt-spoken defense chief had just raised the specter of a broader confrontation, Bush just smiled for a moment and replied, "Good," before turning back to work.

In the aftermath of Baghdad's fall, America's allies and opponents around the world weighed Bush's every word for signs of his future intentions. After all, Iraq had been one of three countries specifically singled out as evil. What did the American military victory there portend for Iran and North Korea, the other regimes in the "axis of evil"? Or Syria, for that matter?

For his part, Bush was insisting that he had no plans for another war. "I have no specific operation in mind at this point in time," he said in late April. "I can't think of a specific moment or incident that would require military action as we speak." Even some of the most ardent advocates of American military action in Iraq were urging caution. After the fall of Baghdad, *The Weekly Standard* ran an editorial making the point that "further countries don't have to be singled out for invasion," and urging the Bush administration to "use the influence gained from the triumph" by employing "psychological leverage." For William Kristol, the magazine's editor, who had long been in the forefront of those urging military action in Iraq, this represented a distinct softening of his position. In the months leading up to the war, Kristol had written a book with Lawrence Kaplan called *The War over Iraq*, which concluded, "The mission begins in Baghdad, but it does not end there."[3]

The truth was that with 240,000 troops serving in the Middle East and Afghanistan, American military forces were stretched thin. By August, some 2,300 American marines were waiting in ships off the coast of Liberia for possible participation in a peacekeeping effort there, following the resignation of President Charles Taylor. The Army had 368,900 soldiers on duty in 120 countries, a number that included 232,759 active-duty troops from a force of 485,000; 74,551 National Guard members from a pool of 352,000; and 61,590 reservists out of a force of 206,000. "Certainly the force is stretched," said General John M. Keane, the acting Army chief of staff.

In sum, there was ample reason for the Bush administration to focus on diplomacy as major combat operations came to a close in Iraq and ample reason to pull back from the strong unilateral stance that had preceded the war. As spring turned to summer, the president kept up his stern warnings to Iran and Syria that they would be "held accountable" if they continued to aid Middle Eastern terrorists or disrupted the occupation of Iraq. In June, Bush said for the first time that Washington and its allies "will not tolerate the construction of a nuclear weapon" in Iran, and White House officials said that they hoped to begin working soon with allies on intercepting ships and aircraft suspected of carrying material that could aid Iran or North Korea in their nuclear programs. Both countries appeared to be accelerating their programs, presumably in an effort to acquire nuclear weapons before the United States could take action against them, as it had against Iraq.

But the prospect of military action against either country was in many ways riskier and more fraught than acting against Saddam had been. Saddam had been an international pariah; by contrast, many nations in Europe and elsewhere have extensive trade relations with Iran and rely on its oil. Iran is also more than three times the size of Iraq, with a population three times as large; invading and occupying it would be a monumental task, even if the full power of the U.S. military had been available. With so much of the force tied down in Iraq, unilateral military action would be all but impossible. Bush had said that he was concerned about keeping weapons out of the hands of Iran's ruling "radical clerics," but most administration officials believed that Iran was determined to pursue a nuclear program, whoever ran the country. The arrival of the occupying Americans next door in Iraq had presumably only strengthened Iranian determination. A senior White House official described the president's warning as a "carefully worded escalation," but Bush had never publicly mentioned any possibility of military action against Iran.

By contrast, Bush had rattled sabers over North Korea. The administration had long suspected that the Communist regime there was not upholding the agreement it had negotiated with the United States in 1994. That agreement had come after North Korea announced its intention to withdraw from the Nuclear Non-Proliferation Treaty and to extract weapons-grade plutonium from its nuclear reactor. The Clinton administration had seriously considered ordering a military strike on the reactor in response, but in the end Washington was able to reach an agreement with Pyongyang to freeze its weapons program in return for assistance from the United States and other nations to cope with its fuel shortages, and to aid construction of two civilian nuclear power plants. The Bush administration declared soon after taking office in 2001 that it would not conduct further negotiations with North Korea until it had completed its own review of existing policy, and a year later, Bush branded the country as part of the "axis of evil" because of what he said was its continuing desire to develop nuclear weapons. The following October, North Korea precipitated a new crisis by admitting that it had indeed built a secret weapons program in violation of the 1994 agreement.

One rationale for taking military action against Iraq had been to keep Saddam Hussein from developing a nuclear weapon, which would have made him infinitely more dangerous to the region and the world. And so in March, before the war in Iraq began, Bush warned the North Korean leader, Kim Jong Il, that if the options "don't work diplomatically, they'll have to work militarily." But American policy makers also knew that whether or not North Korea already had nuclear weapons capability, the situations call for more delicate handling— and the help of allies like Japan and strategic cooperation from China and Russia. Going it alone was the last thing the Bush administration wanted to do with North Korea.

By the summer of 2003, Colin Powell was acknowledging that "no issue is of greater urgency to the U.S. than North Korea's nuclear weapons programs," and that he and the president were seeking broader Asian and international support for isolating the country. President Bush added that America and its allies would work to convince Kim Jong Il "that his decision is an unwise decision." In truth, if North Korea declared itself a nuclear state, Washington would face very unpalatable choices. Strategic air strikes against nuclear facilities remained an option, but the prospects of a full-scale American invasion and potential nuclear war were horrifying. Thousands of American troops still stationed on the Korean peninsula a half century after the end of the Korean War—and millions of South Korean civilians— would be at risk.

In the months since its assertion that it had resumed its nuclear weapons program, North Korea had pressed Washington for one-on-one talks, which the Bush administration steadfastly refused. At the beginning of August, in the face of unrelenting American resistance, North Korea finally agreed to participate in regional, multiparty negotiations with the United States, China, Russia, Japan and South Korea. Bush said he was now hopeful that Kim Jong Il, "because he's hearing other voices, will make the decision to totally dismantle his nuclear weapons program, that he will allow there to be complete transparency and verifiability."

Diplomacy seemed to be bearing fruit. But the story was far from finished.

•   •   •

NO REGION WAS MORE AFFECTED by America's war in Iraq than the Middle East itself. It was there that Paul Wolfowitz's optimistic prewar vision of spreading democracy and building regimes friendly to American interests would be tested. The early results were decidedly mixed. There was every bit as much evidence—if not more—that the war had inflamed anti-American feeling in the Arab and Muslim lands and had put American lives and installations at fresh risk as there were signs that toppling Saddam had made America safer.

In the aftermath of battle, Iraq's neighbors began to come to grips with a new Middle East that was dominated as never before by the United States, and they did so with varying degrees of dread and cautious hope. During the war, many Arab governments effectively encouraged rampant hostility to the United States, as state-supported newspapers and television stations reported that American forces were deliberately killing Iraqi civilians and looting museums. The war also upset the decades-old alliance between the United States and Turkey, which had refused to allow American troops to advance from its soil, and it further exposed a rift between the rich Persian Gulf nations like Qatar, which served as hosts to the American military, and the rest of the Arab world. "Saddam Hussein fomented a miracle: he took history backwards many generations," lamented Talal Salman, the publisher of the respected *Al-Safir* newspaper in Beirut, in a bitter front-page editorial after the fall of Baghdad. "What a tragedy again plaguing the great people of Iraq. They have to choose between the night of tyranny and the night of humiliation stemming from foreign occupation."

But in a nod to Arab sensitivities, the Pentagon announced after the fall of Baghdad that one long-standing grievance would be addressed: All U.S. combat forces based in Saudi Arabia would be withdrawn, ending more than a decade of military operations in that country. American officials now declared that the collapse of Saddam's regime meant that only 400 to 500 American troops would remain in Saudi Arabia, as part of a training program.

Dramatic as it may have seemed, the move would not really affect the American presence in the region, with air operations shifted to Qatar and the certain establishment of some kind of long-term access to bases in Iraq. That implied a whole new range of potential resentments and problems. Hezbollah, the militant Islamic organization backed by Iran and Syria, issued a new call to arms for action against the occupying Americans. "In the past, when the Marines were in Beirut, we screamed, 'Death to America!' " said the group's leader, Sheik Hassan Nasrallah, in a speech just before the war. "Today, when the region is being filled with hundreds of thousands of American soldiers, 'Death to America!' was, is and will stay our slogan."[4]

But in the bitter Israeli-Palestinian conflict, there were faint glimmers of hope in the aftermath of America's military action. In his first months in office, Bush had rejected the pattern of intense involvement and hands-on mediation that he believed had brought the Clinton administration to grief when the Camp David negotiations between Ehud Barak and Yasir Arafat collapsed in 2000. Bush had chosen to offer largely unqualified support for Israel. Washington's Arab allies had long warned the Bush administration that it could not expect their support for a war in Iraq as long as the Palestinian guerrilla war and Israel's occupation of the West Bank and Gaza Strip continued. Wolfowitz and others had just as steadfastly replied that the ultimate road to Middle East peace and security lay through Baghdad. In the months leading up to the war, Bush had offered the strongest rhetorical support for Palestinian statehood of any American president, but he had yet to match his words with deeds. Finally, on the eve of the invasion, Bush had agreed—largely as a favor to Tony Blair—to publicly detail and explicitly support the so-called road map toward peace that had been worked out in months of consultations among the United States, the European Union, Russia and the United Nations.

For Bush, the price of going it alone in Iraq would now be going it together on the Israeli-Palestinian dispute. Although the administration had adamantly insisted on a deliberate timetable, never attempting to move faster or farther than the parties themselves, and on exercising sole power in the region, Bush now acceded to European demands that the United States return to active involvement and apply pressure to both sides to make concessions. To a degree that took some of his sharpest critics by surprise, Bush followed through on his pledge to become more personally involved in pressing for such an Israeli-Palestinian settlement.

In June, at a three-way summit with Bush in Jordan, Israeli prime minister Ariel Sharon and the new Palestinian prime minister, Mahmoud Abbas (who had succeeded the sidelined Yasir Arafat as the chief Palestinian negotiator), made pledges of cooperation. Sharon promised to begin dismantling some "unauthorized outposts" of Jewish settlements in the West Bank, and Abbas declared for the first time that "the armed intifada must end." Bush said that his job would be "to keep the thing moving." The latest rub was Sharon's building of a lengthy concrete-and-wire barrier separating Israel and some Jewish settlements from Palestinian areas in the West Bank. The Israelis asserted that the fence was necessary to prevent further terrorist attacks, but the Palestinians contended that the barrier would cripple their economy and freedom of movement. While acknowledging that the fence might be justified in security terms, Bush also began to press Sharon to hold off on further construction, calling the fence a "problem." And despite a declared cease-fire, Palestinian attacks and Israeli reprisals soon flared again. It was becoming clear to many that Bush would have to get even more involved if the parties were to be moved toward an eventual settlement, a task that could ironically find him playing the same role as Bill Clinton.

FOR RICK SCHWARTZ AND HIS fellow soldiers of the Third Infantry Division, the hot Iraqi summer was brutal. But thanks to Task Force 1-64's efforts, conditions in Falluja were at last more stable in late July. "We are working a tremendous humanitarian push into the repressed community," Schwartz said. "Most people are thankful, but there are those select few that want us out. They are influenced heavily by religious leaders and Sheiks. We go out on patrol every day, and travel throughout the real rough spots. People just want the basics: water, electricity, gas. We deliver free food, gas, school supplies." His biggest worry? Makeshift bombs, or "Improvised Explosive Devices," as the Army calls them. "They are difficult to spot," he noted, "and lethal when employed."[5]

In late July, Paul Wolfowitz made a whirlwind four-and-a-half-day visit to Iraq, at last witnessing firsthand the fruits of his years-long dream of removing Saddam from power. In temperatures sometimes above 120 degrees, Wolfowitz darted around the country, touring the Abu Ghraib prison, witnessing the mass graves in Hilla, interviewing the "marsh Arabs" of southern Iraq whose once-lush lands had been drained by Saddam. He acknowledged that there were huge challenges and much work to be done, but pronounced himself well satisfied with the pace of postwar progress, and in no doubt whatever about the wisdom of the American invasion. Wolfowitz met with the newly elected mayor of Mosul and his council, made up of Arabs, Kurds, Christians and Turkmens. It was just the kind of mix of ethnic and religious groups that Wolfowitz had long argued could thrive if Saddam were gone. "You don't build a democracy like you build a house," Wolfowitz told the group. "Democracy grows like a garden. If you keep the weeds out and water the plants and you're patient, eventually you get something magnificent." When he returned to Washington, however, Wolfowitz did acknowledge that "the pervasive fear of the old regime is still alive in Iraq," and he added, "In many ways, Iraqis are like prisoners who have emerged from years of solitary confinement with no light, no news, no knowledge of the outside world, and they have just emerged into the blinding sun and the fresh air of freedom."

There were some shimmering glints of optimism in Iraq after the fall of Saddam's dictatorship. Hassan Fattah, a young Iraqi-American journalist who returned to Baghdad after the war to start a newspaper called *Iraq Today*, sketched a vision of postwar Iraq as a potential beacon for the Arab world. "Iraqis know Saddam was a fake," he said. "His Arabism came at their expense. For Iraqis it was not Arabism, it was torture and subjugation." After Saddam fell, Fattah said, "There is this feeling that the Arab world has lashed out at us because we did not 'resist' the Americans. It was because Iraqis have learned the lessons of phony Arabism—that Saddam could send $35,000 to the families of suicide bombers" among the Palestinians, "while leaving his own people starving and living on $2 a day. That's why there is a dramatic gulf now between Iraqis and a lot of other Arabs. Young people here want to move on. In ten years, this will be a different place. If I can be a part of it, it will be like Hong Kong or Korea—but with an Iraqi face."

Not all Iraqis felt so liberated. Ethnic feuds, religious rivalries and ancient grudges endured in a country that no American gardener or civics teacher—however well meaning—could quite imagine. So did cruel traditions, which took a toll in the face of continued unease at the American occupation. One morning before dawn, in the Sunni village of Thuluya, Salem Kerbul carried an AK-47 assault rifle on a heartbreaking mission. In June, a force of 4,000 American soldiers had rounded up 400 residents of Thuluya in a strike aimed at tamping down resistance to the occupation. An informer wearing desert camouflage with a bag over his head had pointed out some fifteen prisoners to the Americans. Villagers said they recognized the informer by his yellow sandals and severed right thumb. It was Kerbul's son Sabah, they said. Weeks later, villagers gave Sabah's family a choice: Kill him themselves or face the death of the whole family in retaliation. Sabah's relatives killed him. "I have the heart of a father, and he's my son," Kerbul recalled, his voice almost a whisper. "Even the prophet Abraham didn't have to kill his son. There was no other choice."[6]

BY AUGUST, AMERICAN COMMANDERS HAD decided to end the large-scale raids that had rounded up hundreds of Iraqis, including Baath Party loyalists and other friends of Saddam Hussein's former regime. Lieutenant General Ricardo Sanchez, the new commander of allied forces in Iraq, concluded that the "iron-fisted" approach had run its course. In the process of capturing bad guys, the Americans had alienated many ordinary Iraqis. The attacks on American troops had eased somewhat, and the military decided it could now target its raids, rather than continue the large-scale roundups. Commanders considered it a good sign that the bounty for killing an American had risen from $1,000 to as high as $5,000, because this was a sign that it was harder for Baath Party loyalists to get young Iraqis to take the risk of shooting soldiers.

Rick Schwartz and his Desert Rogues finally returned home in early August—ten months after heading off to Kuwait. Other troops were rotating into Iraq to relieve them and would be expected to serve yearlong tours, perhaps with a brief home leave halfway through. Schwartz's wife, Nancy, waited anxiously at Fort Stewart, Georgia, with their two children, nine-year-old Andrew and Allie, thirteen. "This is the second war we've been through," she said. But this one had seemed "much longer and much more intense" than the Persian Gulf war twelve years earlier.[7]

Intense the war certainly was. It had removed a vicious tyrant, and ended decades of repression. It had demonstrated the possibilities—and some of the limits—of America's finely tooled military machine, and the bravery and skill of the men and women of its armed forces. It had shown the benefits of joint operations between the Army, Navy, Air Force, Marines and Special Operations troops. It had tested a new generation of tactics and equipment.

But as summer shaded into fall, sweeping questions remained. Had the war succeeded according to the terms of the American leaders who had chosen to fight it? Had it made the world a more congenial place for American interests and aspirations? The Iraqi regime had collapsed with surprising speed, a comparative weakling in the face of the American superpower. But was America's own moral position now weakened in some important ways? Had the alliances that had helped defend the United States since World War II been seriously damaged, and how much did it matter if they had?

Definitive answers would surely not be known for some time, perhaps years. It remained possible that in the long run, Iraq could grow more stable and more friendly to American interests. In a region where the raw exercise of power has brought grudging respect as well as resentment, the United States had proven its strength and resolution. But the early hints were not particularly encouraging. The ongoing fighting in Iraq, and the indications that radical Islamic "holy warriors" from around the region might well be joining the fray, seemed to vindicate the warnings of prewar skeptics, who feared the whirlwind that might follow Saddam's demise. A functioning Iraqi government was a long way off, and the challenge of holding together the competing factions of Shiites, Sunnis and Kurds had barely begun. The costly and daunting challenge of rebuilding Iraq's shattered economy, its oil facilities and other infrastructure posed financial and organizational hurdles whose ultimate height could only be guessed at.

After the fall of Baghdad, the Carnegie Endowment for International Peace issued a report noting that the United States had engaged in some 200 military interventions abroad since its founding, sixteen of which could be classified as "nation-building" efforts in which the goal was to change a hostile regime or insure the survival of a friendly regime that might otherwise have collapsed. Of the sixteen attempts, the researchers noted, only four cases—Japan and Germany after

World War II, Grenada in 1983 and Panama in 1989—qualified as successes in which durable, democratic regimes were created. None of those countries bore much resemblance to Iraq. Worse, the study found that when American nation-building efforts foundered, the governments that emerged were often brutal dictatorships or corrupt authoritarian regimes. No one could yet possibly say whether Iraq would follow that pattern, but it was not an impossibility, either.

The early failure to find weapons of mass destruction in Iraq was perhaps the most puzzling, and troubling, postwar reality of all. If the Bush administration and its British allies had exaggerated the threat posed by Saddam, was it deliberate, was it the result of faulty intelligence, or was it simply a reflection of unshakable assumptions that turned out to be wrong? If Iraq did not have the weapons or had destroyed them, as it claimed, was war truly urgent or could containment have been given more of a chance? Given that the shortage of American troops on the ground after the fall of Baghdad had allowed a presumably greater degree of postwar looting and theft, could the disorder also have provided an opportunity for the weapons (or the means and the will to make them) to fall into the hands of the very terrorists or unfriendly regimes that President Bush had so vociferously warned about in the first place?

At a minimum, the sheer demands of America's ongoing military commitment in Iraq, and the complications of dealing with Iran and North Korea, suggested that the Bush Doctrine was not such a neat and easy formulation after all, and that the administration would not always be able to go it alone in the future, even when it wanted to. Every day, the caution of Colin Powell's warning to Bush that America would "own" Iraq for years to come looked more and more justified, as the situation on the ground grew more and more costly in American lives, money and resolve. Depending on where one looked, there were reasons for hope and reasons for doubt, signs of fear and signs of progress. In large parts of Iraq conditions were stable, most of the time, by late August.

General John P. Abizaid, the new head of the U.S. Central Command (Tommy Franks had retired in July), was determined to look at the situation in Iraq with clear eyes. Abizaid, a Lebanese-American from California with a graduate degree from Harvard and fluency in

Arabic, had lived in Jordan and Lebanon and was one of the military's brightest stars, as well as one of Rumsfeld's favorites. He was as polished as Franks was rough-edged, but he was also a ferocious fighter. In the 1973 West Point yearbook, his classmates had called him "an Arabian Vince Lombardi," who "just couldn't accept second place." During the 1983 invasion of Grenada, he commanded a company in the 75th Ranger Regiment and, facing a Cuban bunker, ordered one of his sergeants to drive a bulldozer toward it as his men advanced behind it. Clint Eastwood would re-create the moment in his 1986 film, *Heartbreak Ridge*.[8]

In his first news conference after being sworn in as Franks's replacement, Abizaid summed up the situation in Iraq, as he saw it. "I believe there's midlevel Baathist, Iraqi intelligence service people, Special Security Organization people, Special Republican Guard people that have organized at the regional level in cellular structure and are conducting what I would describe as a classical guerrilla-type campaign against us," he said. "It's low-intensity conflict, in our doctrinal terms. But it's war, however you describe it."

EPILOGUE

Mosul, Iraq
Tuesday, July 22, 2003

The tip came from an Iraqi, a "walk-in" in American police lingo, and it was a hot one: Saddam Hussein's two sons, Uday and Qusay, were holed up in a palatial house in this northern city. Since the fall of Baghdad, Saddam's brutal heirs had been the subject of a manhunt second only to the search for their father. On the pocket-sized deck of playing cards of Iraq's most wanted that had been issued to American soldiers, Qusay was number two, the ace of clubs, and Uday was number three, the ace of hearts. There was a $15 million bounty on each of their heads. Nawaf al-Zidan, the owner of the house where the brothers were reported to be hiding, sat calmly outside the building, smoking, drinking water and eating fruit with American soldiers. Once upon a time, Zidan had bragged of being Saddam's kinsman, but had soured on him after the president threw his brother in jail. Was it payback time? No one was saying, but Zidan was in American custody and troops were moving into position around his house.

By 10 A.M., Special Operations soldiers and members of the 101st Airborne Division had surrounded the house and ordered the occupants to surrender. None did. Ten minutes later, soldiers entered the building and faced fire. Three soldiers were wounded, and the Americans withdrew. Over the next three hours, the Americans pounded the building, shredding its columned walls with grenades and anti-tank rockets, machine-gun fire and ten TOW antitank missiles. They tried and failed to get into a barricaded room on the second floor. Finally, at 1:21 P.M., the Americans stormed a second-floor bedroom, taking fire from and then killing Qusay's fourteen-year-old son, Mustafa. When the shooting stopped, three adults were found dead on a bathroom floor, the Hussein brothers and a bodyguard.

Dental records, X rays from a 1996 assassination attempt on Uday, and personal viewings by four senior members of Saddam's government who were already in American custody all provided irrefutable proof, American military officials said, that the bodies were those of Uday and Qusay. But some Iraqis remained in doubt, so the Americans released grisly photographs, first raw head-and-shoulders views, and then pictures of the faces and bodies after they had been made up by morticians. The first pictures showed that both men were bloated, with heavier beards than either had been known to wear in life. Uday's features were the most damaged, with a long bruise climbing from his mouth across his face.

The arguments began almost immediately. "In a few days, they will show us another fat body with a beard and say it's Saddam," said a laborer named Zohair Maty. "Everyone says they are in Spain."

General Sanchez, the American commander in Baghdad, said he believed that the news of the deaths of Saddam's sons would help curb attacks on American soldiers. "I believe very firmly that this will in fact have an effect," he said. "This will prove to the Iraqi people that at least these two members of the regime will not be coming back into power." But Muhammad Jasim Ali, a police officer in Falluja, predicted just the opposite. "They were the president's sons," he said. "If Uday and Qusay were killed, we will take our revenge. The attacks of course will increase."

There was one other problem with General Sanchez's logic: The whereabouts of Saddam himself remained a mystery.

THE SIGHTING HAD ALREADY TAKEN on a kind of mythic power. At noon on April 9, just hours before his statue fell in Firdos Square, Saddam had appeared in public in the square outside the Adhamiya Mosque in northern Baghdad—at least according to residents who said they were there. "I am fighting alongside you in the same trenches," the president told the cheering crowd, before he and a small group of loyalists climbed into their cars and drove off. Within twelve hours, American aircraft bombed the neighborhood, destroying part of the cemetery behind the mosque. American troops followed up with an assault on the mosque itself in which a shoulder-fired rocket was used to blast open the door to the tomb of Abu Hanifa, an eighth-century Muslim holy man, in the apparent belief that Saddam might have been hiding in the shadows inside. He was not. "Saddam Hussein was our country's leader, he was a statesman, and he was in authority over us," said Maythem Shihab, the custodian of the mosque. "We don't know his whereabouts now, but even if we did, we would not betray him."

Had Saddam been killed in the missile strike on the first night of the war? George Tenet had come to think so. Had he died in the second strike, in the Mansour district on April 7? Dick Cheney thought it was possible. Had he fled to Syria with other members of the regime? He might have. No one could be sure, and in the days after the fall of Baghdad, the senior officials of the Bush administration affected little interest in the question, at least in public statements. "He's either dead or he's going to be caught. We'll find him, the world will find him," Donald Rumsfeld said.

During the campaign against Al Qaeda and the Taliban in Afghanistan, President Bush had declared that he wanted Osama bin Laden, "dead or alive," and the continuing failure to find him was a lingering embarrassment. Now the administration was careful to avoid equating the hunt for Saddam with that for bin Laden. "This is some-body who ruled by traditional means of power: terror, an army, Republican Guard, territory, weapons, wealth, the ability to threaten his neighbors like Adolf Hitler did and Joseph Stalin did," said one administration official. "Without those traditional means, he's got nothing." The official went on to note that Hitler's death had not been conclusively confirmed for years after World War II, remarking dismissively, "Did anybody think that Hitler was still in power?" In fact, the mystery over Hitler's death had allowed for considerable mis-understanding and mischief making in the last days of World War II. Soviet forces were in control of Berlin at the beginning of May 1945, and Joseph Stalin encouraged speculation that Hitler was still alive, perhaps in an effort to gain advantage over the West by leaving open the prospect of a Nazi revival.

Now Saddam, alive or dead, in power or not, kept a hold on the imagination—and the fears—of the country he had ruled for so long. Within days, credible reports began to surface that he had survived the war. On April 18, Abu Dhabi television broadcast a videotape of Saddam greeting supporters in Baghdad, supposedly made on April 9. Tips and rumors about his possible whereabouts began to flood in to the American forces. Intelligence intercepts would later show that fugitive Iraqi officials still loyal to Saddam believed he was alive, and had succeeded in rallying resistance in his name. A London-based Arabic newspaper printed a handwritten letter, purportedly from Saddam, urging Iraqis to rebel against "the infidel, criminal, murderous and cowardly occupier." The note was dated April 28, Saddam's sixty-sixth birthday.

For reasons that remained unclear, American military engineers failed to excavate the site of the April 7 bombing in the Mansour district until June 3, in a belated hunt for possible remains or DNA evidence. Not quite two weeks later, the Americans captured Hussein's top aide, Abid Hamid Mahmoud, number four on the most-wanted list. American forces also believed that they had found most of the $1 billion that Mahmoud and Qusay Hussein had taken from Iraq's Central Bank on the eve of the war. Soldiers had discovered 191 of the 236 known boxes of cash hidden in palaces around Baghdad—about $950 million in all.

Now Mahmoud told American officials that Saddam and Uday and Qusay had all survived the war, and that he himself had fled to Syria with the two sons after the fall of Baghdad, before being expelled by the Syrian authorities. It was the most concrete indication yet that Saddam was still alive. On June 18, two days after Mahmoud's capture, an American Predator drone destroyed a convoy that was believed to be carrying former Iraqi officials to the Syrian border. American officials refused to discuss whether the attack had been aimed at Saddam and the circumstances surrounding it remained murky.

On July 3, Ambassador Bremer offered a reward of up to $25 million for the capture of Saddam or confirmation of his death. "Until we know for sure," Bremer said, Saddam and his family would "continue to cast a shadow of fear over this country." For the Bush administration, it was a reluctant acknowledgment that finding Saddam, one way or another, mattered a great deal.

The next day, an audiotape, purportedly recorded on June 14, was broadcast on Al Jazeera television. The voice on the tape warned, "The coming days will, God willing, be days of hardship and trouble for the infidel invaders." The voice said, "I am with some of my companions in Iraq," and it called on the Iraqis to "protect these heroic fighters and not give the invaders any information about them or their whereabouts." Days later, the CIA concluded that the voice was probably Saddam's.

The Iraqi rumor mill ran rampant. Saddam had been seen in Syria, and in Samarra. He was said to be living in luxury in California, or posing as a taxi driver. "He's in Adamiyah, hiding, wearing an abaya and a veil," said Sura Nuri, an eleven-year-old girl in a Baghdad market, referring to the conservative draped clothing of a Muslim woman. Ahmed Kamal, thirteen, countered: "Nobody can catch him because he has seven masks." A gold merchant named Salah al-Deaicy said there was a simple explanation for all the imaginative scenarios. "It's like being very closed in Saddam's circle for thirty-five years," he said. "You can't see anything but him."

IN FACT, THERE WERE ONLY four possible outcomes in the hunt for Saddam Hussein. The first was that he would be found and, like Uday and Qusay, killed in a final, fierce battle. The second was that he would be captured alive—and the United States had plans for a special tribunal of Iraqi judges to try him for crimes against humanity, should this be the case. The third was that Saddam would resurface elsewhere, in a country outside Iraq, where it might be especially hard for American forces ever to get hold of him. And the last possibility was that months, or years, would go by and his fate would remain a mystery, with unpredictable galvanic power over his followers and enemies alike.

On July 17, the thirty-fifth anniversary of the 1968 Baath Party coup, Al Arabiya satellite television broadcast a five-minute audiotape allegedly made by Saddam, condemning the new Iraqi Governing Council and demanding a "jihad to resist the occupation." Twelve days later, Al Arabiya played another audiotape, in which a voice purporting to be Saddam's mourned the deaths of Uday and Qusay; again, the CIA deemed it "highly likely" that the tape was authentic. The same day, American soldiers conducted dozens of raids and seized more than 175 suspected loyalists of the old regime in Tikrit, in an attempt to flush Saddam out of hiding. One of these men, Adnan Abdullah Abid al-Musslit, was said to be one of Saddam's most trusted bodyguards. On August 1, another purported tape of Saddam's voice surfaced, which said, "We must not let things slip away and our situation become desperate."

The audiotapes notwithstanding, American forces were confident they had Saddam on the run. They thought he might be in disguise, hiding in a mud hut, or in a house somewhere in Tikrit. They suspected that he was moving every three or four hours, at least three or four times a day. American soldiers had detained more than 600 people in Tikrit in June and July, trying to find Saddam. Some residents readily admitted that they assumed he was nearby. "Saddam is with us in Tikrit, and the Americans will not find him," said one tribal elder, Sheik Ismael al-Dibis. "They cannot find him even if they searched for a hundred years."

The Americans knew what a bitter irony it would be if they had finally driven Saddam from power, after twelve years of trying, only to let his ghost live on. As he had been in the days just after September 11, Saddam was once again a hovering presence at top levels of the Bush administration. As debates about the wisdom and the outcome of the war went on, so did the search for Saddam himself. "It is our operational assumption that Saddam Hussein is here," said Colonel James Hickey, commander of a 3,000-member task force in Tikrit. "And if he's here, we'll get him."

CHRONOLOGY

- **September 11, 2001:** Islamic terrorists hijack four passenger jets in the United States; two crash into the World Trade Center's twin towers, a third crashes into the Pentagon, and a fourth into a field in Pennsylvania.
- **January 29, 2002:** President George W. Bush delivers his first State of the Union address and designates Iraq as a member of the "axis of evil."
- **September 12, 2002:** President Bush addresses the United Nations General Assembly to make a case for war against Iraq and to ask for the necessary resolutions from the Security Council.
- **October 2, 2002:** A secret National Intelligence Estimate is circulated, stating that Iraq possesses biological and chemical weapons, and is making efforts to develop nuclear weapons.
- **October 10–11, 2002:** The Senate and the House of Representatives vote to authorize the use of military action against Iraq, should Saddam Hussein refuse to comply with UN resolutions.
- **October 23, 2002:** The United States and Britain formally present Resolution 1441 to the UN Security Council.
- **November 8, 2002:** The UN Security Council passes Resolution 1441 by a unanimous vote of 15–0.
- **November 18, 2002:** UN weapons inspectors arrive in Iraq for the first time in nearly four years.
- **December 7, 2002:** Iraq releases 12,000 pages of files about its weapons programs; the United States concludes that these documents are inadequate and constitute a "material breach" of Resolution 1441.
- **January 20, 2003:** French foreign minister Dominique de Villepin threatens to use France's veto if the United States presses the UN Security Council to authorize military action against Iraq.

- **January 28, 2003:** President Bush delivers his second State of the Union address, in which he warns, "If Saddam Hussein does not fully disarm, for the safety of our people and for the peace of the world, we will lead a coalition to disarm him." Included in the speech is this allegation: "The British government has learned that Saddam Hussein recently sought significant quantities of uranium from Africa."
- **February 5, 2003:** Secretary of State Colin Powell presents his argument for war against Iraq to the UN Security Council.
- **February 15, 2003:** Worldwide demonstrations are organized in major cities across the globe; millions march to protest against a war in Iraq.
- **February 24, 2003:** The United States, supported by Britain and Spain, introduces a second resolution to the UN Security Council, authorizing the use of force against Iraq.
- **March 16, 2003:** President Bush and British prime minister Tony Blair meet in the Azores for a summit with Spanish prime minister Jose María Aznar to urge action by the UN Security Council against Iraq.
- **March 17, 2003:** The United States withdraws its proposed UN resolution, and President Bush delivers a televised ultimatum to Saddam Hussein and his sons stating that they must leave Iraq within forty-eight hours or face war, and declares, "Their refusal to do so will result in military conflict, commenced at a time of our choosing."
- **March 19, 2003:** President Bush addresses the nation and the world to announce the commencement of the war. Bombs and missiles fall on targets in Baghdad, including a location where Saddam Hussein is believed to be staying.
- **March 20, 2003:** Ground forces begin their thrust across Iraq, and meet with little initial resistance; their steady progress is broadcast live in America and throughout the world.
- **March 21, 2003:** The "shock and awe" air campaign begins in Baghdad, as massive explosions rock the capital. British troops reach the outskirts of Basra. The port of Um Qasr is captured by American marines operating under British command.
- **March 23, 2003:** In Nasiriya, members of the 507th Maintenance Company are ambushed; eleven soldiers die, and five are taken prisoner, including Private First Class Jessica Lynch. Eighteen American marines are killed during a separate attack in Nasiriya. Overnight, an Apache helicopter flown

by Chief Warrant Officers Ronald D. Young, Jr., and David S. Williams is forced down near Karbala; the two soldiers are taken into captivity.

- **March 25, 2003**: Members of the Third Infantry Division engage in brutal battles against Iraqi forces and paramilitary irregulars in the Shiite holy city of Najaf.

- **March 26, 2003**: Paratroopers from the 173rd Airborne Brigade land in northern Iraq, to open the northern front. American forces encircle Najaf, after several days of intense fighting.

- **March 29, 2003**: Four American soldiers are killed by a suicide bomber at a checkpoint near Najaf.

- **March 30, 2003**: British Royal Marines launch Operation James, the single largest British operation of the war, in an effort to secure Basra.

- **April 1, 2003**: Private Lynch is rescued from a hospital in Nasiriya. Soldiers of the 101st Airborne Division enter and contain Najaf.

- **April 2, 2003**: Members of the Third Infantry roll through the Karbala Gap.

- **April 3, 2003**: Troops from the Third Infantry reach Saddam International Airport, on the outskirts of Baghdad.

- **April 4, 2003**: Saddam International Airport is occupied by U.S. forces and renamed Baghdad International Airport. Twelve minutes of video that appears to show Saddam Hussein strolling the streets of Baghdad is aired on Iraqi television.

- **April 5, 2003**: U.S. forces from the Third Infantry's 2nd Brigade make their "Thunder Run" into central Baghdad, in a brash display of might and purpose.

- **April 7, 2003**: The 2nd Brigade again penetrates Baghdad, seizing Saddam Hussein's Republican Palace. U.S. forces stabilize Karbala and Najaf, while British forces declare control over Basra.

- **April 9, 2003**: U.S. forces secure Baghdad, and, in a symbolic act of victory, help Iraqis topple a statue of Saddam Hussein in Firdos Square.

- **April 10, 2003**: U.S.-backed Kurdish pesh merga forces move to occupy Kirkuk, following several weeks of strategic caution.

- **April 11, 2003**: Mosul falls to Kurdish pesh merga and U.S. Special Operations troops.

- **April 13, 2003**: Seven American prisoners of war are discovered in Samarra and rescued by American marines. U.S. forces attack Tikrit.

- **April 14, 2003:** The Pentagon declares major operations in Iraq over.
- **April 15, 2003:** A group of more than seventy notable Iraqis representing a variety of interests meet at Tallil Air Base, near Nasiriya, to discuss the creation of an interim government.
- **April 16, 2003:** General Tommy Franks visits Baghdad. President Bush pronounces, "Thanks to the courage and might of our military, the Iraqi people are now free," and urges the United Nations to lift sanctions.
- **May 1, 2003:** President Bush, speaking from the deck of the USS *Abraham Lincoln*, announces the official end of combat operations in Iraq.
- **May 12, 2003:** Ambassador L. Paul Bremer III arrives in Baghdad as the U.S. civilian administrator, replacing retired lieutenant general Jay Garner.
- **May 22, 2003:** The UN Security Council grants the United States and Britain the authority to administer postwar Iraq.
- **May 29, 2003:** The BBC reports that the government of Tony Blair had exaggerated intelligence reports about Iraq's weapons of mass destruction in a dossier released in September.
- **July 13, 2003:** Twenty-five prominent Iraqis from a range of political, ethnic and religious backgrounds form the Governing Council, the first interim government of the new Iraq.
- **July 18, 2003:** David Kelly, a scientist at the British Ministry of Defence, is found dead in an apparent suicide, two days after having undergone tough questioning during a parliamentary inquiry on Iraq's weapons of mass destruction.
- **July 22, 2003:** Saddam Hussein's sons, Uday and Qusay, are killed by U.S. forces in a raid in Mosul.
- **August 7, 2003:** A car bomb explodes outside the Jordanian embassy in Baghdad, killing seventeen Iraqi civilians (including five police officers) and marking the first terrorist attack following the fall of Saddam Hussein's regime.
- **August 19, 2002:** A huge truck bomb explodes outside the UN headquarters in Baghdad. The suicide attack kills 23 people, including Sergio Vieira de Mello, the UN envoy to Iraq, and wounds at least 100, in an escalation of the security threat to all who would work to rebuild Iraq.
- **August 29, 2003:** A powerful car bomb explodes outside the Imam Ali Mosque in Najaf, Shiite Islam's holiest shrine, killing nearly 100 people, including Ayatollah Muhammad Bakr al-Hakim, the most prominent Shiite cleric cooperating with the U.S. administration in Baghdad.

NOTES

PROLOGUE

1. John Daniszewski, David Zucchino and Tony Perry, "U.S. Thrust Meant to Send Message," *Los Angeles Times,* April 6, 2003, p. A1.

2. David Zucchino, "A Daylight Dash: The Army's Brazen Tank Attack Stunned Even the Commanders Who Carried It Out," *Los Angeles Times,* April 6, 2003, p. A1.

3. Drew Brown, Juan O. Tamayo and Martin Merzer, "Tanks Roll into Iraqi Capital," Knight Ridder Tribune News Wire, April 5, 2003.

CHAPTER I: TWELVE YEARS IN THE MAKING

1. Wolfowitz's aides have since insisted that he had meant to say "ending state sponsorship" of terrorism. Whatever he meant, his words reverberated at the time.

2. Bob Woodward, *Bush at War* (New York: Simon & Schuster, 2002), pp. 74–91; author's interviews with senior administration officials.

3. Nicholas Lemann, "The Redemption," *The New Yorker,* Jan. 31, 2000, p. 48.

4. Paul Wolfowitz, "Remembering the Future," *The National Interest,* No. 59 (spring 2000), cited in Ivo H. Daalder and James M. Lindsay, *America Unbound: The Bush Revolution in Foreign Policy* (Washington, D.C.: The Brookings Institution, April 2003).

5. Cited in Staff of Reuters, *Saddam's Iraq: Face-off in the Gulf* (London: Reuters Books, 2002).

6. Paul Wolfowitz, "Victory Came Too Easily," *The National Interest,* No. 35 (spring 1994), p. 91.

7. Council on Foreign Relations, "Live from the Convention," Aug. 9, 2000, cited in Daalder and Lindsay, *America Unbound.*

8. Condoleezza Rice, "Promoting the National Interest," *Foreign Affairs,* January-February 2000, p. 47.

9. Glenn Kessler, "U.S. Decision on Iraq Has Puzzling Past," *The Washington Post,* Jan. 12, 2003, p. A1.

CHAPTER 2: THE AXIS OF EVIL

1. Kenneth M. Pollack, *The Threatening Storm: The Case for Invading Iraq* (New York: Random House, 2002), p. 117.

2. Ibid., p. 122.

3. Sandra Mackey, *The Reckoning: Iraq and the Legacy of Saddam Hussein* (New York: W.W. Norton, 2002), p. 325.

4. Elaine Sciolino, *The Outlaw State: Saddam Hussein's Quest for Power and the Gulf Crisis* (New York: John Wiley & Sons, 1991), p. 61.

5. Stanley A. Renshon, ed., *The Political Psychology of the Gulf War* (Pittsburgh: University of Pittsburgh Press, 1993), cited in Pollack, *Threatening Storm,* p. 149.

6. Cited in Sciolino, *Outlaw State,* p. 65.

7. Gary Milhollin, prepared testimony before House Committee on International Relations, Subcommittee on Middle East and South Asia, October 4, 2000, cited at www.iraqwatch.org/government/Index_US_hearings.htm.

8. Pollack, *Threatening Storm,* p. 17.

9. Gary Milhollin, "Saddam's Nuclear Shopping Spree," *The New Yorker,* December 13, 1999, p. 44.

10. Pollack, *Threatening Storm,* p. 175.

CHAPTER 3: THE BUSH DOCTRINE

1. David Martin, "Plans for Attack Began on 9–11," *CBS News,* Sept. 4, 2002, cited in Micah L. Sifry and Christopher Cerf, eds., *The Iraq War Reader* (New York: Touchstone, 2003), p. 213.

2. Michael Elliott and James Carney, "First Stop Iraq," *Time,* March 31, 2003, p. 172.

3. Robert V. Remini, *John Quincy Adams* (New York: Times Books, 2002), p. 58.

4. Brent Scowcroft, "Don't Attack Saddam," *The Wall Street Journal,* Aug. 15, 2002, p. A12.

5. Henry Kissinger, "Our Intervention in Iraq," *The Washington Post,* Aug. 12, 2002, p. A15.

6. Woodward, *Bush at War,* pp. 331 ff.; author's interviews with senior administration officials.

7. Colin Powell with Joseph E. Persico, *My American Journey* (New York: Random House, 1995), p. 540.

8. Glenn Kessler and Peter Slevin, "Cheney Is Fulcrum of Foreign Policy," *The Washington Post,* Oct. 13, 2002, p. A1.

9. Woodward, *Bush at War,* p. 348.

CHAPTER 4: RESOLUTION 1441

1. Author's interviews with senior Bush administration officials.

CHAPTER 5: THE FAILURE OF DIPLOMACY

1. Robert Graham and James Harding, "War in Iraq: How the Die Was Cast Before Transatlantic Diplomacy Failed," *Financial Times,* May 27, 2003, p. 15.

2. Author's interview with a senior French official.

3. Author's interviews with senior Bush administration officials.

CHAPTER 6: THE WEEK OF WAITING

1. John Daniszewski and Edwin Chen, "Hussein Rejects Ultimatum," *Los Angeles Times,* March 19, 2003, p. 1.

2. Ron Martz, "Soldiers Unfazed by Prospect of War," Cox News Service, Dec. 19, 2002.

3. John Hendren, "Ready and Raring to Go to War," *Los Angeles Times,* March 4, 2003, p. 1.

CHAPTER 7: BEST-LAID PLANS

1. Peter J. Boyer, "The New War Machine," *The New Yorker,* June 30, 2003, p. 61.

2. Tom Brokaw, interview with George W. Bush, NBC News, April 24, 2003.

3. Brokaw interview.

CHAPTER 8: THE ELEMENT OF SURPRISE

1. Brokaw interview.

2. Ibid.

3. Rick Atkinson, Peter Baker and Thomas E. Ricks, "Confused Start, Decisive End," *The Washington Post,* April 13, 2003, p. A1.

4. Mark Magnier and Sam Howe Verhovek, "Villagers Count Their Losses, Say Promised Medical Aid Isn't There," *Los Angeles Times,* March 23, 2003, p. 3.

CHAPTER 9: SHOCK AND AWE

1. Robert Burns, "Tomahawk Missiles and Stealth Fighter-Bombers Open the War to Remove Saddam Hussein," Associated Press, March 19, 2003.

2. Martha Brant, "Front Lines: High-Tech Battle Planning," *Newsweek* (online edition), March 12, 2003.

3. Laurie Goering and Ray Quintanilla, "Ground War Heats Up," *Chicago Tribune,* March 23, 2003, p. 1.

4. Verbatim accounts of Young and Williams from CBS News, 60 *Minutes II,* with Dan Rather, May 14, 2003.

5. Lisa Rose Weaver, Karl Penhaul and Paul Reid, "Shooting Was Coming from Everywhere," *Atlanta Journal-Constitution,* March 25, 2003, p. A5.

6. Pentagon briefing, May 7, 2003.

7. John J. Lumpkin, "Iraqi Air Force Not a Force in War Yet," Associated Press, March 25, 2003.

CHAPTER 10: A TURN FOR THE WORSE

1. United States Army report on the ambush of the 507th Maintenance Company, Executive Summary, at www4.army.mil/ocpa/reports/.

2. Juan O. Tamayo, "Oh My God, I'm Home," *The Philadelphia Inquirer,* April 14, 2003, p. A1; also Dana Priest, William Booth and Susan Schmidt, "A Broken Body, a Broken Story, Pieced Together," *The Washington Post,* June 17, 2003, p. A1.

3. Susan B. Glasser and Rajiv Chandrasekaran, "Clashes at Key River Crossing Bring Heaviest Day of American Casualties," *The Washington Post,* March 24, 2003, p. A1.

4. Graham Rayman, Thomas Frank and Hugo Kugiya, "Fierce Ambushes:

'It Was Just Bodies Everywhere' as Iraqis Surprise Marines," *Newsday,* March 24, 2003, p. W5.

CHAPTER 11: THE BRITISH IN BASRA

1. Martin Bentham and Ewen MacAskill, "Desert Rats Under Fierce Onslaught," *The Guardian* (London), March 25, 2003, p. 7.
2. David Williams, "Urban Guerillas Stall the Advance," *Daily Mail* (London), March 25, 2003, p. 6.
3. Richard Norton-Taylor and Rory McCarthy, "British Plan to Take Basra By Force," *The Guardian* (London), March 26, 2003, p. 4.
4. Keith Dovkants, "Bloodbath in Basra," *The Evening Standard* (London), March 26, 2003, pp. 4–5.
5. Susan B. Glasser and Richard Leiby, "British See Uprising by Civilians in Basra," *The Washington Post,* March 26, 2003, p. A1.
6. Rory McCarthy and Richard Norton-Taylor, "Battle as Iraqis Break Out of Basra," *The Guardian* (London), March 27, 2003, p. 1.
7. Keith B. Richburg, "Near Basra, British Purvey Juice, Milk and Artillery," *The Washington Post,* March 28, 2003, p. A25.
8. David Fox and Paul Harris, "Crisis in Basra," *The Independent* (London), March 28, 2003, p. 1.
9. Mark Magnier, "In Basra, Panic as a Tactic of War," *Los Angeles Times,* March 31, 2003, p. A1.
10. Tim Butcher, "Marines: Commandos Launch Battle for Basra," *The Guardian* (London), March 31, 2003, p. 7.

CHAPTER 12: SECURING THE NORTH

1. Steve Vogel, "Troops Parachute In to Open a New Front," *The Washington Post,* March 27, 2003, p. A1.
2. Damien McElroy and Karen McVeigh, "US Air Drop Adds to Pressure on Iraq and Turkey," *The Scotsman* (Edinburgh), March 28, 2003, p. 2.
3. Mackey, *Reckoning,* p. 64.
4. Atkinson, Baker and Ricks, "Confused Start, Decisive End."
5. Thomas E. Ricks, "War Could Last Month, Officers Say," *The Washington Post,* March 27, 2003, p. A1.
6. Boyer, "New War Machine," p. 67.
7. Atkinson, Baker and Ricks, "Confused Start, Decisive End."

CHAPTER 13: SAVING PRIVATE LYNCH

1. David Zucchino and Tony Perry, "Allied Forces May Be Quicker to Fire," *Los Angeles Times,* March 29, 2003, p. A3.
2. Peter Baker, "A Turkey Shoot, but with Marines as the Targets," *The Washington Post,* March 28, 2003, p. A1.
3. Priest, Booth and Schmidt, "Broken Body."
4. Ibid.
5. Ibid.
6. Ibid.
7. Ibid.
8. Ibid.
9. Jerry Adler, "Jessica's Liberation," *Newsweek,* April 14, 2003, p. 42.

CHAPTER 14: THROUGH THE KARBALA GAP

1. Lieutenant Colonel Eric C. Schwartz, e-mail to author, July 21, 2003.
2. Rajiv Chandrasekaran and William Branigin, "Suicide Bombing Kills 4 Soldiers," *The Washington Post,* March 30, 2003, p. A1.
3. Atkinson, Baker and Ricks, "Confused Start, Decisive End."
4. Boyer, "New War Machine," p. 69.
5. Rick Atkinson, "Najaf Besieged in Reinvigorated Army Offensive," *The Washington Post,* March 31, 2003, p. A15.
6. William Branigin, "A Gruesome Scene on Highway 9," *The Washington Post,* April 1, 2003, p. A1.
7. Rick Atkinson, "Army Enters Holy City," *The Washington Post,* April 2, 2003, p. A1.
8. Atkinson, Baker and Ricks, "Confused Start, Decisive End."
9. James Kitfield, "Baghdad's Liberation," *National Journal,* April 12, 2003, p. 1133.

CHAPTER 15: THUNDER RUN

1. American commanders initially denied any responsibility for the blackout. Later, they acknowledged it might have been the result of allied bombing that inadvertently toppled transmission towers.
2. Kitfield, "Baghdad's Liberation," p. 1134.
3. Ibid., pp. 1137–38.

4. Ibid., p. 1134.
5. Schwartz e-mail to author.
6. Zucchino, "Daylight Dash."
7. Ibid.
8. National Public Radio, Weekend Edition, "Entry of the Third Infantry into Baghdad," April 6, 2003.
9. Zucchino, "Daylight Dash."
10. Ibid.; Schwartz e-mail to author.

CHAPTER 16: THE FALL OF BAGHDAD

1. Peter Maass, "Good Kills," *The New York Times Magazine,* April 20, 2003, p. 32.
2. Peter Slevin and Dana Priest, "Wolfowitz Concedes Iraq Errors," *The Washington Post,* July 24, 2003, p. A1.
3. Dennis Steele, "Baghdad: The Crossroads," *Army Magazine,* June 2003.
4. National Public Radio, April 7, 2003.
5. Schwartz e-mail to author.
6. William Branigin, "3 Key Battles Turned Tide of Invasion," *The Washington Post,* April 20, 2003, p. A20.
7. Ibid.
8. Anonymous e-mail by embedded Army historian, posted on www.strategypage.com/iraqwar/taking_baghdad.asp.
9. Branigin, "3 Key Battles."
10. Anonymous e-mail, www.strategypage.com.
11. Branigin, "3 Key Battles."
12. Ibid.
13. All of this battle account comes from Maass, "Good Kills."
14. New York Times Television, "Hunting Saddam," July 27, 2003.
15. Jon Lee Anderson, "The Collapse," *The New Yorker,* April 21–28, 2003, p. 70.
16. Schwartz e-mail to author.
17. Atkinson, Baker and Ricks, "Confused Start, Decisive End."

CHAPTER 17: THE AFTERMATH

1. Barton Gellman, "U.S. Has Not Inspected Iraqi Nuclear Facility," *The Washington Post,* April 25, 2003, p. A14.
2. Barton Gellman, "Seven Nuclear Sites Looted," *The Washington Post,* May

10, 2003, p. A1; Barton Gellman, "Odyssey of Frustration," *The Washington Post,* May 18, 2003, p. A1.

3. Peter Baker, "Rescuers Nearly Called Mission Off," *The Washington Post,* April 16, 2003, p. A1.

4. Peter Baker, "Days of Darkness, with Death Outside the Door," *The Washington Post,* April 14, 2003, p. A1.

5. Ibid.

6. Ibid.

CHAPTER 18: CATASTROPHIC SUCCESS

1. Alan Sipress, "Commander Pays Triumphant Visit to Baghdad," *The Washington Post,* April 17, 2003, p. A25.

2. Frederick W. Kagan, "War and Aftermath," *Policy Review* (The Hoover Institution), August–September 2003, p. 4.

3. David Zucchino, "Iraq's Swift Defeat Blamed on Leaders," *Los Angeles Times,* Aug. 11, 2003, p. A1.

4. Rajiv Chandrasekaran, "Blackouts Return, Deepening Iraq's Dark Days," *The Washington Post,* July 3, 2003, p. A1.

5. Mark Fineman, Robin Wright and Doyle McManus, "Preparing for War, Stumbling to Peace; U.S. Is Paying the Price for Missteps Made on Iraq," *Los Angeles Times,* July 18, 2003, p. A1.

6. Greg Miller, "Head of Joint Chiefs Defends Use of Cluster Bombs in Iraq," *Los Angeles Times,* April 26, 2003, p. A8.

7. Niko Price, "AP, In First Nationwide Tally of Iraqi Civilian War Deaths, Counts At Least 3,240," Associated Press, June 11, 2003.

8. Fineman, Wright and McManus, "Preparing for War, Stumbling to Peace."

9. Timothy Carney, "We're Getting in Our Own Way," *The Washington Post,* Outlook, June 22, 2003, p. B1.

10. Fineman, Wright and McManus, "Preparing for War, Stumbling to Peace."

11. Dave Moniz, "Ex-Army Boss: Pentagon Won't Admit Reality in Iraq," *USA Today,* June 3, 2003, p. 1A.

12. Kagan, "War and Aftermath," p. 27.

CHAPTER 19: SMOOTH LANDING, ROUGH TAKEOFF

1. Sydney J. Freedberg, Jr., and Corine Hegland, "Reinventing Iraq," *National Journal,* March 22, 2003, p. 899.

2. Donald L. Barlett and James B. Steele, "Iraq's Crude Awakening," *Time,* May 19, 2003, p. 49.

3. Sudeep Reddy, "Gauging Iraq's Untapped Oil Potential," *The Dallas Morning News,* March 30, 2003, p. 1H.

CHAPTER 20: CASUS BELLI

1. CNN, "Wolf Blitzer Reports," May 30, 2003, Transcript 053000CN.V67.

2. Barton Gellman, "Odyssey of Frustration: In Search for Weapons, Army Team Finds Vacuum Cleaners," *The Washington Post,* May 18, 2003, p. A1.

3. Bob Drogin, "Iraq Had Secret Labs, Officer Says," *Los Angeles Times,* June 8, 2003, p. A1.

4. *Vanity Fair* interview with Paul Wolfowitz, May 9–10, 2003, cited on Pentagon Web site www.defenselink.mil/transcripts.

5. Ibid.

6. Nicholas Lemann, "How It Came to War," *The New Yorker,* March 31, 2003, p. 36.

CHAPTER 21: THE PRICE OF GOING IT ALONE

1. Brokaw interview.

2. James Dobbins, "We've Been Down This Road Before," *Los Angeles Times,* July 17, 2003, p. B15.

3. Cited in Ronald Brownstein, "Those Who Sought War Are Now Pushing Peace," *Los Angeles Times,* April 17, 2003, p. A1.

4. Josh Mcyer, "Hezbollah Vows Anew to Target Americans," *Los Angeles Times,* April 17, 2003, p. A1.

5. Schwartz e-mail to author.

6. Anthony Shadid, "For an Iraqi Family, 'No Other Choice,'" *The Washington Post,* August 1, 2003, p. A1.

7. Catherine E. Shoichet, "Warriors Return to Fort Stewart," *The Atlanta Journal-Constitution,* August 8, 2003, p. C1.

8. Thomas E. Ricks, "Centcom's Renaissance Man, New Chief Abizaid Is Departure from Previous Army Leaders," *The Washington Post,* August 3, 2003, p. A18.

ACKNOWLEDGMENTS

In 1952, my aunt Bobbie, my mother's older sister, sailed to Europe on the *Queen Elizabeth* and was asked to dance by King Faisal II of Iraq. He was a good dancer, she said, but apparently not light enough on his feet to keep from being killed in a coup six years later. For much of my life, that's about all I knew about Iraq, unless you count painting plywood and muslin to look like Baghdad for a Western Illinois University Theater Department production of *Kismet* when I was in eighth grade. In recent years, like most Americans, I have learned a great deal more about a country that has been a center of civilization, commerce and conflict for thousands of years, though I was still an unlikely candidate to write this book when Susan Chira, *The New York Times*'s editorial director of book development, approached me about the project last winter. I thank her for her friendship, kindness and wise counsel to a first-time author who has never been to Iraq, never covered the military, doesn't speak Arabic and still knows a lot more about *Kismet* than the Koran. Fortunately, dozens of my colleagues at the *Times* are experts on everything from military tactics to the Middle East. It is their reportage—over the dozen years from the end of the Persian Gulf war to the present—that forms the backbone of this book.

As a diplomatic correspondent in the *Times*'s Washington bureau in 2002, I covered a part of the story myself, and I have supplemented our published work with additional interviews with senior American, British and French officials (many of whom I can best thank by not naming them), and the excellent reporting of other publications and books, acknowledged in the endnotes. My tireless researcher and friend

Karen Avrich did more than find the right piece of information and the best bit of context, wherever she could and whenever I needed it. She read over my shoulder, checked my facts, compiled the chronology that appears at the end of the book and generally provided the kind of experience and professionalism that any author would envy. I thank her from the bottom of my heart. Any mistakes are mine.

Among my *Times* colleagues, I owe special gratitude to Steven Lee Myers, whose coverage of the Third Infantry's advance across the desert set the standard for all other embedded reporters; John F. Burns, whose brilliant reporting on the siege and fall of Baghdad held readers spellbound; Dexter Filkins, who bravely followed the Marines and other stories wherever they took him as a "unilateral" reporter without military protection during and after the war; Jim Dao, whose coverage of Special Operations forces provided some of the book's most compelling scenes; C. J. Chivers, who spent six unbroken months providing fearless coverage of the conflict in northern Iraq; and especially Eric Schmitt and Thom Shanker, whose whip-smart, tireless coverage of the Pentagon helped clarify the fog of war, and whose reading of the manuscript saved me from many errors. David Sanger, Elisabeth Bumiller, Steve Weisman, Dick Stevenson, Julia Preston and Felicity Barringer covered the Bush administration's months of politics and diplomacy with a depth and clarity that made my work easier at every turn. So did Jim Risen's dogged decoding of the controversies over intelligence on Iraq's weapons programs. Jim Dwyer, with the 101st Airborne Division, and Mike Wilson, with the Marines, brought sharp eyes and vivid prose style to everything they wrote. Elaine Sciolino's personal support—and her coruscating coverage of France—gave me courage to carry on. The analytical reporting of Michael R. Gordon, the chief military correspondent of the *Times,* was my constant guide, and I am grateful for his support despite his commitment to his own ambitious book on the war. John H. Cushman, Jr., the son and grandson of Army generals, is not only a former *Times* Pentagon correspondent and a wonderful editor; he also took the time to explain many basics of tactics and strategy to me, amid all his other duties as weekend editor in the Washington bureau. Patrick E. Tyler's daily lead-all accounts of the war, and his coverage of postwar Baghdad, were a continual source of important information. I have drawn on several compelling articles by Peter Maass, a contributing writer for *The New York Times Magazine*. The fabulous Monica Borkowski and Barclay Walsh in the Washington bureau library dug up great nuggets, as always. Karen Cetinkaya, the foreign desk weekend picture editor, chose the marvelous photographs—many of them by *Times* photographers acknowledged below—and Joe Burgess drew the maps that accompany the battle accounts.

Other *Times* correspondents, columnists and photographers provided vital help, including Edmund Andrews, R. W. Apple, Jr., Neela Banerjee, Elizabeth Becker, Richard Bernstein, William J. Broad, John Broder, Frank Bruni, Lynette Clemetson, Adam Clymer, Barbara Crossette, Steve Crowley, Monica Davey, Shaila K. Dewan, Maureen Dowd, Steven Erlanger, Alan Feuer, David Firestone, Ian Fisher, Ruth Fremson, Thomas L. Friedman, Jeffrey Gettleman, Chris Hedges, Tyler Hicks, James Hill, Warren Hoge, Steven A. Holmes, Carl Hulse, Michael Janofsky, Douglas Jehl, David Johnston, Sarah Kershaw, John Kifner, Peter T. Kilborn, Nicholas D. Kristof, Vince LaForet, Mark Landler, Charlie LeDuff, Chang Lee, Eric Lichtblau, Sarah Lyall, Neil MacFarquhar, Robert D. McFadden, Donald G. McNeil, Jr., Judith Miller, Doug Mills, Alison Mitchell, Ozier Muhammad, Adam Nagourney, Naka Nathaniel, Richard A. Oppel, Jr., Jane Perlez, David Rohde, Susan Sachs, William Safire, Marc Santora, Craig Smith, Don Van Natta, Jr., Amy Waldman, Bernard Weinraub, Jodi Wilgoren and Jim Yardley.

Among journalists at other publications, I must single out four at *The Washington Post:* Rick Atkinson, a veteran military-affairs writer and historian to whose coverage of this war I often turned; Peter Baker, my old White House colleague, who hustled for scoop after scoop from Kuwait to Baghdad; William Branigin, whose vivid accounts of some key engagements of the Third Infantry were unrivaled; and my classmate and friend of more than twenty years, Bart Gellman, who relentlessly covered the frustrating hunt for Iraq's weapons of mass destruction. In addition, the *Post*'s overall package of superbly edited stories and graphics rounded out my understanding of the war, and I am proud to acknowledge that debt.

This book would never have been possible without the support of my bureau chief, Jill Abramson, who encouraged me to write it and released me from regular duties to allow me to finish it. I thank my friend Rick Berke, the Washington editor, for more than he will ever know. Howell Raines, then executive editor, approved my assignment to write this book, for which I am grateful. Howell's predecessors Max Frankel and Joe Lelyveld, and his successor, Bill Keller, have each taught me in turn the meaning of integrity in journalism, and I am especially in debt to Bill for his profiles of Paul Wolfowitz and Colin Powell.

James B. Steinberg, former deputy national security adviser, now vice president and director of foreign policy at the Brookings Institution, read much of the manuscript and offered very helpful criticism. I also extend sincere thanks to Lieutenant Colonel Eric C. Schwartz, the commander of Task Force 1-64 of the 2nd Brigade of the U.S. Army's Third Infantry Division, for his help in reconstructing key engagements of his unit, and for the evident bravery he and his troops displayed.

My friend and seatmate Robin Toner suffered through my odyssey with good cheer, as did my former colleague Betsy Kolbert. For listening above and beyond the call of duty, I thank Harry R. Brickman. John Harris offered valuable advice on book writing, as did Steve Oney. The members of the California Tiki Militia, an elite group whose purposes are obscure but whose members are wonderful, provided long-distance moral support and friendship. My agent, Bob Barnett, and his associate, Ana Reyes, looked out for my interests on a small project that was barely worth their time. John Sterling, president and publisher of Henry Holt and Company, encouraged me to try my hand at this book when I was nervous about doing so, and kept encouraging me just when I needed it most. Paul Golob, editorial director of Times Books, provided terrific guidance, good questions, great patience, necessary prodding, superb blue-pencil work, at least one all-nighter—and the title. I could never have made it to the finish line without him. Heather Rodino kept cheerful track of the paper flow. I thank Chuck Thompson, the proofreader, for spotting— and saving me from—numerous errors of military terminology and fact.

My parents, Connie and the late Jerry Purdum, worked hard to give me and my sister, Edie, and brother, Steve, every advantage, but most of all their love. Whatever I may yet grow up to be is largely their doing, and I thank them all. My in-laws, Steve and Judy Myers, have taught me priceless lessons about war, naval aviation, martinis, Manhattans and life. To my newborn son, Stephen, whose gestation coincided with this book's, I hope *A Time of Our Choosing* may provide an answer, however disappointing, to the question of what his daddy did in the war. To my daughter, Kate, who spent too many evenings and weekends without me while I wrote it or otherwise toiled for "The Pooh Pork Times," I can only say, "I'm back!" And to their mother, Dee Dee Myers, I owe all that is good and right and fun and exciting in life, and I promise to keep striving to deserve it, always.

T.S.P.
Washington, D.C.
September 2003

INDEX

Page numbers in *italics* refer to maps.
Abbreviation: WMD = weapons of mass destruction

ABOUT THE AUTHOR

Todd S. Purdum is a correspondent in the Washington bureau of *The New York Times,* covering topics from politics and policy to culture. He was born in Macomb, Illinois, and educated at St. Paul's School and Princeton University, where he wrote his senior thesis on the loyalty-security program in the Eisenhower-era State Department and was the campus stringer for *The New York Times.* After graduation, he joined the newspaper as a copyboy in 1982, and later served as a police reporter, City Hall bureau chief, chief metropolitan political correspondent, White House correspondent, Los Angeles bureau chief and diplomatic correspondent. He has reported from more than twenty-five countries and has won various state and national awards. He lives in Washington, D.C., with his wife, Dee Dee Myers, the political commentator and former White House press secretary, and their two children. This is his first book.